PHOTOGRAPHY BY
LEE LOCKWOOD/
BLACK STAR

LITTLE, BROWN
AND COMPANY
BOSTON/TORONTO

CROCKETT'S VICTORY GARDEN

BY
JAMES
UNDERWOOD
CROCKETT

Library of Congress Catalog Card
No. 77-72669

Twenty-Second Printing

Photographs copyright © 1977 by
Lee Lockwood/Black Star

Photographs on pages 226 and 227
are reproduced courtesy of Photo
Researchers.

Drawings by George Ulrich.

Cuts from old seed catalogues
courtesy of the Massachusetts
Horticultural Society Library

Designed by Christopher Pullman,
WGBH

Design implementation by
Designworks

Published simultaneously in Canada
by Little, Brown & Company
(Canada) Limited

WAK
Printed in the United States of
America

Acknowledgements   No book is entirely the work of one person, if only because the individual learned from others throughout his lifetime. But in this volume I am indebted to many persons too numerous to list. However, certain men and women were particularly helpful in bringing this book from the idea stage to its present reality. Foremost must come my heartfelt thanks to Russell Morash, without whose inspiration the book would never have been written; next, I owe a debt of gratitude to Marjorie Waters, who oversaw the translation of the materials from the television format to the printed page. No book can exist without an editor, and much of the flavor and zest for gardening that shows through these pages is due to the gentle yet firm guidance of William D. Phillips of Little, Brown and Company; he is a man of boundless energy and enthusiasm that is communicated to all who work with him. Lee Lockwood, a photo-journalist who has covered the world in happy times and sad ones, is responsible for the photographs that allow the reader to see for himself how much fun and how rewarding gardening can be. Chris Pullman, the designer, is an amazingly creative gentleman who has taken my dirt-gardener approach to vegetable culture and turned it into a thing of beauty. There are so many others behind the scenes that I want to thank publicly for their efforts in my behalf. They include Mike Mattil, the copyeditor, Peter Carr, General Manager of Manufacturing, and Donna Baxter, production assistant, all from Little, Brown; George Ulrich, the illustrator; Dianne Smith, of Designworks, who was in charge of design implementation; Karen Green, typist; Lewis Lloyd, Administrative Manager, WGBH; and Donald Cutler, my literary agent.

PREFACE

I first met Jim Crockett on a cold, rainy day in December 1974. Along with some of my colleagues at WGBH, Boston's public television station, I had begun to work out plans for a gardening show that we would tape in our own backyard. The timing for the show seemed perfect. The nation was battling back from the oil boycott and self-sufficiency was both practical and fashionable, even if it meant digging up the front yard to plant tomatoes. We hoped to build the show around a professional horticulturist. Jim had written several excellent gardening books. It only remained to see if he was interested in the idea.

I liked Jim immediately, as everyone does. He's a warm and friendly man. So after we talked about the show's concept for a while, we arranged a time when he would tape a short screen test. Then he'd have a chance, along with us, to see whether he liked the electronic experience. I had already wrested from our buildings and grounds department the garden site: a 75 × 75–foot square of sodded ground just outside our studios. It would receive 8 to 10 hours of summer sunshine and it was close enough to the control rooms to make hauling the equipment easy.

On the day Jim arrived for his test, a light, freezing rain was falling. We planned to have him look into the camera, tell us a bit about himself, and then plunge his spade into the soil while describing the vegetables he intended to grow there all summer long. Although there was no frost in the ground, I could see him wince with pain as he plunged his spade to the earth. "My God, this soil is like concrete."

Jim made a splendid appearance on his test, agreed to do the series, and hurried off to a previously planned trip to the West Coast, where he'd be until two weeks before the first taping. "But do something with that soil, Russ, it's awful." We learned later that in its former years our garden plot had been a flood plain for the Charles River, the town dump, the site where the contractor who built the WGBH studios had chosen to bury the construction rubble, and, most recently, the parking area for the station's trucks.

So there I was, four months short of the first show, with a crusty, impenetrable square of land and my expert thousands of miles away. In the time since Jim's test, the ground had frozen solid, delaying any soil preparation until the spring thaw. We spent those intervening weeks praying for a March day warm enough to pull the garden into shape in time for the scheduled first taping in mid-April. We were lucky; it was a reasonably dry winter and an early spring, allowing our contractor to truck in some much-needed topsoil. Despite the favorable weather conditions, we were taking the chance of working the soil too soon. But we had no choice: the production schedule was staring us squarely in the face.

I remember one hysterical day late in March as we surveyed the newly surfaced garden, watching our beautiful greenhouse, a gift from Lord and Burnham, going up, it

began to snow. I wondered what vegetables Jim could get to grow under that.

About fifteen days before the first taping, Jim returned from California. The listings had gone out to the newspapers and we were committed to delivering a thirty-minute program about vegetable gardening to viewers up and down the East Coast. I will never forget the day Jim returned, looked at the soil, and said, "Looks fine, but now we've got to get the rocks out." That meant digging over every square inch of garden by hand. "And, we must have more organic matter." We'd already turned in about six bales of peat moss, a very generous amount by my pre-Crockett standards, but Jim was asking for another twenty bales. No wonder his garden does so well, I thought, it's all peat. But, I kept a civil tongue and spent the next ten days, along with Jim and two other stalwarts, building up the soil. We rototilled, we dug rocks, we found a lovely old bottle, circa 1900, a not-so-lovely muffler, and a 1959 Indiana license plate. Finally, after every inch of the garden had been picked over and personally certified as suitable by Jim, I allowed myself a tentative grin, confident that the garden at last was ready.

"Looks fine, but now there's too much soil, Russ. We'll have to build it into beds." Oh no. Four days to go until the taping, two of them over a weekend. I put in a panicky call to some carpenter friends, who built the four lovely beds that hold our precious soil which nourishes the Victory Garden crops. We nicknamed the central path Main Street and the intersection Crockett Plaza. We paved one with concrete to support our heavy camera equipment that rumbles along following Jim through the garden.

So, with only minutes to spare, with the garden finally ready, the greenhouse finished, the concrete a bit damp but serviceable, a marvelous gentleman with a wireless microphone tucked in his back pocket peered out from under his trifocals to announce for all to hear that he was Jim Crockett and this was *Crockett's Victory Garden*.

There are dozens of reasons for the popularity and success of *Crockett's Victory Garden*. We've had the assistance and support of scores of people, here at the station and elsewhere. WGBH's enthusiastic programming executives, Mark Stevens, Henry Becton, and Peter McGhee, helped breathe life into the idea early on, and stood by with words of

Russell Morash, creator and producer of Crockett's Victory Garden

encouragement at every critical bump and curve. Deborah Johnson and Jo Madden, each in her turn as the show's production assistant, kept the many loose ends involved in television from frazzling at the last minute. Gary Mottau deserves a special medal for his tireless efforts at keeping the garden and greenhouse beautiful from week to week. Nathan Hasson made valiant efforts to keep the mail opened and answered. Our long-suffering crew learned to distinguish carrots from cucumbers, and the engineering staff had their hands full with the sometimes cranky equipment on which television depends. Robert J. Lurtsema, maestro of our classical music program on WGBH-FM, selected our theme music, a song called "Gaspe Reel," composed and played by Bill Spence and available on his album *The Hammered Dulcimer*. We are indebted, too, to dozens of individuals at Wilson's Farm, at Littlefield-Wyman, at John D. Lyon, Inc., and at Weston Nursery, and so many others who provided us with their best advice, their finest plants, and their newest products.

But mostly, of course, the program succeeds because of Jim himself. He's a born teacher, a man who is willing to share his knowledge because he knows that gardening can give people pleasure, and can actually improve their lives. On more than one occasion, as I hacked away at some gardening chore, Jim would appear at my side, quietly working along with me but doing the job correctly. We've all learned so much from this modest, unpretentious man, as gentle off camera as on. I'm proud to know him.

In fact, if I have any regrets, it's only this: that the show has cost Jim his privacy, has exposed him to any number of requests for gardening advice, from any quarter at any time. I remember during one particularly blistering day, as I baked inside our control room during the taping, I felt a bit dizzy and sat down rather unceremoniously, just as the show was in its final minutes. Before I had time to protest, I found myself entering an ambulance feet first, with Jim by my side. On the way to the hospital, when I managed to convince my worried companions I would survive to tape another show, the ambulance attendant turned to Jim and said: "Listen, as long as we've got some time, I wonder if you can help me. My mother's fuchsia is covered with red spider mites . . ."

Russell Morash,
Producer-Director,
Crockett's Victory Garden

May your garden, like mine, give you "Victory" over the high cost of fresh vegetables as well as the joy and good health that come from living close to nature.

Jim Crockett

Crockett's Victory Garden

TWELVE MONTHS IN THE VICTORY GARDEN

In this book's preface, Russ Morash has told you how *Crockett's Victory Garden* came to be, but he's left out part of the story. He doesn't tell you how frightened I was at first by the impersonal glass eye of the camera. Nor does he know how exposed and vulnerable I felt in those first days as an audience gathered at the garden fence, watching my every goof as I learned to cope with this new experience. He only mentions that I have written a number of books about gardening and that one of them led him to my door.

He didn't know about the quietness of my private life. How, with our four children grown, Margaret and I had time

to travel and do the things we had planned for so many years. He didn't know he was dealing with an introvert. After all, I am a writer and a gardener, and both of these occupations are usually pursued in private, alone at a typewriter or pulling weeds in the garden. (Everyone leaves you alone if there are weeds to pull.) He wouldn't know until months later that I nearly panicked on an early show, as I wondered how I ever allowed myself to be put in such a position. But I'm sure he does remember the number of times he said, "Loosen up, Jim. You look scared to death."

When I began my television career with *Crockett's Victory Garden*, I had written fifteen books covering a substantial range of gardening subjects. Still, we were deluged with requests from viewers who wanted a book that accompanied the show, a month-by-month gardening guide as easy to follow as the show itself.

This is it, and its origin in the television show distinguishes it from other gardening books. I've set out in the show to teach the fundamentals of gardening, to let the camera follow me week after week through the cycles of preparation and planting and harvesting. But I've done some of the learning as well as the teaching. Every week letters pour into the station from novice and veteran alike. These letters have convinced me that gardeners need more than clear how-to information: they need to know why a certain procedure is recommended and how it works; they need advice, and cautions, and logical explanations. I think it's the teaching and learning, for viewers and for me, that make this book special.

Unlike so many gardening books that are organized either by theme or alphabetically by plant, I've organized this book by the months of the year, because time and the weather are the critical factors in gardening. *Crockett's Victory Garden* is designed to help you plan, time, and carry out the year's many gardening tasks. Considering the amount of labor that goes into your garden, it's probably the most valuable real estate you own, so it should pay you back with constant and bountiful production all year long.

Which leads to another important point. Like the show, this book covers twelve months because the gardener's year is a circle that has no absolute beginning or end. You and I both know gardeners who go out one spring weekend and "plant" their entire garden for the one and only time all season. When their carrots have been pulled there isn't another young crop to follow. Because they plant only one variety of main-season tomato instead of a few early and midseason plants, their first ripe tomatoes appear when tomatoes are a drug on the market. It's a boom-and-bust approach that leads to unmanageable surpluses followed by bare or weedy ground for the rest of the season.

My philosophy is that a garden should be in production for as long as possible, from the early spring into the winter. This means working all year long, preparing the soil in the fall, ordering seeds and planning the garden in the winter, getting the seedlings started in January, and planting and harvesting all through the growing season. I've started this book with the March chapter because in the Victory Garden and all but a few favored sections of the South and South-west, March is the beginning of the gardener's year. But as you read through you will notice that every month has its own special role. It doesn't really matter when you begin; you can pick up the cycle of the seasons at any time and begin from there. I'm ready when you are.

This book is based on the experience of the Victory Garden, a small demonstration plot outside the WGBH studios in Boston, Massachusetts. But this doesn't mean the information here won't apply to you if you live in another part of the country. My purpose is not to teach local gardening but to teach the fundamentals, and these do not change from region to region. In the Victory Garden are principles and procedures that apply to every garden, whether in Arizona or

Pennsylvania or Oregon. To help you make the minor adjustments in timing I've provided a regional chart on page 306. You should also, as I do, consult with your local gardening center or agricultural extension service for specific information particular to your area.

This book is distinguished, too, by the number and diversity of plants it covers. I've never grown an all-vegetable garden in my life, and I think that's true of most gardeners. You will find here everything we grow in the Victory Garden: a hundred different varieties of vegetables, in addition to annuals and perennials and herbs and berry bushes and trees and house plants. The book concentrates on vegetables because to my mind there's nothing to compare with hot buttered corn picked only minutes before, or a homegrown tomato, full of juice and warm from the garden. There's more than quality of flavor involved here, though; there's the economics of gardening, too. According to a state university survey the average gardener can grow about five dollars' worth of vegetables for every hour spent in the garden. And that's all nontaxable income.

A word now about the book's chapters. They begin with a checklist of the monthly jobs, each of which receives special attention within the chapter. A short introduction outlines the weather conditions we expect in the Victory Garden during the month and notes the general progress in the garden and greenhouse. Then there are separate listings, arranged alphabetically, for any crop or plants that need attention, whether the job is planting or propagating or pest control. At the end of each chapter, just as at the end of the shows, are some of the month's questions to the Victory Garden. I've included them not only because they provide helpful if sometimes obscure information, but because, frankly, I think this communication among gardeners is useful. The last pages of each chapter are devoted to monthly features, where I've given simple instructions for the critical gardening jobs, information useful not only for that month, but throughout the year. Whenever you begin the gardening cycle, it will be useful to familiarize yourself with these features.

As a closing thought, let me offer some encouragement. I've noticed that many of the people who write to the show are worried about their prospects for success. For these people, in fact for all gardeners, I recommend plain uncomplicated faith, or if faith is lacking, then elementary logic. There is no mystery about gardening, just the wondrous fact that seed time and harvest occur each year, generation after generation, wherever the soil is tilled. If gardeners do their part they can confidently expect the miracle to continue as it has through all time.

Planting lettuce seedlings

MAR

Plant
Leeks
Lettuce
Onion sets
Peas
Radishes
Spinach
Turnips

Transplant
Begonias
Broccoli
Cabbage
Cauliflower
Celery
Chives
Onions

Start Seedlings
Broccoli
Cabbage
Cauliflower
Leeks
Parsley

Thin
Lettuce

Special Events
Azaleas
Dahlias
Fruit Trees
Hollyhocks
Irises

MAR

March holds a singular position in the gardener's year. In spite of the sudden snowstorms that occasionally bury us here, the longer days bring warmer temperatures and, if we're lucky, dry weather, leaving the soil ready to work. In the Victory Garden we're ready to go as soon as the soil is, because we always do our soil preparation in the fall (see "Soil Preparation," pages 246–249). But if for some reason you find yourself with March approaching and your soil unprepared, by all means prepare it now. The additives won't have as much time to work into the soil but it's far too important a step to skip. If I make no other point in these pages, let this message be clear: nothing, but nothing, matters as much as soil preparation.

There's a simple test for soil readiness: if a handful of soil remains in a moist ball after it's squeezed, the soil is still too wet to work; if it crumbles like chocolate cake, it's ready. Working wet soil compacts it and can ruin the structure completely, so it doesn't pay to work the soil before the chocolate-cake stage. But as soon as it is ready, I plant some of the cool-weather crops, peas, turnips, and onion sets among them. An occasional blast of cold weather doesn't hurt them in the least.

This is the month we empty our cold frames (see this month's Feature, pages 26–27) of the last of the spring-flowering bulbs, which we bring inside for forcing. Then we turn the frames over to one of the major spring jobs: providing the warm days and cool nights that will harden off the cell structure of young seedlings. We put in the everbearing strawberry plants, sown in December and moved to 3-inch pots in February, along with most of the young seedlings in the greenhouse and hotbed. By the end of the month the cold frames are packed with seedlings being prepared for setting out into the garden in April.

Important as March is, though, our year really has no beginning or end. Gardening is a continuous cycle and all the months are equally important if not, I admit, equally hectic. In the March greenhouse there is progress to report on dozens of plants, sown or propagated or repaired over the winter. Some of the lilies come into bloom, notably the spectacular Gold Coast lily planted in December. The browallia comes into flower, too. And we have healthy new seedlings of ageratum coming along. The chionodoxa, also known as glory-of-the-snow, open their lovely blue star-shaped flowers. One March, after months of waiting, we were at last able to show some healthy growth on our coffee seedlings, which had refused to germinate until we provided them with sultry 80-degree temperatures. We have growth out in the garden in March, too, when the crops sown in the hotbed in February have germinated. There's even a sign of life from the daffodil bulbs that I naturalized in a grassy corner of the garden one October.

It's a month of promise as well as progress. A month when I can put my hands to the garden soil for the first time since the snows fell.

An azalea forced into bloom in early spring

Azaleas The azalea is one of those plants that have dominated the florists' bestseller lists for the past few years, a result of plant scientists' successful efforts to manipulate the plant's growth and dormancy periods, extending the blossoming period to run from November through May; as the plants normally bloom only in April, this is really a remarkable feat. In Japan these plants live in pots for a century or more but I can tell from the questions sent in to the Victory Garden that many American gardeners lose their plants after their first blossom period because they don't know how simple it is to save them.

I had an azalea in the Victory Garden one spring that had blossomed earlier and was about to produce its next season's foliage and flower buds. The plant had been in the same pot all through the year, so just after flowering it was ripe for repotting and a light pruning to keep the plant in shape.

There were 3 or 4 stems on the plant that seemed headed off in the wrong direction, which is about the average number of mavericks on an azalea. So I snipped these stems off, hiding the blunt snipped ends by making the cuts within the foliage and just above a leaf. Then I removed all the old flowers from the plant as well as the young seed pods that sometimes appear as the little flowers fade.

An azalea plant usually needs to be potted into a 1-inch-larger pot every spring to accommodate the enlarging root system. So after I pruned the foliage I knocked the plant out of the pot and set it into a larger one that had an inch of drainage stones at the bottom. Azaleas grow best in an acid medium, so I filled it around the roots with peat moss (sometimes I use half peat and half sand), making sure that the plant was not set in any lower than it had been in its previous pot.

Then I watered it, adding a little house plant fertilizer to the water. I fed it again in a couple of months and a third time in midsummer, when the beautiful, full growth had matured, the dark green foliage developed, and the flower buds formed, taking special care to water frequently. It is very important to keep the soil under azaleas moist all the time.

A midsummer cluster of wax begonias in bloom

Begonias I sow the seeds of the beautiful, long-flowering wax begonia in January. Rather slow to grow when young, they are only 1 inch tall at most by March, but it's time to move them to individual compartments in six-packs. These are tender plants that can't take the open garden until nighttime temperatures remain above 50 degrees, so I leave them in the greenhouse until then.

Broccoli Broccoli, cabbage, and cauliflower, while each unique in looks and flavor, are all members of the cabbage family; technically, they're known as brassicas. They mature at slightly different rates, cauliflower being the slowest, but they thrive in the same conditions and suffer the same pests and diseases so in the garden they're treated individually but identically.

I sow the first of my broccoli, cabbage, and cauliflower seeds in March. I only need about a dozen plants of each vegetable, so I allow for a percentage lost to poor germination and weaklings, and sow about 18 seeds of each vegetable in 4-inch pots filled with commercial potting soil. I set the pots in the bright warmth of the greenhouse or hotbed, and when the seedlings are about 1 inch tall I transfer them to individual places in six-packs. They grow very quickly in indoor heat, so toward the end of the month I move the six-packs to the cold frame to harden-off. They will continue to grow there, but more slowly, and will be ready for the open ground in April.

Cabbage and Cauliflower Like broccoli, these vegetables are members of the cabbage family. The information for them is given in the broccoli entry for March.

Celery In the month since their sowing in February, the celery seedlings have grown to be about 1½ inches tall, and they're ready for transferring to six-packs. Celery produces flowers rather than edible stalks if it's subjected to cold temperatures early in its life, so I leave the seedlings in the cosy greenhouse or hotbed until the night temperatures can be counted on to stay above 55 degrees. In the Victory Garden it's usually late May or early June before they can be safely planted outdoors.

Chives We began our first season in the Victory Garden with a grand scheme to grow the WGBH station logo in living plants. It was a little more ambitious than we'd bargained for, so we adjusted our sights and decided to surround the show's end credits with a bed of chives. All summer long the plants grew and grew. We would cut them back to the soil line now and then and they would quickly grow again. Finally when we moved inside for the show's winter season we left them out in the cold and forgot about them.

The following March we took two of these plants, cut

the greenery back to the soil line, and put them into the garden's perennial border, spacing them about a foot apart. Even after a cold winter they flourished when they were put into the fertile soil in the garden. By the middle of May they were about 18 inches tall and dense with grand lavender blossoms.

Dahlias Dahlias are the national flower of Mexico. As hot-weather flowers, it may be surprising to find any activity at all for them in March. Ordinarily, if dahlia tubers are of common, inexpensive varieties, I simply plant them outdoors at about the time the last frost is due. But some of the new varieties are very expensive, so I want to pass along a way to multiply a single tuber into dozens of plants and get around the impossible price tags that accompany these prize plants in the garden centers. Dahlias come in many different sizes, petal formations, and in every color but blue. They thrive in the garden and they're beautiful cut flowers too, so this March routine is well worth the minimal time involved.

A single dahlia tuber, planted in the ground, can only produce a single plant. So I multiply the yield of each tuber by planting them in pots in March and taking cuttings in April for setting out as growing plants in May. These cutting-grown plants will each produce flowers as big and plentiful as a planted tuber, and may actually come into flower earlier.

I usually begin with a clump of tubers that I dig up in November and winter-over in a cool cellar. At this time of the year there are latent buds at the crown, and this new growth is the source of next season's stems. So as I divide the clump into individual tubers, I make sure that each carries with it a bit of the crown's healthy, growing tissue.

Then I plant the single tubers (or one I've bought from a garden center) in potting soil in 5- to 7-inch pots, leaving the crown tip barely exposed above the soil. In less than a week, dark spots appear on this tip, signaling the beginning of the new growth. Next month when the new stalks are about 3 or 4 inches tall, I'll cut them off and root them.

Dahlia

Fruit Trees *Pruning old trees:* We have four crab apple trees along our north border that were planted long before anyone ever dreamed of *Crockett's Victory Garden*. They had suffered first from years of neglect and then from a hasty and overambitious pruning that distorted the trees' natural oval shape. They needed pruning badly when we began the show so I waited until one March, when the weather was warm enough to work outdoors but the buds had not yet begun to swell on the trees, and then took a serious look at the situation.

Most orchard trees produce suckers, or water sprouts; they're pencil-thin limbs that shoot straight up out of the tree. They're never particularly attractive, but thanks to the improper pruning there were so many of them on these crab apple trees that they were nothing short of ugly. They made the trees look like a row of witches' brooms. If allowed, suckers would eventually mature, but their nearly vertical stance would make them hopelessly weak, much too weak to hold fruit. They should always be removed.

I used pruning shears to cut the suckers off, making sure to remove the slightly swollen base of the sucker clean to the trunk. If that swelling isn't removed several more suckers will sprout from the spot, making the problem worse than it had been to begin with. Because the suckers are so slender I don't treat the small cut surfaces left behind, as they'll heal by themselves.

At this point I stood back to evaluate the trees' older

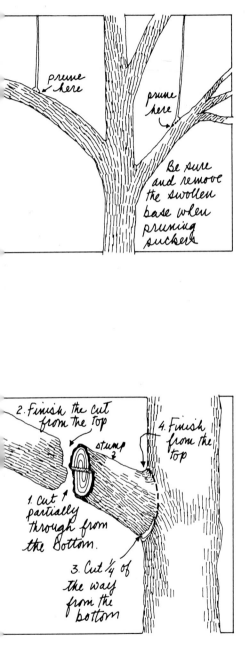

prune here

prune here

Be sure and remove the swollen base when pruning suckers

2. Finish the cut from the Top

stump

4. Finish from the Top

1. Cut partially through from the Bottom.

3. Cut ¼ of the way from the bottom

growth. It's a rule of pruning that placement of limbs should be evaluated when they're young; they should be pruned if necessary, and never be allowed to grow so they rub against each other. Eventually their outer skin wears away, giving disease a perfect raw entry spot. Unfortunately, several large branches on these trees were rubbing so hard that the bark was damaged; pruning with a saw was required.

While it's possible to use a standard carpentry saw for pruning, there's quite a bit to recommend the specialized pruning saw. For one thing, the teeth are sharpened in such a way that the saw cuts on the pull stroke rather than the push. This, in combination with the saw's bowed design and the wide set of the teeth, prevents sticking and eases the cutting motion. Another advantage is that some pruning saws are narrow and fit into the small and awkward places that bedevil the pruning operation. Finally, with a pole saw, it's possible to attach long handles to the saw and prune growth 20 feet above the ground without ever climbing a ladder.

The major problem in pruning large branches from a tree is weight. If I were simply to slice down through the branch's junction with the trunk, it's very likely that the weight of the branch would bear down before the slice was completed, ripping a strip of bark from the tree and inviting disease and rot. I solve this problem by cutting large limbs off in two sections. With the first section I remove about 90 percent of the branch but leave a stump on the tree that can be delicately removed later. The first cut need not be particularly neat, but the removal of the stump should be clean and as close to the trunk as possible so that neither bulges nor gouges are left to disfigure the tree. (Sometimes I find that it helps to trace the cut out beforehand with the saw.) As to the cutting operation itself: I always start with a small cut up from the bottom, about ¼ of the way through the branch; then I make a final cut from the top down, meeting the first cut. This further protects the tree from the risk of torn bark.

Most trees need a yearly trim in the spring, before the buds swell. (Black walnut, birch, and maple trees are exceptions; their sap will bleed in the spring, so they should be pruned in the early fall.) The side shoots, dead and unwanted branches should all go. If an orchard tree is still young, some careful attention will save it from the kind of fate that struck my crab apples. First of all, the strength of a fruit tree's branch is determined by the angle at which the limb meets the trunk. The wider the angle the stronger the tree's wood and the abler it is to support heavy crops without breaking. Young trees should be pruned to make the most of that wide growth, and also to thin out the interior branches of the tree so that sunshine can easily reach all the fruit. Tree fruit needs sunshine for sweetness.

Grafting: One March I was given a young apple tree by a friend. It was the perfect time of year for grafting, so I decided to set the tree in the Victory Garden to demonstrate the techniques on the show. Although it seems to scare gardeners away, grafting is a simple job with a great payoff: a single tree that produces several different varieties of the same fruit. It's a great idea for gardeners who crave variety but don't have the space for five different trees. I will admit that they're rather peculiar looking when the branches blossom at different times through the spring, but that's part of the fun of it.

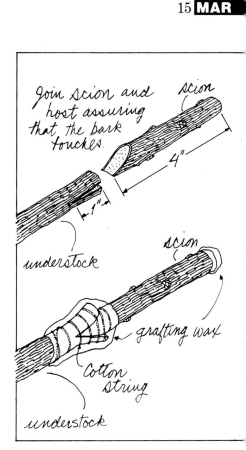

I brought in the tips from several branches of trees in my own yard — McIntosh, Gravenstein, Blue Pearmain, Golden Delicious, Roxbury Russet — none larger than a pencil, to graft to this young tree. These branch tips are called scions; you probably have a friend who owns an apple tree who would gladly share one of these tiny branches with you. If you're interested in the old-time varieties, they're available through the Worcester (Massachusetts) Horticultural Society.

I picked out five well-spaced branches around the periphery of the tree so the new varieties would be evenly distributed around the tree. Then I grafted each of the five branches, one at a time. First I removed all the spurs from the branch so that the energy would go to the grafted variety. I cut off the top half of the branch, which in the case of this tree was about 12 inches, and used a very sharp knife to slice down carefully through the center of the branch about 1 inch deep. (Take it easy with this cut. Don't graft your fingers, too.) Then I cut a 4-inch section from the center of the scion and sharpened the bottom end of this section into a wedge 1 inch long, taking care to leave the bark along the sides of the wedge, and I inserted the wedge into the slice on the stem. The object here is to put growing tissue in contact with growing tissue, with the bark as protection, so the bark of the scion and the bark of the twig should touch, at least on one side. I secured the union by wrapping a length of cotton string around it, and then painted the entire area with hot grafting wax to seal out the air. I touched a little of the wax to the tip of the grafted section, too, to prevent loss of moisture. (This wax congeals very quickly, so I use a charcoal burner in the garden to keep it hot and liquid.)

Throughout the first growing season I removed all the buds from the parent branches in order to force the tree's energy into making these grafts develop into branches. During that first summer the grafts grew nearly 2 feet, and they began to bear fruit during their second year.

Hollyhocks I'm hard-pressed to think of a summer flower more commanding than the hollyhock, with its 5- to

Majorette hollyhock, an annual variety

Opposite: A late summer harvest, with giant Musselburgh leeks in command

7-foot spikes of white, yellow, pink, or deep maroon blossoms that open over a two-month period. But there won't be a single healthy hollyhock in the perennial border in the summer unless I give them some special care the minute the snow is off the ground in March. I take off all the leaves, even those that are beginning to grow, and remove all this foliage from the garden. Then when the new growth appears I spray once a week for six weeks with agricultural sulfur, Maneb, or Ferbam, any of which is available in a garden center. I repeat this routine in the fall just before the ground freezes, and the hollyhocks will be free of the much-feared rust that raises brown spots all over the leaves and ruins so many of these plants.

The annual hollyhocks that I sowed in February are ready to harden off in March so I set them out into the cold frame to adjust to the cool weather.

Irises The iris borer is a dreaded pest in the Northeast: it can easily devastate whole plantings of iris, particularly the very vulnerable bearded iris. Left to its own devices the borer pupates in the summer and emerges as a moth in the fall to lay vast numbers of minute eggs on the outer leaves of the iris plant. By May of the next year the plant's new leaves look watery. For many gardeners this is the first sign of trouble, and it's already too late for a solution: it means that the borers are at work within the leaves and are chewing their way down to hollow out the plant's fat roots, known as rhizomes. As if that weren't bad enough, the roots then fall prey to a secondary infection that produces an evil-smelling rot.

I use a two-part defense to protect the perennial border's bearded iris from this unhappy fate. In March, before the plants begin to grow, I pick up all the fallen foliage from the ground and cut the plants back to about 4 inches from the ground. Then once a week until the flowers open I spray with malathion or diazinon, directing the spray toward the bottom half of the leaves. A little liquid soap or detergent added to this solution helps it adhere to the foliage. In November I clean the area again and burn all the dead leaves to destroy any eggs that have been deposited on the foliage during the fall.

Leeks Any week during the summer that I harvest a leek on camera, I am guaranteed to receive dozens of comments from awed viewers. Big as baseball bats (well, nearly), with long white tips, they really are an eye-popping crop. And one of the reasons is that I give them a good jump on the growing season by sowing seeds in the hotbed in February, and sowing another crop indoors in early March.

For my demonstration purposes I only need about a dozen plants, so I put only a few pinches of seeds into a 6-inch pot filled with commercial potting soil or soilless mix. Later in the month I transplant the seedlings into a seed flat at 1-inch spacing. Most of these seeds germinate, so the transplanting of these tiny individual blades is a tedious job if the seeds have been sown too close together. The seedlings will grow rapidly in a sunny spot in the greenhouse or hotbed.

Because leeks do so well in the hotbed, I usually plant an insurance crop right in the hotbed soil in March. Later in the month I thin the seedlings to 1-inch intervals and leave them in the hotbed until they're ready for transplanting into the open garden in April.

Lettuce This is one of the standby crops of the early spring Victory Garden. Every variety of lettuce grows quickly and thrives in the cool weather, so I always make sure to have small crops on hand to move into the garden whenever I can.

Our lettuce season begins in February, with a sowing in the hotbed. In March I sow a second crop, putting about a dozen seeds into a 4-inch pot filled with potting soil and covering them lightly with ⅛ inch of milled sphagnum moss. Bottom-watered, drained, and kept indoors in the sun, the seedlings will be up in just a few days. Lettuce also does beautifully in the hotbed, so I sow a sparse, short row there, too. Whether in the greenhouse or in the hotbed, the little seedlings will need to be transferred to individual compartments in six-packs or thinned after a couple of weeks to prevent crowding.

Onions There are three ways to grow onions in the garden: from seeds, from transplants, and from sets. We've tried all three in the Victory Garden, and we've found that each has its advantages and disadvantages.

I don't sow seeds of ordinary onions directly into the open soil in the Victory Garden because the soil dries out too quickly to produce a good crop. But I do sow the fast-maturing bunching onions, or scallions, outdoors in early April. If we want full-sized onions from seed we have to give the crop a two-month jump on the growing season by starting the seedlings in the hotbed or greenhouse in February. The advantage to starting from seed, whether in February or April, is that seeds are much cheaper than sets, and all varieties are available.

Onion sets are immature onion bulbs. They're grown from seed one year, harvested early and stored under controlled conditions, and then sold in the spring. They're expensive, and only those varieties that tolerate long periods of storage can be handled in this way, so the choice is limited. But they're easy and foolproof, and they're the first of the season's harvest. All in all, they're probably the best bet for home gardeners.

I plant the sets in March. First I work 5-10-5 into the soil. Then I plant 2 rows, 2 inches apart, gently pressing the sets down into the soft soil at 2-inch intervals until the tips are just under the surface. This is a dense planting, but we pull every other one as scallions later in the spring, leaving half the crop to mature into full-sized onions. After planting, I water the row with a diazinon and water mixture to protect the crop from the ravages of the root maggots.

The pots of seedlings that I sow in February need a little attention in March: I transplant the seedlings into large containers, setting them in with 1 inch space all around so they won't be crowded as they wait for the weather to become warm enough for outdoor transplanting.

Parsley This is not only one of the most familiar and popular of the herbs, it is one of the most prolific. It is in fact a biennial but it's grown as an annual: we harvest the leaves

A pot of parsley

all summer long and then pot the plants up to produce their tender foliage indoors through the winter.

Parsley seeds are slow to germinate; sometimes it can be three weeks or more before there's a sign of growth above the soil. So to encourage them to sprout more rapidly I soften the seeds by soaking them in lukewarm water for several hours before planting. Then I put 3 or 4 seeds into 3-inch peat pots filled with soilless mix and keep them moist during their entire germination time. In early May, when they are bushy young plants, I set them out into the garden.

Peas I don't think there's anything more satisfying for me than walking out into the garden in March, through the last few patches of snow, to plant the year's first crop of peas. The cold weather won't hurt them at all, and planting them this early means they'll mature before the onslaught of hot weather, and they'll be all the sweeter for it. Like corn, peas begin to lose their sweetness the moment they're picked, which is why frozen and canned peas are usually better tasting than old but "fresh" peas that occasionally show up in grocery store produce sections.

As with all legumes, peas can take nitrogen directly from the air by enlisting the aid of soil bacteria, so before I plant them I moisten the seeds with water and then dust them with a powdered legume inoculant, which gives the seeds ready access to those needed soil bacteria. (Various legume inoculants are available at garden centers and through seed catalogs.) This is all the nourishment the crop will need beyond the fall soil preparation, so I don't add any additional commercial fertilizers before planting.

Pea seeds planted tightly in a trench

Most seed catalogs and gardening literature advise a thin sowing of peas, but you'll never hear me say that. I've been planting them close together in thick rows since I was a child, and I've learned that if you are stingy with your peas they'll be stingy with you. Not only is the yield greater with the thicker sowing, but the dense foliage forms its own natural support as the peas grow, and needs only a minimum of help on that score from the gardener.

So I begin with a trench about 4 inches deep and 6 inches wide, sowing the seeds across the bottom of the trench so that some actually touch each other and others are no more than 1 inch apart. Then I use a hoe to pull about 1 inch of soil over the seeds, and tamp the soil down. The dwarf varieties, which grow only 15 inches tall or so, need no further support than their own dense growth provides. And the taller varieties do very well with an old country trick known to experienced gardeners as "pea brush." Just after I sow the seeds and hoe the soil over, I stick the dead, leafless branches of deciduous trees or shrubs into the soil through the middle of the

A young crop of peas with pea brush

pea trench, forming a continuous natural trellis. As the plants grow they wind around the brush, making expensive wire or plastic netting unnecessary.

As the season advances and the plants grow, I pull soil in from the sides of the trench to keep the roots cool and deep. Let me pass along a tip for an early pea harvest: cultivate lightly at least once a week, keeping the top ½ inch of soil around the plants loose, and pull some of this soil up around the base of the plants. I find it speeds the pea harvest by ten days or so.

Of course a pea trench is only a possibility in March if the soil is dry enough to work, and that is not always the case, so I take precautions against a wet spring by preparing a row in the fall for a simplified, and early, planting of peas. In November, I prepare the soil in a row that borders one of the Victory Garden's paths. Then in the spring, as soon as the soil is thawed enough to work (even if it's still quite wet), I lay the pea seeds over the soil, making sure they're treated with captan to prevent rotting, and push them in with my finger until they're about 1 inch deep. The cool, wet soil won't harm the seeds in the least, and this method of planting won't harm the soil.

Commercial growers have their own method of pea-sowing. It requires far more space than I have in the Victory Garden, but it is perfectly suited to home gardeners if there's room enough, and it produces the highest yield of any sowing method. There is no trenching involved. Instead, after the soil is thoroughly prepared for planting, the seeds are broadcast throughout an entire area with no thought to rows or pattern. Then the seeds are covered by drawing a cultivator through the bed; some of the seeds are left exposed, but the loss is negligible. If you're thinking of giving this a try, use low-growing varieties that are easily self-supporting. When the peas are ready, just walk into the patch and pick your bountiful harvest. Don't worry about the damage your feet may be doing; the yield is so great with this approach that the loss is easily affordable. After the final harvest, either till or dig the vines into the soil, or pull them and add them to your composter.

Radishes For years I gave up growing early radishes at all because I could never seem to win the battle against root maggots, the scourge of many early root crops. But with the coming of diazinon, the one and only root maggot insecticide I've found effective, I've changed my spring planting lineup to include radishes. In fact, I even start the first crop in March, although in New England the crop needs protection from the weather this early in the year, so I plant either in a hotbed or under a cloche. (For more on both of these weather-beaters, and the cold frame as well, see pages 26–29.)

For the cloche planting I begin by working 10-10-10 into the soil, and then sprinkling the seeds down a ½-inch-deep furrow, keeping the row to a short 5 feet so the harvest is manageable. Then I water the row with a diazinon mixture after I close the furrow, and I repeat the diazinon again in 3 to 5 days. For most crops I continue the diazinon applications at 10-day intervals throughout the growing season but radishes mature so quickly and diazinon stays active for so long (during which time the crop is inedible), that I forgo the repeated applications and hope the double dose at planting time will take care of the maggots.

Spinach This vegetable can stand any amount of cold weather. I put in the first of our crop as soon as the ground can be worked in the spring, but spinach is so hardy that if planted in the fall it winters-over just waiting for the first warm weather in the spring, when it begins to germinate. It doesn't grow during freezing weather, but it isn't

Spinach seedlings

damaged either. On the other hand it has no tolerance for hot weather at all; it goes to seed as soon as the summer days arrive. So we grow it in the Victory Garden during the spring and fall and satisfy our summer spinach cravings with New Zealand spinach, a heat-tolerant spinach substitute.

I buy new spinach seeds every year, as they do not store well for long periods of time. Before I sow them I sprinkle 10-10-10 fertilizer through the row to supply the high nitrogen the crop will need for healthy leaf growth. Then I sow the seeds lightly about 1 inch apart into a ½-inch-deep furrow. I say lightly because next month's thinning will be a chore if the seeds are sown too close together. After sowing I close the furrow and water the row.

Turnips Somewhere along the line, sad to say, turnips have developed something of a peasant reputation, and although many people are familiar with these vegetables, few gardeners grow them anymore. Which is a shame, as they're a simple crop, and tasty, and they provide the spring garden with one of its first stripes of green.

As with so many root crops, turnips will be devoured by root maggots unless something is done to prevent this, so after I sow the seeds at 1-inch intervals along a ½-inch-deep furrow, I water the row with a mixture of water and diazinon. This keeps the maggots at bay for the first week or two but then it loses its strength, so I repeat the diazinon applications at 10-day intervals throughout the growing season. This is far too important to be careless about; the maggots develop from eggs laid by an inconspicuous ¼-inch fly, and diazinon is, in my opinion, the most effective defense against them. It does require cautious use though; the crops can't be eaten within two weeks of a diazinon application, so I stop the diazinon routine two weeks shy of harvest.

Q&A

Q: Last summer I pulled up a lot of witch grass and put it in my compost pile. Can I put this compost on my garden this year, or will the witch grass start growing all over again?

A: I'd suggest that you sift your compost to remove the roots of the witch grass. They're white, about $1/16$ inch in diameter, and there are buds at close intervals. Bury them deep in a new compost pile to give them another season of decay. If you don't you will indeed have witch grass in your garden again this year.

Q: We live on a hillside facing south and west in western Massachusetts. I'm having a hard time convincing my father that nut trees would be a good investment.

A: I'm with your father. In your climate, although you'll be able to grow a Carpathian walnut, a hickory, a butternut, or a black walnut, the squirrels will make off with whatever insignificant yield you may have. Nut trees just can't be grown commercially so far north.

Q: I have a dozen tulip bulbs that I never got around to planting last fall. They wintered in my unheated garage. Can I plant them now and expect flowers?

A: Yes, you can plant them; no, you can't expect flowers. But you may produce enough foliage to mature the bulbs so you can store them properly until planting time next fall and have flowering bulbs next year.

Q: I'm starting my first vegetable garden this year. Can you give me any advice about siting the garden in my yard?

A: The primary thing you need is sunshine, at least 6 hours a day and the more the better. Orient the garden's rows on a north-south axis so each crop will have the benefit of full sun. Avoid nearby trees, not only because they'll shade your plants but because they'll soak up an enormous amount of the soil's moisture. Make sure there's adequate drainage to the site: low, swampy areas dry out slowly if at all. Locate your garden with a watering source nearby so it'll be simple to keep the soil properly watered.

UNDER GLASS

The growing season is never long enough. No matter where they live, gardeners are forever searching for ways to earn another few weeks, another month. One way to do this is by setting out 6-week-old seedlings, rather than sowing seeds outdoors as soon as weather permits. It's possible, of course, to buy seedlings from garden centers. I've had to do this at times myself, but I much prefer, for several reasons, to start my own seedlings. It's inexpensive both in money and time, and it allows you to grow those special varieties you can't always buy at garden centers. Frankly, it's more satisfying too.

The logical location for fledgling plants is on the sunniest windowsill in the house, and in fact this spot has seen gardeners through many a spring, and continues to do so. But it's not really the best of all possible worlds. For one thing, the space is limited. For another, no matter how sunny the window is, it can only be sunny for part of the day, and plants prefer full days of sunshine. Another drawback is that the plants grow in constant warmth. To do best, they need warm days and cool nights to develop rugged growth. Seedlings demand constant moisture, too, which is hard to manage in the dry atmosphere and heat indoors.

All of which brings me to three pieces of simple, inexpensive and portable outdoor equipment that provide the

temperature and light the seedlings need. We use all three in the Victory Garden, each to meet different needs.

Cold frame Of all these tools I'd have to say that the cold frames are the most indispensable in the Victory Garden. They're really no more than glass- or plastic-covered boxes that store the sun's heat while giving the gardener some control over temperatures with

ventilation. We have several cold frames in almost constant use all year long. In the spring we use them to harden-off seedlings; the cool weather will toughen their cell structure and give them more of a chance in the garden. We also use cold frames all through the growing season for growing plants on from smaller containers, and we often use the cold frames as nursery beds during the summer, too. During the winter we

Materials

½-inch exterior-grade plywood	4' × 4' panel (for box)
1" × 1" common pine	2 1-foot lengths (for ventilator stakes)
1" × 3" common pine	4 4-foot lengths (for cover frame)
26-inch-wide translucent or clear stock corrugated fiberglass	2 4-foot lengths (for cover surface)
Stock corrugated redwood molding to fit fiberglass	3 4-foot lengths (for cover frame)
1½" half-round molding	2 4-foot lengths (for cover frame)

Hardware

2" × 2" loose-pin backflap hinges (use galvanized or brass hardware to prevent rust)	8 (for corners of box)
2" angle irons	4 (for corners of cover frame)
4" loose-pin strap hinges	2 (to secure cover to box)
¾" flat head stove bolts/washers	(for hinges)
¾" #8 round head wood screws with washers, or pan head screws	(to secure fiberglass to corrugated molding at front of cover)
1¼" #8 flat head wood screws	(for redwood molding)
¾" #8 flat head wood screws	(for angle irons)

Building the Cold Frame

The cold frame is nothing but a box with a hinged lid. The walls of the box are cut as shown from a sheet of ½-inch exterior plywood and assembled with two 2" × 2" loose-pin hinges at each corner. Ventilation is provided by two stakes, screwed in slightly off-center to allow the stakes to swivel into two different positions.

The cover is a sandwich of sorts, assembled on a frame of 1" × 3" pine. The second layer consists of two lengths of corrugated redwood molding along the top and bottom and halfround redwood molding along the sides. The third layer is two panels of fiberglass, overlapped in the center. Finally, the sandwich is secured with a 4-foot length of corrugated redwood across the top, fastened to the back of the box with large loose-pin hinges. The hinges have to be bent to a 90-degree angle to wrap around the top of the cover; smaller hinges will fit more neatly but won't be sturdy enough. (The design for the cold frame has evolved over several seasons in the Victory Garden. The only remaining hitch is that the cover will not flip all the way back to rest on the ground, so we drive stakes into the soil behind the frame; the fully opened cover rests on these stakes and takes the pressure off the hinges.)

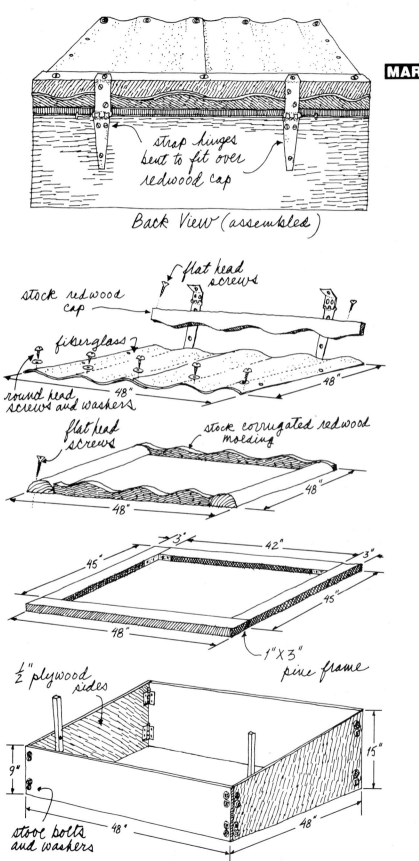

Back View (assembled)

strap hinges bent to fit over redwood cap

flat head screws

stock redwood cap

fiberglass

round head screws and washers

48"

48"

flat head screws

stock corrugated redwood molding

48"

48"

3"

42"

45"

3"

45"

48"

1" × 3" pine frame

½" plywood sides

15"

9"

stove bolts and washers

48"

48"

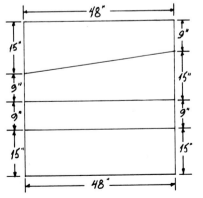

48"

15"

9"

9"

15"

9"

15"

15"

48"

store tender plants in cold frames, and give spring-flowering bulbs such as tulips, hyacinths, daffodils, and crocuses the controlled temperatures they need to make strong roots so we can bring them indoors and force them into bloom in midwinter.

In the spring, temperature is the critical element in the cold frame. To keep plants growing well, I want to maintain night temperatures of about 45 degrees and daytime readings in the mid 70s. Rather than guessing at the temperature, I keep a thermometer inside each of the frames and check it regularly.

If the day is sunny and the temperature is in the 40s, I open the vent about 6 inches. But if the outdoor temperature is around 60, I open the cover completely. Then, toward the middle of the afternoon, I close the cover to trap the day's heat and, in freezing weather, pull a water-repellent insulator over the top to keep the heat inside.

I use the cold frames all winter long, too. This not only gives me a place to winter-over some of the bulbs, herbs, and perennials, but it leaves the cold frames in place so they're all set and ready to go first thing in the spring. During the winter months the goal in cold-frame culture is to maintain temperatures just above freezing. This low-temperature storage holds plants in a sort of suspended animation until spring. Heat from the sun should be prevented from entering; otherwise plants begin to grow prematurely. So along in October I hill-up around the outside walls of the frames with soil or leaves. Then I watch the weather forecasts closely. Just before the ground freezes, I cover the frames with sturdy water-repellent tarpaulins as protection against the snows.

This outer insulation is enough for many of the wintering-over plants, but if I feel the need for one last precaution, I mulch the plants inside the frames with peat moss or salt marsh hay or leaves.

Hotbed We're blessed with a beautiful greenhouse in the Victory Garden but for many gardeners this is a luxury beyond reach. Happily there's an inexpensive alternative, and while hotbeds are nowhere near the size of greenhouses, they can be used in the same way.

A hotbed is simply a cold frame with heat. Years ago a layer of fermenting horse manure provided this heat; now the job is done by plastic heating cables. We selected a bright, sunny spot in our garden for the hotbed and began by excavating an area 4 feet square and 1 foot deep. On the bottom we put 4 inches of coarse gravel to provide drainage. Ordinarily the heating cable is laid directly on the

gravel, but I've found that the stiff plastic is difficult to arrange evenly and keep in place. To solve this problem, I laid a sheet of ⅛-inch pegboard over the gravel, treated side down, then stapled the cable to the pegboard to keep it in place.

To protect the cables from an unwitting jab with a trowel or spade I laid a 4-foot-square sheet of ½-inch galvanized hardware cloth over them. This isn't an absolute necessity, but I highly recommend it. Over the hardware cloth I spread 2 inches of coarse builders' sand to help distribute the heat evenly through the 6 inches of planting medium, a combination of equal parts peat moss, topsoil, and sand, that I add as the final layer.

Then when the cold-frame structure is placed over the heated foundation, the hotbed is ready for seeds. I sow many of the early spring crops here as early as February, so I can set out sturdy seedlings as soon as the weather permits. I usually

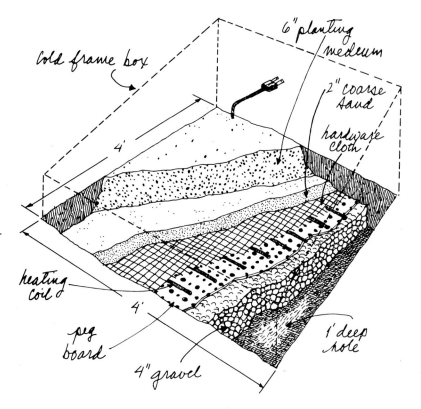

fill the hotbed with these crops planted in short, closely spaced rows. The plants are here for such a short time that they don't need much room, and every bit is precious.

Hotbed cables have thermostats that prevent the temperatures from falling below 68 degrees, but they have no way to take care of overheating in sunny weather, so the hotbeds need the same ventilation attention the cold frames do. They also need the added insulating carpet at night to trap the heat being produced. And because the bottom heat dries the soil quickly the hotbed crops need a watering check every day. Those seeds just can't be allowed to dry out.

Cloche A cloche is a protective structure for an entire garden row. It's a particularly handy piece of equipment because it makes it possible to sow a crop in its permanent garden location long before the weather is in fact suitable. Cloches have been in use in England and on the Continent for many years but are just now being discovered by American gardeners. They are especially helpful for plants that don't take well to transplanting .

But the cloche crops do need some watchful attention.

For instance, cloches need ventilation to prevent overheating on sunny days. They can be lifted off entirely or the ends can be removed to allow hot air to escape. What is more, the cloche warmth is persuading the soil that late spring has arrived, and the soil dries out

quickly as a result. So I raise the cloches every couple of days to make sure that the seeds are getting the moisture they need.

The cloches in my garden are of a very inexpensive and simple construction based on a design borrowed from my counterparts at the BBC. Essentially, when in use the cloches constitute a tunnel constructed in sections. Each section is made from a 26 inch × 4 foot panel of corrugated fiberglass, secured into a semicircular position with stiff wiring. The fiberglass transmits light nearly as efficiently as glass and is all but unbreakable. The wiring projects off the bottom edge of the fiberglass to give each section legs to stick into the soil to hold it in place. A pair of crosswires keeps the fiberglass bowed into the shape of a Quonset hut.

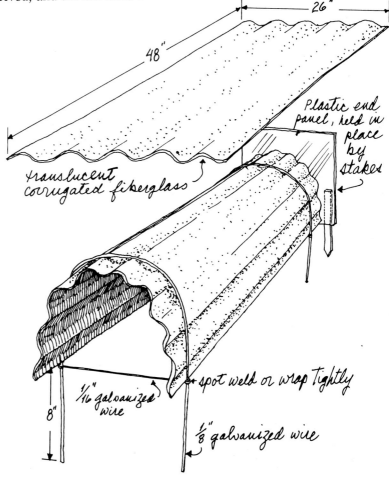

26"

48"

Plastic end panel, held in place by stakes

translucent corrugated fiberglass

spot weld or wrap tightly

1/16" galvanized wire

8"

1/8" galvanized wire

Buttercrunch and Ruby lettuce

APR

Plant
Beets
Carrots
Corn
Dill
Endive
Gladioluses
Jerusalem Artichoke
Kohlrabi
Lettuce
Parsnips
Peas
Potatoes
Radishes
Spinach
Swiss Chard

Transplant
Beets
Broccoli
Cabbage
Cauliflower
Clematis
Daylilies
Foxglove
Fruit Trees
Leeks
Lettuce
Onions
Pansies
Raspberries
Roses
Strawberries

Start Seedlings
Cucumbers
Eggplants
Melons
New Zealand Spinach
Okra
Onions
Peppers
Squash
Tomatoes

Thin
Kohlrabi
Onions
Spinach
Swiss Chard

Special Events
Spring Lawn Care

APR

April begins in the Victory Garden with cool, moist weather. Early in the month the rain is abundant and the temperatures range from the upper 40s during the day down to the chilly 20s at night. Toward the end of the month, the average day and night temperatures will have risen ten degrees, and the rain will taper off. On cloudless days the sun is strong and hot.

This is perfect planting weather, making April one of the busiest months in the Victory Garden, May being the only other candidate for this honor. Busy as this month always is, though, I hope I never have another April like our first. The show was scheduled to go on the air on April 16, but I didn't return from a business trip to the West Coast until April 1, and for both the show's producer, Russ Morash, and me, the intervening two weeks are nothing but a blur now. The greenhouse that had been loaned to us was only partially (or, as the joke goes around the station, parsley) finished. We did have our seeds on hand, but we hadn't had time to start our own seedlings and had to buy them from a garden center. Worst of all, the soil hadn't been prepared. I hope no one ever encounters such obstinate clay, so many rocks, so much broken glass, or the bricks, mortar, and other debris — including a tire and muffler — that we hauled from the soil. Every day we worked on the soil, from dawn till darkness and then some, but the show went on as planned, one exhausted man in front of the camera and one behind.

Beets Beets can go into the Victory Garden anytime in April and I usually plant several early varieties, along with a main season variety. If beets are to be tender and juicy rather than tough and woody, they have to be well fed and well watered, so before sowing I work 5-10-5 fertilizer into the soil. To increase garden production, I sow two ½-inch furrows 4 to 6 inches apart, and space the seeds at 1-inch intervals. As with all seeds, I'm especially careful to keep the soil moist through the germination time.

In addition to the beets I sow directly into the open garden in April, it's time to transplant the beets I sowed in the hotbed in February; they have had two months of warm, pampered growth and are a sturdy 2 inches tall. With this head start they'll be ready for harvest and fresh borsch by early June. I put the seedlings in at 3-inch intervals and in

Freshly picked beets at their tenderest size

order to get the most from the garden, I plant them in double rows 6 inches apart. They'll be in a slight state of shock after this move, but a drink of transplant solution will help them get over it.

Broccoli   Broccoli is a part of the cabbage family, and like its relatives it's a plant the old-time gardeners call a gross feeder: it produces succulent growth only if the soil has been given a strong boost. So I begin by digging in about 2 inches of well-rotted cow manure and then add 10-10-10 fertilizer (5 pounds to 100 square feet) to provide continuing food for the plants as they grow. Broccoli is vulnerable to a disease called clubroot, so I add additional ground limestone to the soil, about 4 handfuls to a 6-foot row, which inhibits the clubroot growth.

Then the soil is ready for the husky seedlings that have been in the protection of the cold frame since March. I set them into the soil at 18-inch intervals because they are well nourished, and will spread wide when fully grown. (In the Victory Garden I plant only one row of broccoli, but if I were to plant more, I'd space the rows 3 feet apart.) While the broccoli plants are young, there is space available between them, so I alternate each broccoli with a lettuce seedling that will be harvested before the broccoli demands the space.

Cabbage-family crops have their difficulties with a variety of pests, but if the right precautions are taken, the plants will do just fine. The cutworm is particularly dangerous to the tender stems of young seedlings, so after I've set the seedlings in, I give each a cutworm collar. Then to protect the plants from an insidious April arrival, the imported cabbageworm caterpillar, I spray the plants with *Bacillus thuringiensis* at 7- to 10-day intervals, a routine I continue until the harvest. The root maggot is our main worry in the Victory Garden: given free rein, it would easily demolish the roots of 40 to 80 percent of our crops. The whole country suffered from root maggot problems until diazinon came along. So I add diazinon to the transplant solution when the plants are newly set in, and then repeat the diazinon applications at 10-day intervals to keep the problem under control. For gardeners who would prefer not to use diazinon, a chemical, on their garden, the root maggots can also be controlled with a root maggot mat, a physical barrier that will control cutworms too. There is more information about these pests and the defenses against them on pages 152–157.

All the cabbage family crops are at their most tender if they've grown with a healthy supply of nitrogen, so I sidedress all the cabbage-related crops every 3 or 4 weeks through their growing season. I use about ½ pound of 10-10-10 to a 10-foot row, scattering it in two broad bands on both sides of the row. If there's a mulch on the soil the fertilizer will sift down through it; if not, I barely scratch the fertilizer into the soil and then water the row to dissolve it and make it available to the plants. All the cabbage plants have shallow root systems, so the cultivation around them should never go any deeper than ½ inch.

A young cabbage plant about to head up

Cabbage Cabbage needs nutritious soil if it is to produce a delicate, tender head, so I work in 2 inches of well-rotted cow manure or compost, and 10-10-10 fertilizer (5 pounds to 100 square feet) to keep the plants well fed during their entire growth. Then to help the plants ward off clubroot disease, I work ground limestone into the soil, about 4 handfuls to a 6-foot row, and the ground is ready.

The cabbage seedlings I set out in April have been in the cold frame since March. I put them in at 18-inch intervals with 3 feet between the rows, as they will demand all this space when they have their full growth. In the meantime, there is ample room to grow a lettuce crop between the cabbage plants.

Cabbage plants face the same dangers that broccoli does, so I give these plants the same protection: a cutworm collar to defend the plants' tender stems; *Bacillus thuringiensis* at 7- to 10-day intervals to control the cabbageworm caterpillar; and diazinon at 10-day intervals to control root maggots. I've had good luck with a root maggot mat, which controls not only the maggots but the cutworm and replaces chemical insecticides. All these insects, and the preventive routines, are described in more detail on pages 152–157.

Once the seedlings are set in, I give each plant a drink of transplant solution. If I'm using diazinon, I put it right in this solution to make sure the plants are well protected as soon as they're in the garden.

Carrots Many seed catalogues don't mention this, but the long, slender carrot varieties produced by commercial growers require a soil so soft, deep, and smooth that they are all but impossible for many home gardeners to grow. In the Victory Garden, where the soil contains not only rocks but impervious blue clay, it would be folly even to try these varieties. Instead, I plant one of the solid, chunky, blunt-tipped carrot varieties of the type known as Half-long. These stubbier varieties are every bit as tender and tasty as the longer ones.

Carrots can be sown as early in the spring as the soil can be worked, which, in this garden, is March or April. I dig the soil over, the full depth of the spading fork — at least 8 inches — loosening it and removing any rocks bigger than 1 inch in diameter. Then I work 5-10-5 fertilizer (5 pounds to 100 square feet) into the top 4 or 5 inches of soil. After raking, the soil's ready for planting, but as an added precaution against compacting the soil I lay long boards between the rows to distribute my weight as I work. (I leave these boards here for the entire growing season.)

I sprinkle the seeds into a ½-inch furrow, or "drill" in garden terminology, trying to space them every ½ to ¼ inch or so. This is no mean task. The seeds are tiny and they cling to everything, including my hands. It's well worth the effort to space them carefully, though, as this cuts down on the thinning operation, which can be arduous.

There won't be a sign of these carrots for at least three weeks, but there certainly will be weeds. So I sow a few radish seeds in the furrow, right along with the carrot seeds. The radishes will be up in a week, identifying the carrot row so I won't pull the young carrots as I weed. About a week after the carrot tops break through the soil, the radishes will be ready for harvest.

Cauliflower Cauliflower is another member of the cabbage family, and is treated precisely as are broccoli and cabbage. The soil is prepared with 2 inches of well-rotted cow manure or compost, 10-10-10 fertilizer (5 pounds to 100 square feet) to provide the plants with continuing nourishment, and ground limestone, 4 handfuls for a 6-foot row, to help the plants fight clubroot disease.

The seedlings I set out in April were sown in early March and have been in a cold frame to toughen their growth or "harden-off." I plant them at 18-inch intervals, 3 feet between the rows, to give them room to grow. Then I set in lettuce seedlings between the cauliflower; the lettuce will be on the table before the cauliflower begins to need the space.

Then I begin the routines to protect the plants from the varieties of voracious pests that will demolish the crop if allowed. I put a cutworm collar around each plant. I give each plant a dose of *Bacillus thuringiensis*, a regimen I continue at 7- to 10-day intervals until harvest to control the imported cabbageworm caterpillar. Then to protect the crop from the most dangerous of all the pests, the root maggot, I add diazinon to the transplant solution, and repeat the diazinon applications at 10-day intervals throughout the growing season. I've been pleased with the results of the root maggot mat, a nonchemical alternative to the diazinon applications. This will not only control the maggots, but the cutworms as well, making the collar superfluous. (All these pests, and the defenses against them, are described on pages 152–157.)

A healthy young cauliflower plant ready for blanching

Clematis Of all the flowering vines, the clematis is one of the best for the home gardener. It will grow in either sun or light shade. It is rarely attacked by insects or diseases. And the abundant blossoms last for several weeks, in colors ranging from lavender and purple, through pink and red, to yellow and white.

There are two types of hybrid clematis, but I can grow only one of them in the Victory Garden. I can't grow the type that produces blossoms on the previous year's growth because the Victory Garden is in the part of the country where winter temperatures fall below zero degrees Fahrenheit. Such cold weather is just too much for this type of clematis: it would in all likelihood die back every winter, so I would get foliage year after year, but never see any blossoms. Instead I plant the type that produces blossoms and foliage in a single year; these vines are a little sparse in their first year, but in later years as they develop stronger crowns and root systems they just blaze with color.

I planted these vines along a border of the garden that hadn't received the soil attention that the other areas had. The first thing I did was dig a big hole for each plant, 18 inches across and 12 inches deep. Next I mixed with the soil an amount of compost equal to the bulk of the soil. Then because clematises grow best in a near-alkaline soil (pH 6.0 to 7.0), I sprinkled a dusting of ground limestone into and around the planting hole. Clematises, as the old-timers would say, like their heads in the sun and their feet in the shade, so I plant them in a sunny spot and either mulch the soil at the base of the vines or plant low annuals around them to shade and keep the roots cool.

Clematises, and other vines as well, need a support to climb on, even when they are small. Left to ramble on the ground, they make but fitful attempts at growing. When given a support they immediately take a real interest in life and grow at a gratifying rate.

Corn I know there are many home gardeners who argue that the yield of a corn crop doesn't justify the amount of room the plants take up in the garden, but that's an argument I don't swallow. This vegetable begins to lose its sweetness the moment it's picked, so even corn bought at a farmer's roadside stand won't measure up to homegrown. If you've never tasted corn a short ten steamy minutes from the stalk, by all means plant a crop and prepare for a treat.

Corn is a very heavy feeder. In fact, three hundred years ago Indian women taught the Puritan settlers to plant corn by putting a dead fish into the soil with every kernel, to feed the growing plants. Fish are in short supply in the Victory Garden but corn's need for food continues, so I dig

Clematis Jackmani in its first season

the soil over and add as thick a layer of compost as we can spare. To this, I add 10-10-10 fertilizer (5 pounds to 100 square feet).

The trick to corn production is in the planting of rows. Corn is pollinated by the wind: the pollen falls from the male tassels onto the female silk. If the corn is planted in single rows, the wind is apt simply to carry the pollen away, and the result will be corncobs incompletely filled out. So I always plant at least four rows of each variety; even so, there are problem plants at the ends of rows, where fertilization fails to occur.

In the Victory Garden, I plant several different varieties of corn, which will mature over a period of 6 weeks or

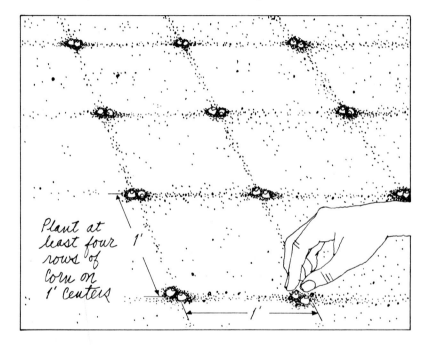

Plant at least four rows of Corn on 1' Centers

more. I love the early corn — I've waited nearly a year for it — but the later corn is sweeter. The actual planting is simple. I lay a couple of kernels on the soil about 1 inch apart, and repeat this at 12-inch intervals, spacing the rows 12 inches apart, too. Then I push the kernels about 1 inch into the soil with my finger, cover, and water.

Cucumbers Toward the end of May the weather in the Victory Garden will be mild enough to set out cucumber plants, so in mid-April I start the seeds indoors in individual peat pots. If they are to be really superior, cucumbers must grow quickly, developing mature fruit in a matter of 10 weeks. They like heat, food, and moisture, and I make sure they get them all. I sow 2 seeds ½ inch deep in a pot and keep them moist, in a warm spot (70 degrees); the seedlings pop up in about 5 days.

Dahlias Prize dahlia tubers can be extremely expensive, so I use a professional technique for getting the most from each purchased tuber. In March, I plant the tubers indoors in individual pots. Now, in April, each tuber has produced good healthy plants with several stems, which I cut and root. By the time the weather is warm enough to set the dahlias out, in May, I have at least a dozen plants from each tuber that I bought originally. They will all flower beautifully and make handsome plants just as large and attractive as though each had been grown from a costly tuber rather than from a homegrown cutting. What's more, each plant will present me in the fall with a cluster of tubers that can produce hundreds of plants another season.

Dwarf dahlias in the annual border

Daylilies Wild daylilies are graceful perennials that bear either yellow or orange blossoms. From these, plant breeders have been able to produce creams, maroons, and pinks, as well as different shades of yellow and orange, and they've also managed to extend the season, which now runs from early summer until the fall. Since these plants are so hardy and grow well in all parts of the country, the only concern in selecting them is getting the color you want.

Daylilies multiply quickly, soon making large clumps, so I put just one in my rather restricted perennial border. It will begin to bear blossoms in July and will continue to flower for a month or more, though, as the name implies, each flower lasts but a single day.

Since the soil in the perennial bed has been enriched and dug over, planting a daylily is simplicity itself. I dig a hole big enough to accommodate the root ball and position the plant, matching the soil line of the ground to the crown of the plant. All newly set plants should have the soil firmed around them. On plants as large as daylilies, I use my feet to be sure the soil is well compacted around the roots.

Dill Dill is another herb that has undergone a revolution in popularity in the last few years. It's a fragrant, flavorful plant grown both for its seeds and its leaves, and although it's costly in the markets, it's easy to grow in the garden.

Dill plants, unlike parsley and some other herbs, are annuals: after they set flowers and seeds, they die. Once a single generation of plants is allowed to go to seed in the garden, the plants will continue to come up spontaneously from year to year. For some strange reason, these bonus crops are usually stronger than those carefully sown by the gardener's hand.

Dill thrives in any well-drained, well-prepared garden soil, so long as the site is sunny. To sow the seeds I scratch a little patch of soil and scatter a few seeds over it, cover them about ¼ inch deep, and keep them moist. The plants grow to about 3 feet tall, so they may need staking in windy areas.

This April planting of dill will be ready for cucumbers and sour cream in June (what a cool summer treat that is), so I'll continue sowing a few seeds every 3 weeks or so to guarantee a fresh crop of dill all summer long.

Eggplants Eggplants are native to tropical Asia; there and in the Near East they are among the most prized of all vegetables. Most eggplants, known as aubergines to the British, have deep purple skins, but some varieties are white. They're a warm-weather crop and can't be set outdoors in the Victory Garden until June, when our evening temperatures can be expected to stay above 55 degrees. By starting the

A flourishing eggplant in flower

seeds in the greenhouse in April, 2 seeds to a pot, ½ inch deep, I can gain a good six weeks on the growing season. The seedlings will be up in about a week and a half; when it is apparent which seedling is the stronger, I clip off the weaker of the two so that only one plant will grow in each pot.

Endive Endive, sometimes called escarole, is a leafy green plant that grows and looks something like lettuce and even tastes a little like it. Grown without blanching, endive has a sharp, bitter flavor, but given the proper care it is a delicious salad green and relatively easy to grow.

Because this crop grows best in cold weather, our most successful crop is the one sown in August for harvest right up until the ground freezes, but I do plant a crop in the spring, and it does just fine as long as I sow it early enough and the weather stays cool. One year we missed being able to show the blanching technique on television because of a busy schedule; by the time we got to it, hot weather had arrived and the plants bolted and went to seed.

So in April I plant the seeds in highly organic garden soil laced with a handful of 10-10-10 for every 10 foot row. I

The productive, closely spaced Victory Garden rows

drop a pinch of seeds together at 8-inch intervals. Endives are unique in that they sprout best when the seeds are not covered; I simply press them onto the moist soil surface. In May the seedlings will be ready for thinning to 1 plant at each site.

Foxglove   Foxglove is a biennial. It produces only leaves in its first year. The plant lives over the first winter and sends up flower stalks the second year. Then it blossoms, ripens, seeds, and dies. Its botanical name is *Digitalis* and it's the source of the medicinal extract of the same name, but of course we grow it for the spectacular reward of 5-foot-tall flower spikes that appear in June and July.

Foxglove is one of a scattering of biennials that I've put into the perennial border to provide a variety of shape and color. I set in a cluster of three one-year-old plants, just about to enter their flowering stage. After setting the plants into their hole, I pressed the soil down firmly with my feet to make sure there was firm contact between the soil and the roots.

Fruit Trees   As part of my plan to make the Victory Garden more of a typical backyard plot rather than just a vegetable garden, I planted a young peach tree one April. The most important fruit tree information for the home gardener is this: buy dwarf trees, not standard-sized ones. A standard apple tree can grow to be 25 feet tall and spread 30 feet across, and will be years before it even begins to set fruit. On the other hand, dwarf trees start to bear within two or three years, and the fruit is just as big and delicious as that of the larger trees. Dwarf trees are only 6 to 8 feet tall at maturity, so you can spray and prune easily and reach almost all of the fruit just standing on the ground, which takes the hazard out of picking.

A fruit tree will be in a garden for years, and if the soil is well prepared, will produce sweet, juicy fruit year after year. So first I dig a hole that's at least a foot wider than the root ball of the tree. Then I enrich the soil I've dug out: I mix in sphagnum peat moss, at the ratio of about 1 part peat to 2 parts soil, and add a handful of 14-14-14, a slow-release fertilizer. I set the tree in the hole so that the bud union, the crook on the stem, is just above the final grade. I add about one third of the soil mixture, firming it down with my foot; then I add the rest of the soil, and firm it down. Obviously this firming process is critical — no plant will grow if the soil is loose around the root. Once the tree is settled I build the excess soil into a sort of shallow bowl around the base of the tree's trunk to hold the water that I give it at planting and regularly every week during its first summer.

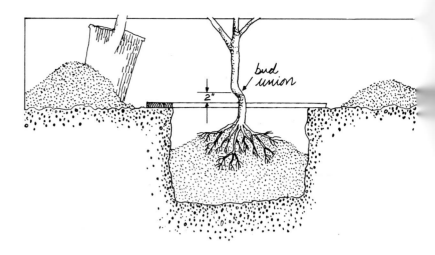

bud union

2"

Now for the part that makes many a gardener cringe: I cut the branches of the tree back so they are no more than 2-inch stubs growing from the main trunk. If I didn't, the tree wouldn't make it through the summer, because the root system has been radically abbreviated during removal from the nursery and can't continue to support this extensive top growth. All stone fruit trees — plums, nectarines, peaches, cherries, apricots — must be pruned severely at planting time for this reason. No cause for despair, though, as the tree will respond to this surgery with a new spurt of growth and an early production of fruit.

Gladioluses Near the end of April I put in my first gladioluses, and I continue to plant a few more every couple of weeks until early July, which gives the Victory Garden a continuous display of glads for most of the summer and early fall. In our fertile soil these natives of South Africa will reach a height of about 5 feet at maturity. A single plant will bloom for about a week or 10 days, losing the lower florets on the stem as upper ones open.

Gladioluses grow from corms that are sometimes mistakenly called bulbs. The concave side of the corm is the bottom, but if it's planted upside down it will still grow.

Three times the thickness of the corm: that's the easy formula for determining the right planting depth of glads. First I scatter a small handful of bone meal (0-14-0) over the soil and use my trowel to make the planting holes. I arrange the holes randomly, about 4 inches apart, so the glads will grow in clusters, not rows. After a couple of weeks they send their straight green swords up through the ground.

Jerusalem Artichokes The Jerusalem artichoke is not an artichoke and it isn't from Jerusalem. It's a rank, weedy-looking, tuberous-rooted sunflower that grows in the wild over much of the North American continent. It was a favorite among the Indians and is popular abroad, but it's only recently being rediscovered by American gardeners. The edible part of the plant is the nubby root, or tuber, 3 to 4 inches long and thinly covered with a fragile tan or lavender skin. It can be cooked a number of ways, but I'm partial to those that are slowly roasted with lamb.

These plants thrive along roadside ditches and in meadows, but their roots won't grow large unless they are planted in rich soil and given enough moisture. One year a single one-ounce tuber planted in the fertile soil next to the Victory Garden's compost pile yielded ten pounds of roots at harvesttime in the fall. And this from a tuber we bought from a grocery store produce department (though seedsmen do occasionally stock them).

I chose a sunny isolated spot at the north side of the garden for our Jerusalem artichokes because they can easily grow to 8 feet tall, shading nearby small plants. I plant the tubers about 2 feet apart and about 4 inches deep. Once planted they live indefinitely because it's nearly impossible to find all the tubers in the fall digging, and those bypassed will sprout spontaneously the following spring.

Jerusalem artichokes in flower in late summer

Kohlrabi Most gardeners' familiarity with kohlrabi is limited to what they read in seed catalogues, and that's too bad because this odd-looking member of the cabbage family is tasty and easy to grow. The edible portion of the plant is its swollen stem, which is ready for harvest when it grows to

about the size of a tennis ball. Kohlrabies grow throughout the summer, so I plant my first crop in April, followed by small plantings at 2-week intervals until late August.

The best kohlrabies are those that grow fast in highly organic, well-fertilized soil, and are kept well watered. When I plant a row of kohlrabies, I sow a pinch of seeds ½ inch deep at 6-inch intervals. They're ready for thinning to single plants at each 6-inch spacing in 2 weeks, and for harvest in 10 weeks. If they take longer than 10 weeks to mature, they have not had sufficient moisture and fertilizer and they will be tough and poor of flavor.

Lawn Care There was an untended corner adjacent to the Victory Garden that looked the way untended lawns usually look. There was a scattering of perfectly respectable grass — a mixture of fescue and Kentucky bluegrass — generously dotted with plantains, dandelions, and chickweeds, and, of course, a few hard, bare spots. The first thing I do with a lawn in this shape is to give it a 30 percent test: if at least 30 percent of the lawn is covered with permanent grass, and if it's the grade and elevation I want, I don't dig it over. Surprising as it may be, if 30 percent of the lawn is good grass, I can bring the other 70 percent up to par with a combination of ground limestone, fertilizers, weed controls, and new seeds. (If your lawn fails the 30 percent test, see September for guidance in the reclamation process.)

The soil in the Victory Garden is quite acid, as is the case for most of the area east of the Mississippi. This is due to the leaching action of regular rainfall throughout the centuries. Since grasses grow best when the soil is only slightly acid or neutral in reaction, my first step in reclaiming this lawn was to add ground limestone (35 to 50 pounds to 1,000 square feet). West of the Mississippi where normal rainfall is light and where alkalinity may be a problem, the soil often needs sulfur (20 pounds to 1,000 square feet) to lower its alkalinity. It would have been best to add the lime in the fall to give it more time to work but the spring came and the lawn looked dreadful, so the lime went on in April. Better late than never.

Fertilizers are more than the key to healthy grass — they are the key to weed control, because well-fed grass is stronger than weeds. In particular, grass craves nitrogen, so the fertilizer I use is high in nitrogen, 20-10-5. This is unlike most garden fertilizers: it is made to release its nutrients slowly, feeding the lawn continuously for several months. An application in the spring and another in the fall will keep the grass fed for the entire year.

Fertilizer will keep weeds under control in a well-maintained lawn, but when I first approached this corner of the Victory Garden, the weeds had the upper hand. I hesitate to use chemicals in gardening, but there are times when there is no other choice, and this was one of them. I don't advise spreading a weed-killer over an entire lawn, because it can kill desirable plants if it touches them. Instead I use one of the types that can be put directly on individual weeds. A couple of weeks after spot weed control, most weeds will have withered away.

The lawn's bare spots were hard and crusty and needed a fresh start with new seeds. But even more than seeds, the soil needed additional organic matter to loosen it and help it hold moisture. The organic material I used was sphagnum peat moss, available at any garden center. I spread about 3 inches over each spot and worked it into the top 6 inches of soil. Grass seeds need to rest on firm soil, so I pressed the worked-over soil down with my feet. To smooth the surface for seeding I lightly drew an iron rake over each spot; on the final pass I raked in one direction only, leaving tiny parallel grooves in the soil, a slightly rumpled bed for the seeds to fall into.

Now a word about grass seeds. It's important to know that the grass seeds that are cheapest by the bag are not necessarily the most economical. For example, the mix with the lowest price tag may also have the highest percentage of cheap annual rye grass seeds that produce a limited number of fast-growing, short-lived plants. I prefer planting a mixture of two kinds of grasses for a permanent lawn: fescue, which does well in either sun or shade; and Kentucky bluegrass, which does best in sun. These grasses generally are satisfactory in all but the warmest parts of the country.

I sowed the seed lightly across the bare spots, and then raked each spot again, perpendicular to the direction I raked earlier. This turned most of the seeds into the soil, but many of those left on the surface sprouted too, because the soil was kept moist. I like an oscillating sprinkler for moistening the soil, since its gentle side-to-side motion allows the water to soak into the soil slowly. I don't allow puddles to form on the surface, as this can cause seeds to float away.

Leeks Leeks are unique in the onion family. Rather than producing a bulb, they form a thick white stem that has a mild onion flavor. They have been one of our most spectacular crops in the Victory Garden, impressive in size and sublime in flavor.

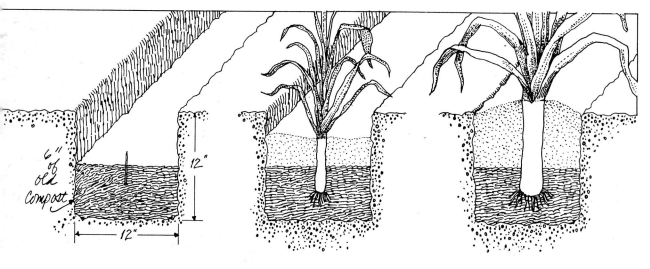

The longer the white portion of the leek, the greater the yield of edible vegetable. And the way to grow those long white stems is to transplant seedlings into a deep trench so that their initial growth occurs well below the normal garden surface. They will even survive the winter here in Boston, providing us with half the fixings of leek and potato soup to warm a cold day.

Toward the middle of the month I set out leek seedlings that were started indoors in March. Before setting them out I dig a trench 12 inches deep and just about as wide. But I don't plant my leeks at the 12-inch depth. Instead, I fill in the bottom of the trench with a 6-inch layer of old compost. This is a secret weapon that will make all vegetables thrive, leeks in particular. Then I use my trowel to make holes in the bottom of the trench, and set in the seedlings about 6 inches apart, giving each a drink of transplant solution. When they are transplanted, they look like slender blades of grass about 3 to 4 inches tall. As they grow, I pull extra soil from the sides to fill in the trench, keeping the tip of the growing stem always above the soil level. Each time, before I pull soil around them, I scatter 5-10-5 fertilizer along the row (5 ounces to a 10-foot row).

Six-packs of young lettuce seedlings ready for transplant

Lettuce It comes as a bitter disappointment to many gardeners, but head lettuce, commonly called Iceberg, will not grow in most parts of the United States because the summer nights are too hot; the plants will bolt, that is, produce flowers and seeds rather than form heads.

That holds for the Victory Garden, too. So I plant leaf lettuce instead, and the results are spectacular. In the spring I plant varieties such as Black Seeded Simpson, a beautiful lime-green, cool-weather favorite; Ruby, a dark red, somewhat later variety; and Buttercrunch, a delicious semi-heading tender beauty. I sow lettuce seeds directly in the garden, and I also set them in as transplants whenever I can find the space for one or more plants. I always have a young generation of seedlings ready for transplanting. In April, for instance, the March sowing is ready to be transplanted to the garden at 10-inch intervals, then showered with transplant solution.

I think it's a mistake for gardeners to plant enormous crops of lettuce. It doesn't store well in the ground or anywhere else, and I suspect that many gardeners harvest the extra forty heads in the dead of night and feed them to their compost piles. You'll have lettuce all summer long if you'll plant small rows — mine are about 4 feet long — and plant every week or ten days.

I prepare the seedbed by scratching in a handful of 10-10-10 fertilizer, and lime if a soil test indicates the need. Then I drop a pinch of seeds (4 or 5) into a ½-inch furrow at 10-inch intervals. I try to keep this "pinch" under control: if too many plants grow together, thinning is a chore. After covering the seeds firmly, I water the row and continue watering frequently, from then on, to prevent the young seedlings from drying out.

New Zealand spinach

Melons In our first season we grew a dozen or more varieties of melon, selected from different seed catalogues. Our casaba, Crenshaw, honeydew, and watermelon produced fruit that was only fair in flavor because it ripened after the arrival of cool fall weather. But our cantaloupe did beautifully. This did not come as much of a surprise to me: cantaloupes, often known as muskmelons, are usually the most successful of the melon crops for the home gardener.

If there is a trick to growing melons, it is to start them early and then to set them into warmed soil. Many gardeners overlook these steps, and wind up with fruit barely worth the eating. I start the melon seeds indoors in a pot in April: 2 seeds to a pot, 1 inch apart and ½ inch deep. When the seedlings have grown to about 2 inches tall, I cut off the weaker of the two so that only one sturdy seedling remains in each pot. In mid-May, about two weeks before the seedlings are to go into the garden, I mulch the soil with black plastic, which draws and holds the sun's heat, giving the crop a warm head start.

New Zealand Spinach Despite its name, New Zealand spinach is not really spinach. It thrives in hot weather, when real spinach either goes to seed or won't grow at all. But for spinach lovers it's a great substitute: its taste is very similar, and the harvest of the tender leaves can begin in

June and continue well into the fall. On top of that, the plant is a real producer — 4 or 5 plants are plenty for a family of four.

The weather will be warm enough in May to set seedlings out, so I start the seeds indoors in April. The seeds' tough outer layers have earned them a reputation as reluctant germinators, but there's a solution for that. I scrape each seed across a file or sandpaper to scratch a hole in that outer covering and then I soak them overnight to soften them; they sprout within 10 days without further problems. To lessen transplanting shock, I plant my seeds in flowerpots, sowing 2 seeds ½ inch deep to each pot. When the seedlings are about 1 inch tall, I cut off the weaker one in each pot, allowing the stronger plant to grow without competition.

Okra In the south, okra is a familiar vegetable; unfortunately it's rarely found in gardens in the colder parts of the country, but I've grown some handsome plants in the Victory Garden. The plant is a member of the hollyhock family, and the edible portion is the long, pointed immature seed pod.

I start the okra seeds in peat pots, 2 seeds to a pot, in mid-April. The surface of these seeds is a little tough, which makes them reluctant germinators, so I rub each seed across a file or a piece of sandpaper before planting. This wears away some of the seed's surface, and allows sprouting to occur easily. After they begin to grow, I snip off the weaker seedling in each pot, leaving the remaining plants to grow stronger than ever.

Onions Sowing onion seeds in the open ground is a rather risky business because the young seedlings look very much like tiny blades of grass and so are easy prey for the unsuspecting cultivator, and because, with their shallow roots, they are even more sensitive to drying out than most seedlings. But it can be done if the soil is moist and high in organic content. I often sow bunching onion seeds — Beltsville Bunching is my favorite variety — in April. They do fine because they will grow quickly and are harvested young.

Onion seeds are tiny, so sowing them thinly ½ inch apart and ½ inch deep requires a steady hand and patience. Once they're in the soil and covered, I drench the seed row with a solution of water and diazinon to discourage the fly of the onion maggot from laying her eggs. At the end of the month the seedlings are ready for thinning to 1-inch intervals. In May I'll thin them to 2-inch intervals and eat the tasty pulled scallions.

The seedlings I set out in April are the ones whose seeds I sowed in February. Some of these I'll harvest as scal-

lions, so I set them in double or triple rows at 2-inch intervals. Others I'll let mature to full onions, so I'll set them in single or double rows at 4- to 6-inch intervals. After setting in, I give all the seedlings a drink of transplant solution fortified with diazinon to control onion maggots.

Pansies The Victory Garden pansies begin to flower in early April, long before pansies are expected in this area. The reason is that I bed them down for the winter under a snug mulch of pine needles so that I don't lose a single plant to cold weather. (For more information on pansy culture, see July, August, and November.)

Now in April I just dig up the clumps of pansies and relocate them where I want them in the garden, planting them in holes deep enough so the plants will sit in the soil at the same depth they had in the nursery bed. I firm the plants in, give each a treatment of transplant solution, and stand back to appreciate this early splash of color.

I can keep these pansies in blossom throughout most of the summer just by picking off the faded blossoms so that the plants are not allowed to set seed. Once it has produced its progeny, a pansy plant considers that its mission in life is fulfilled, and it dies; if I want the plant to continue blooming, I have to interrupt that cycle by snipping off the blossoms as they begin to wither.

A parsnip harvest

Parsnips A mature parsnip looks like an enormous white carrot and has a delightful, sweet flavor. Parsnips are ready to harvest late in the fall, about the time the ground freezes, but if they are left in the soil over the winter, they are even sweeter the following spring.

If the root is to be uniform and straight rather than bumpy and crooked, the parsnip must grow in soft, smooth, rock-free soil. Since that in no way describes the soil in the Victory Garden, although every inch of it has been dug over again and again, I had to prepare a special growing space for each individual parsnip. This may sound like more trouble than it's worth, but a few plants will satisfy a family's needs, so I think it pays off handsomely.

To provide the soft growing space for each parsnip, I use a crowbar to make a cone-shaped hole, jamming it down into the soil 10 or 12 inches deep and rotating it until the top of the hole is some 4 inches across. Then I fill this hole with soil that I've sifted through a ¼-inch hardware cloth screen. This soil is so soft and rock-free that any root crop would grow in it, and parsnips in particular will thrive. I make a series of holes at 8-inch intervals along the garden row, one for each plant that I want. Then I drop 3 or 4 seeds onto the surface of the sifted soil, push them down to a depth of ½ inch, and firm them in. I buy fresh parsnip seeds every year because they don't have much tolerance for storage.

Parsnips are not only slow to mature, but they are slow to germinate as well. Because weed seedlings often sprout quicker than parsnips, I mark the row by dropping in a

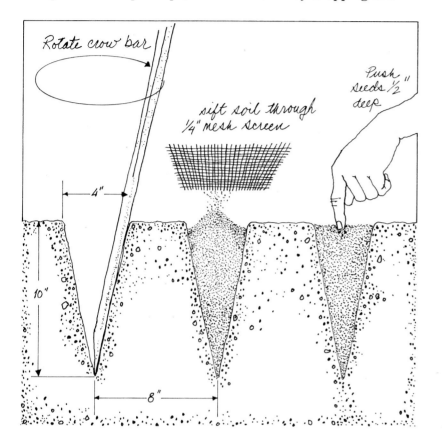

Rotate crow bar

sift soil through ¼" mesh screen

Push seeds ½" deep

4"

10"

8"

few radish seeds between the parsnips. The radishes sprout even quicker than weeds, allowing me to hoe between the rows without worrying about hurting the parsnips, which still have not emerged. The radishes will be ready for harvest within a week of the time the parsnip shoots appear.

Peas Most gardeners are pea lovers, so April is an exciting month because the March sowing of peas breaks through the soil and begins sturdy growth in the cool spring weather. The March sowing includes regular or English peas as well as edible podded peas, more commonly known as Chinese pea pods or snow peas. I follow this first planting with another sowing of peas in early April. Because my garden is only for demonstration purposes, I put in short rows, about 10 feet long, that will provide a substantial harvest beginning around the middle of June. If our summers didn't get so hot (85 to 100 degrees) so quickly, I'd be able to harvest the peas over a much longer time.

It is not too late toward the latter part of April to plant any kind of peas in the Victory Garden, but to be certain of success in my final planting, I choose a variety such as Wando, which will mature even if the summer weather arrives early. (For more on peas see March, June, August, and November.)

Peppers Pepper plants love the heat, so they shouldn't be planted outside until June, when the night temperatures can be counted on to stay above 55 degrees. However, they need such a long growing season that it isn't practical to sow them from seeds in the open garden, so I start the seedlings indoors in April, 2 seeds to a pot, ½ inch deep, and keep them in a bright, hot spot (about 75 degrees) to insure good germination and strong seedlings. When the seedlings first show their heads, about 10 days after sowing, I begin a regimen of weekly feeding with a solution of water and liquid fertilizer. When it is apparent which seedling in each pot is the stronger one, I cut off its neighbor so that all of the nutrients will go toward producing superior seedlings, one to a pot.

Potatoes Space is precious in the Victory Garden. I just don't have enough room to plant more than a few demonstration potato plants, but each plant will yield 6 or 8 full-sized potatoes and sometimes several smaller ones, so even this modest planting will be worth the effort. I find that a few early-variety potatoes, ready for digging in midsummer, are a special treat, far tastier as "new" potatoes than those grown for winter storage.

Potatoes like full sun and a light, sandy soil. They also want an acid soil, as alkalinity will promote the development of a skin disease called scab. So I've made a point of keeping the potato area free of lime. If your garden has been limed and you still want to grow potatoes, add sulfur at the rate of ½ pound over the surface of a 15-foot row to lower the pH of the soil to between 4.5 and 5.5, which is just right for potatoes.

Potatoes are grown from sections of mature potatoes, but those bought in a grocery store may not work; these are often treated with a sprout-inhibitant to keep them salable longer. I buy certified seed potatoes by the pound from a local garden center, so I can rest assured that I have untreated potatoes of varieties that I know can be successfully grown in my area.

I could just plant the whole potato, but I can get more for my money, and a larger yield, by cutting the potato into sections about the size of an egg, making sure each section has two or three eyes. I plant each of these sections separately, and each will produce a strong potato plant.

Potato sections treated with fungicide before planting

     Before the sections go into the ground I dip them in sulfur or captan (fungicides) to prevent rotting of the cut surfaces. Then I leave them exposed to the sunshine and air for 3 or 4 days. This dries out the cut surfaces as a further precaution against rotting when the sections hit the cold, damp soil of early spring.

     The first year in the Victory Garden I decided to try three different planting methods: the traditional way, in which the sections are buried a few inches below the ground; and two easier ways, using mulch to cover the sections, rather than soil. The two mulch methods were less than a glorious success. The warmth and dampness of the mulch attracted slugs that made off with a good third of the crop. The traditional method produced a healthier and fuller crop, so the second year I abandoned the mulch approach completely. Nevertheless, there is something to be said for mulching: it requires both less time to plant and less time (almost none) to maintain. I'll give directions for all three, and let you decide between high yield and low effort.

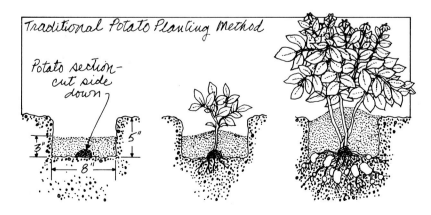

Traditional Potato Planting Method

Potato section— cut side down

5"

3"

8"

When the potato foliage dies back, the crop is ready

Traditional method: I dig a flat-bottomed trench 6 to 8 inches wide and 4 to 5 inches deep. Then I sprinkle in 3 good handfuls of 5-10-10, an excellent potato fertilizer, in a 15-foot row and scratch it into the soil so it won't be in direct contact with the potato sections. I put the potato sections in, cut sides down, about a foot apart in the trench and cover them with about three inches of soil. As the plants grow, I'll pull soil in from the trench to keep the plants cool, a procedure known as hilling or mounding.

Mulch methods: For the two mulching methods there was no hilling or cultivation involved. I simply set the potato sections on the surface of the soil about a foot apart. For the plastic mulch, I covered the row with a strip of agricultural-grade black plastic, 18 inches wide and as long as the row, and made sure that all the edges of the plastic were buried in the soil to hold it in place. Then, over each potato section I sliced into the plastic an X, about the size of the potato, to give the sprouts an exit. In my opinion the plastic mulch method, developed in England where summers are cool, is suitable to cloudy, cool areas such as the Pacific Northwest, but wherever summers are hot the black plastic causes the soil to become too warm for this cool-weather vegetable.

For the hay mulch, I just covered the cut potatoes, spaced every 12 inches along the row, with 6 or 8 inches of hay, and kept the hay moist. The shoots grew right through the hay. There were no weeds and no further work.

Radishes One of my favorite viewer letters came from a would-be gardener who confessed that while radishes were known to be "absolutely foolproof," hers had failed miserably. Well, radishes are *not* that easy. For one thing, they need at least 6 hours of sunshine a day or they'll make all tops and no bottoms. For another, like peas and spinach, they do best in the cool bright days of early spring and fall. The midsummer crops are often hotter than firecrackers. But unfortunately on those cool bright days of spring there lurks in the soil the dreaded root maggot, which will chomp its way through the radish crop, leaving the tender roots scarred and tunneled. So whoever started the rumor that radishes are a cinch had full sunshine, cool days, and no maggots.

I plant my first sowing of radishes in the open garden in April, though I usually plant some in March in the hotbed or cloche. First I work a handful of 10-10-10 fertilizer into soil limed and manured the previous fall. I sow the seeds in a ½-inch-deep furrow about ½ inch apart along a 5-foot row. (Radishes are at peak flavor for such a brief time that I never plant more than I can use.) To protect the radishes from the root maggots I drench the row with diazinon and water. Then I keep my fingers crossed and hope. With luck I'll have radishes in 25 to 30 days. To have tender radishes most of the summer and fall I plant successive crops every week or so except during June and July.

Raspberries Of all the delightful fruits for the home garden, none is more productive than raspberries. That's a special bonus, because growing raspberries at home is about the only way to get them to the table in perfect condition; they are extremely difficult for the commercial market to raise and ship since they are so easily damaged in handling.

Ordinary raspberries ripen in midsummer on canes that grew the previous year, but we chose for the Victory Garden a variety called Durham, an everbearing type that produces two crops of berries annually, one in early fall on the

A Durham raspberry

current season's growth and another the following summer from the same canes.

I set the young bushes, which we bought in a local nursery, into our ordinary garden soil that had been enriched with cow manure and peat moss. Then I sprinkled a little 10-10-10 fertilizer around each plant after setting it out, to get it off to a speedy start.

I don't expect more than a handful of fruit from raspberry bushes in their first year, but after a year or two in the soil they'll yield bountifully for many seasons.

Roses If you've never grown roses before, let me offer a word of encouragement. Roses grow wild in every part of the United States and Canada, so it's quite likely they will grow in your garden.

I like to plant roses off by themselves because they are susceptible to particular diseases, respond to particular fertilizers, and are attacked by particular insects. When they are grouped together in their own garden I can give them the special attention they need. Nevertheless, I set five bushes into the Victory Garden's perennial border and they've done fine. (For more information see the perennial border feature in the September chapter.)

Because I put the roses in the perennial border, which had been thoroughly dug over, with compost and cow manure added, no further soil preparation was needed. But if I were planting these bushes in unworked soil, I would dig a hole at least 2 feet across and 2 feet deep, and work in cow manure, peat moss, and lime before setting the plants in.

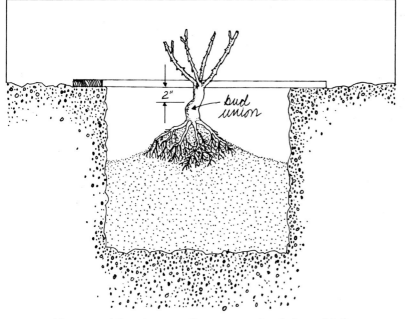

Almost without exception, a rosebush bought from a garden center is a composite plant produced at a nursery by joining the bud of a fine-flower variety to the root of a type known for its vigorous root system. This combination assures a sturdy plant and abundant flowers. The union, where the bud and root join, appears as a bulge and is quite visible. This is the bush's weak link, and the future success of the rosebush depends on that union being planted at the right planting depth. This depth varies in different parts of the country. In the Victory Garden, and in other areas where the winters are severe, this bulge must be planted 2 inches below the surface of the soil where it will be protected from the killing cold. In the South, where the plant will be inclined to send out suckers from the root stock itself, the bulge should be planted 2 inches above the soil.

Spinach By the end of April, spinach plants grown from seeds planted in early March begin to become crowded and compete with one another for space. When this happens I thin them to about 5-inch intervals. I don't throw these pulled seedlings away, though, or put them in the composter; they're wonderfully tender at this age and just right for salads.

April is the last opportunity to plant another crop of spinach until the fall, because those plants that are still in the ground when the hot Boston weather arrives will go to seed. I sow the April crop in a ½-inch furrow, about ½ inch apart, and they'll be ready for thinning in about 6 weeks.

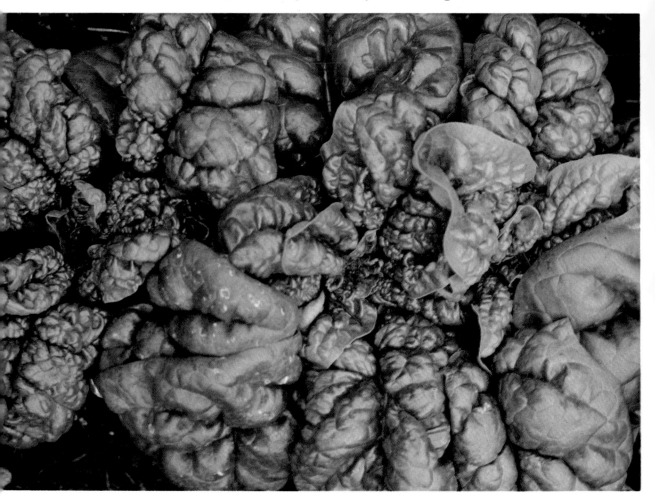

Spinach ready for harvest

Squash In the Victory Garden's first year I planted more than a dozen different kinds of zucchinis and summer squashes under the greenhouse windows — the hottest part of the garden. By midsummer they had grown so vigorously that it looked as if they might overtake the whole garden. One reason that they were so successful is that I started them indoors in late April, 6 weeks ahead of planting time, 2 seeds ½ inch deep in a pot. I kept the pots in a warm, sunny spot, and when the seeds sprouted about a week later, I cut off the weaker seedling in each pot and let the other develop into a husky plant.

Strawberries Strawberries grown in the home garden are usually sweeter and richer than any that can be bought in stores; commercial growers are often forced to grow varieties that travel without bruising, which eliminates Fairfax, Sparkle, and Sure-Crop, all of which I put into the Victory Garden.

I set my June-bearing strawberry plants into the ground as early in the spring as possible so that they could become well rooted before the warm weather. I prepared the soil the previous fall by covering it with a layer of 2 inches of cow manure and 4 inches of compost. In the spring I dug both these materials into the soil. Then I spread 10-10-10 fertilizer on the surface (2½ pounds to 100 square feet). It wasn't necessary to add more lime because a soil test indicated a pH of 5.7, the slightly acid condition ideal for growing strawberries.

I ordered my strawberry plants through the mail. They arrived looking as if a truck had run over them, and I had to throw at least half of them away. There wasn't time to order replacements so I took my chances with the remaining sorry specimens; happily, because they were planted early, most of them survived.

Strawberries multiply by sending out runners, or aboveground stems, from the main plants. At approximately every 12 inches along the runners a new plant grows and sets down roots into the soil. For this reason I plant strawberries in what's known as a matted-row system: the plants grow throughout a 3-foot-wide row.

Strawberry plants have long roots and they need to be planted carefully into a deep slitlike hole. If planted too deeply, the crown is likely to smother and rot; if set too high, the crown will dry out and the plant will die. The idea is to set the plants in the slit so that one-half of the crown is buried below grade, one-half above. I make the hole with a flat-bladed spade, which I insert 8 inches deep at 2-foot intervals along the row. As I slip the plants in, I fan the roots out slightly to separate them and give them a better chance to

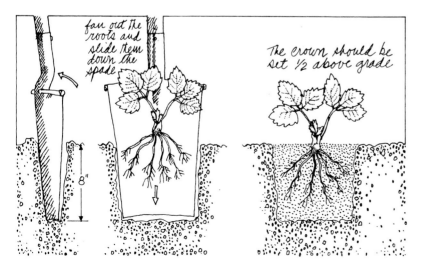

fan out the roots and slide them down the spade

8"

The crown should be set ½ above grade

grow. Then I firm them in and give them a good drink of our transplanting elixir, water and liquid fertilizer.

June-bearing strawberry plants are undoubtedly the most familiar variety of strawberry, but they are not the only variety, and they're not, in my opinion, even the best. Ever-bearing, or Alpine, strawberry plants are substantially different from their June-bearing counterparts: for one thing, as the name implies, they produce fruit all season long, from the spring through to the first frost; for another, they do not produce runners and so remain as tidy handsome plants throughout their lives; finally, their tartly sweet fruit is beautifully shaped and a rich, deep red. I'm at a loss to explain their obscurity, given this commendable list of traits.

I began the Victory Garden's everbearing strawberry crop during our first December, and nursed the plants along through the spring, finally setting them into the cold frame in March for a few weeks of hardening-off. Then in April I set plants into soil that had been prepared with the usual doses of lime and peat moss, along with an added boost from a layer of compost. I spaced the plants about 6 inches apart, gave them a drink of transplant solution, and they were off.

It's best to replace strawberry beds every two or three years, because the plants and the soil nutrients will have become too exhausted to produce good crops.

Swiss Chard Swiss chard is part of the beet family, but it's grown for its succulent, vitamin-rich greens rather than for its roots. With just minimum attention throughout the summer, it will have a long, productive life: as the plant matures, I harvest the outer leaves and allow the crown and roots to stay in the ground, where they will continue to produce new growth until the ground freezes. In some of the

warmer parts of the country, Swiss chard will even last the winter, producing new growth until spring. Then the plant, which is a biennial, sends up a flower stalk. So no matter where you live, you have to make a new planting of Swiss chard each year.

I sow the seeds directly into a ½-inch-deep furrow, dropping a pinch at 12-inch intervals. Late this month when the young plants grow to about 1 inch tall, I'll sacrifice all but the most vigorous seedling at each spacing. If I want more plants I can transplant the pulled seedlings to another spot in the garden.

Tomatoes In January we generally receive the first questions from viewers, asking if it's time to plant tomatoes. In February, the question is asked again and again, and in March the chorus grows louder. But this early in the season I resist the pressure because I know I won't gain so much as a day in the growing time. Tomatoes love hot weather, and they'll just sit there until it comes. So in early April I sow tomato seeds indoors. (For information on sowing seeds indoors, see pages 284–285.) I like to sow a few seeds of various types, specifically early, mid-, and main-season varieties. That will give me fruit very early in the summer, and after the early varieties finish fruiting, I'll have massive crops right up until frost in the fall.

To get the small number of tomato seedlings I need, I sprinkle 6 or 8 seeds in a 3-inch pot of soilless mix, lightly cover them with milled sphagnum moss, and label the varieties. After watering I set the pot in a warm sunny spot — at least 70 degrees.

It is necessary to keep the soil barely moist at all times to insure good germination and growth. This is critical, and I check the surface more than once a day, watering with tepid water as needed. Late each afternoon I allow the soil surface to become nearly dry to discourage attacks of the damping-off fungus.

In two weeks, when the seedlings are about 1½ inches tall, I transplant them into plastic six-packs or individual pots filled with soilless mix. After watering with tepid transplant solution, I set the six-packs in a shady place for a day to prevent the plants from wilting in the hot sun. Then it's back to a sunny location to grow into stocky plants, ready for setting out in the garden in May.

Q&A

Q: I have barely adequate light indoors for my broccoli, cabbage, and cauliflower seedlings. Would it speed their growth to put them outdoors, even while it's still chilly?

A: It certainly would. If you try to grow your seedlings indoors with poor light, they will be weak, spindly, and barely capable of supporting their own weight. On sunny days, when the temperature is at least 45 degrees or higher, move them outdoors into the sun in a place protected from the wind, then bring them in at night. Your plants will be much stronger when they go into the ground.

Q: Would planting a border of flowers around a vegetable garden help keep the woodchucks away?

A: Nice thought, but it won't work. The solution for the woodchuck problem, and rabbits too, is to put up a 1-inch-mesh chicken-wire fence, 3 feet tall. Bury the fence 1 foot into the ground, and support the top 2 feet with stakes. Even taking precautions, you should expect these ingenious vegetarians occasionally to make off with a plant or two.

Q: My asparagus rows are about 2 feet apart. Can I plant strawberries between the rows?

A: No, strawberries need full sun and the asparagus plants will shade them. Let me add that your asparagus rows should be 4 feet apart. Why not set out another row of asparagus plants (see May chapter for guidance) which would have the correct spacing? In the long run, you will have a much better crop.

Q: Can lime and fertilizer be put on the garden at the same time, or do they neutralize each other?

A: Lime and fertilizer can go on at the same time, but with much less effect than if the liming is done in the fall and has several months to react to sweeten the soil. Then add fertilizer just before planting time to get the maximum benefit; fertilizer added in the fall is apt to leach out of the soil by spring planting time.

Q: I have an area that gets one or two hours of sunlight a day. What vegetables can I plant there?

A: I would plant shade-loving wildflowers. Most vegetables wouldn't have a chance there, though you might take a gamble with pumpkins.

Q: The winter has broken the larger branches of my junipers. Can I tape and repair them, or are they permanently damaged?

A: You should cut them back to the point of damage. It may be a couple of years before your plants are fully recovered.

PLANTING AND TRANS- PLANTING

The primary job of the April gardener is getting the crops in the ground, either as seeds or as young seedlings. I'll give the general information for this here, and the specifics with the alphabetical entries.

First, I always begin the planting and transplanting regimen by marking the rows with string. This may strike beginning gardeners as needlessly fussy, but straight rows are more than good housekeeping — they make for good garden production because spacing can be arranged so that each kind of plant uses its space most efficiently.

Sow dry and set wet: this pearl of gardening wisdom is the old-time shorthand meaning that seeds should be sown in dry soil, and seedlings set into damp soil (the old adage errs here slightly, as wet soil would be overdoing things). The reason is that tiny seeds are easier to handle when there's no moisture involved, while damp soil is kinder to the roots of seedlings.

I use a planting board to make the furrow for small seeds. At this time of the year, when the soil is still so cool and moist, I make the furrow as deep as the minimum depth suggested on the seed packages. When the summer weather is here, from June on, and the soil is hot and dry, I double this depth to keep the seeds protected from the baking sun.

The spacing of the seeds in the furrow depends on the size of the mature plant. If the grown plant's foliage will spread 12 inches in all directions, as for instance with broccoli, I plant the seeds in clusters of 2 or 3, spaced every 24 inches, thinning to the

strongest plant in a cluster when the seedlings appear. Slimmer vegetables, like carrots or radishes, can be planted close together, and the excess seedlings pulled to thin the plants to a 1- to 2-inch spacing.

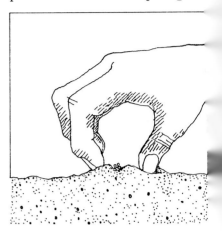

Once the seeds are in the furrow I cover them by squeezing the dry soil from both sides with my fingers. I tamp the soil down to put the soil and the seeds in close contact with each other and then water the furrow. This watering is the most important element in the young plant's life. If the seed row dries out even once before the plants are well rooted, it will spell the end of those seeds. If your soil is heavy and apt to form a crust when it dries, cover your seeds with sand or a soilless potting mixture so the seedlings can emerge from the soil without difficulty.

I am asked again and again for watering formulas in planting seeds, but they just don't

Transplanting seedlings with a planting board

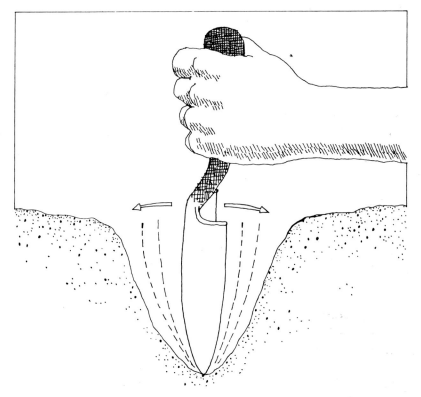

exist. The amount of water a garden needs depends on the soil and the weather. My advice is to learn to read soil by its look and feel. Dry soil is lighter in color than moist soil, so paleness is a signal to water. If you don't trust your eye, there's another test. Squeeze a handful of soil. If water drips out, that soil is too wet and will have to dry out before it can be worked. Like wet soil, moist soil will stay in a ball when the squeeze is released, but the ball will disintegrate with the flick of a finger into what looks like the crumbs of a chocolate cake.

I wait for a late afternoon or an overcast day before putting my seedlings into damp soil; this spares them from the hot sun in their first hours outside. I make a hole for the seedlings with a trowel, spacing the holes according to the ultimate size of the plant. I always make sure the depth of the hole will accommodate the entire root ball comfortably because crowded roots will have trouble reaching for water. Then I

press the soil firmly around the roots with my hands to establish the close contact needed between the soil and the roots. The seedling should be so firmly in the ground that if one of the leaves were pulled, the leaf would break but the plant stay put. Once the seedling is in I make a little saucer of soil at the base of the stem to hold water and funnel it to the roots. I give the plant a drink of transplant solution, a mixture of water and water-soluble fer-

tilizer (I use 23-19-17) in the proportions recommended on the label. To give the plants a little more protection from the brutal sun, I spread hay or straw lightly over the tops of the plants.

Finally, for both seeds and seedlings, I label the rows with the plant's variety and planting date, and I hope you do too. It's a good way to check on a plant's performance under the particular conditions that exist in your garden.

Radishes

MAY

Plant
Asparagus
Basil
Beans
Broccoli
Cabbage
Carrots
Cauliflower
Dahlias
Garlic
Lettuce
Potatoes
Radishes
Shallots
Squash

Thin
Beets
Broccoli
Cabbage
Carrots
Cauliflower
Corn
Endive (see April)
Kohlrabi
Onions (see April)
Squash
Turnips

Transplant
Cucumbers
Dahlias
Melons
New Zealand Spinach
Parsley
Petunias
Rhododendrons
Silver Fleece Vine
Squash
Sweet Potatoes
Tomatoes

Harvest
Asparagus
Lettuce
Onions
Radishes
Spinach
Turnips

Special Events
Chrysanthemums
Fruit Trees
Roses
Strawberries
Tulips

MAY

May is the first harvest month in the Victory Garden. It's not a bountiful harvest, but it's enough for a fresh salad of lettuce, radishes, scallions and incredibly succulent spinach; and the early turnips are ready too.

More than anything else, though, May is a working month. There are more tasks to be done than there are hours in the days to do them. The March and April plantings need attention. Aphids and leaf miners make their unwanted appearance, and our defenses must be at the ready. Our weather in May is far from predictable. May is the bridge month between the cool spring and the hot summer, and often its early days offer a little of both. By later in the month the soil begins to feel the effects of the warming sun, and, depending upon soil and weather conditions, a serious watering routine may have to begin.

Still, the major job of the month is planting. More crops are planted in May than in any other month so that by the first of June nearly every inch of garden soil is working. Even this early in the spring I can begin multiple cropping, replacing each harvested plant with another crop so the precious Victory Garden real estate is always at work.

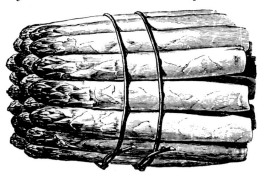

Asparagus Once during a trip to England I visited the garden of Sir Joseph Hooker, the first curator of Kew Gardens, and found an asparagus bed that was 118 years old and, thanks to Sir Joseph's diligent soil preparation, still producing. You may not plan to pass your asparagus bed along to your children and grandchildren, but even the short-term success of your asparagus will be in direct proportion to the care you take in preparing the soil.

Asparagus matures very slowly. It's three years from seed to the first light harvest, so planting seed in the garden is the longest possible route to fresh, homegrown asparagus.

Instead, I cut a full year off the maturation time by planting one-year-old roots, available from garden centers and by mail at this time of year. Two-year-old roots are also available, but I prefer the younger ones: when the two-year-old roots are dug from the nursery, so much of their root structure is left behind that they are slow to recover from the shock of relocation.

Asparagus roots need a thick layer of soil protection, both from the elements and from the hazards of cultivation, so they have to be planted deeply. I dig a trench 12 inches deep and 18 inches wide, with a distance of 4 feet, center to center, between the trenches. At the base of the trench I loosen the soil to the depth of the spading fork — 8 to 10 inches or so — and add ½ pound of 10-10-10 fertilizer to each 10-foot stretch of trench. Asparagus thrives in a neutral soil, with a pH of about 7.0, so if a soil test shows this deep trench soil is too acid, I sweeten it with ground limestone. Then I add my secret weapon: 4 inches of old compost in the bottom of the trench, to keep the plants well fed for years.

After I've spaded the soil and added the fertilizer and compost, the soil in the bottom of the trench is very loose. To give the roots a solid base to rest on, I walk over the soil to firm it, and then rake it to make it level, leaving the trench 8 or 10 inches deep, and ready to receive the asparagus roots. I fan the roots out like the arms of an octopus, lay them at 2-foot intervals along the floor of the trench, and cover them gently — these are fragile roots — with 2 inches of garden soil. As the summer progresses I'll pull in more soil from the sides of the trench until I've filled it in completely. Every three months or so I'll side dress the rows with 10-10-10 fertilizer, using about a handful for each plant.

In May, two years after planting, these one-year-old roots will have produced a healthy crop, ready for harvest when the stems are about 8 inches tall and ½ inch or greater

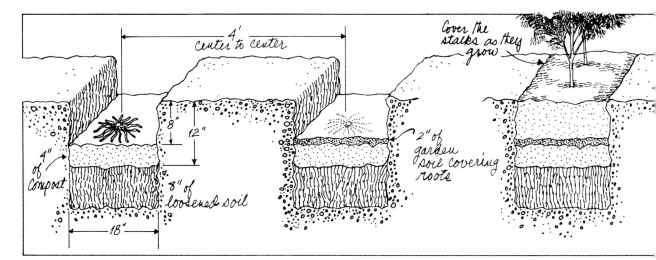

in diameter. I keep this first harvest to a minimum, so that as many stems as possible will grow on and nourish the plants in the following years. But I do make sure to pick the harvest on time, as the growing stems quickly send out side branches and foliage, and when that happens the harvest opportunity is lost. I don't use any tool for the harvest: I just bend the succulent stems until they break, because any portion of the stem that's too tough to break is too tough to eat.

On the sad day that I notice there are no asparagus stems fatter than ½ inch in diameter, I know the season's harvest is spent, and the plants are about to enter their revival period. I help them along in this by fertilizing the bed with 5-10-5 or 10-10-10 immediately after the harvest, and again in mid-July and mid-August.

Basil Basil has lately climbed out of relative obscurity into the herbal limelight, and it's about time. This is a delicious herb, especially with fresh tomatoes or in sauces. Only its outer leaves and stems are picked, and these are quickly replaced as the plant grows, so basil is productive and handsome throughout its life.

Basil plant, bird's-eye view

Story has it that herbs grow in poor soil. I'd like to modify that somewhat: some will grow in poor soil, but they grow better in prepared soil. I sow my basil seeds in a ½-inch furrow in soil that's been limed and manured and enriched with 5-10-5 fertilizer. The seedlings will be ready for thinning in June.

Beans In order to demonstrate as many gardening techniques as possible, I've planted quite an assortment of beans from time to time in the Victory Garden. The shell beans and the ornamental scarlet runner beans produced acceptable but unspectacular results: the shell bean seeds, bought from a hardware store seed rack, germinated poorly; the scarlet runners produced promising blossoms, but followed with stringy pods.

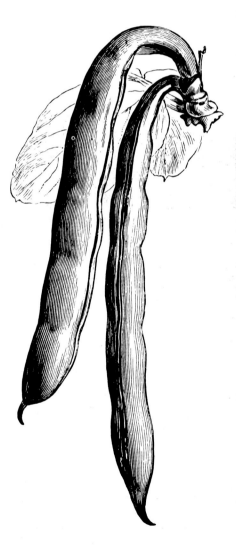

Our best crop is the bush or snap bean. One year, for the sake of comparison, we planted several varieties of pole beans in addition to the bush varieties, and the bush beans won the contest hands down: they produce their entire yield over a short period of time, so the dead stalks can be removed after harvest and a new crop planted; because they grow and are harvested quickly, they rarely have disease or pest difficulties; and their flavor's considerably better than the pole bean as well. By contrast the pole beans have to be provided with something to crawl on and building these structures can be costly, both in time and money. Moreover, toward the end of their long season, the pole bean plants are apt to develop unsightly foliage due to disease that attacks the leaves, especially in rainy weather. On the other hand, pole beans do have their good points: they use much less garden space than bush beans, and they produce a constant, though relatively small yield through the entire summer. But all things considered, it's understandable that almost no commercial growers produce pole beans. My advice for gardeners who plant pole beans is to try some of the modern bush bean varieties instead; they are much easier to grow and far tastier as well.

With most bean varieties, there is no percentage in planting too early. The seeds will just sit in the soil waiting for it to warm up, and may rot in the meantime, though this problem has been all but eliminated by the many reliable seedsmen who coat their seeds with a fungicide to prevent rotting. So I plant my earliest beans in mid-May, when the soil in the Victory Garden has reached 55 degrees. (There are two exceptions to this: the fava or English broad bean, a Canadian and European favorite, which thrives in cold weather and should be planted as early in the spring as possible; and the lima bean, which likes a warmer soil and which I plant in the Victory Garden in June.) I know the soil temperature precisely because I test it, burying a regular outdoor thermometer vertically in the ground for an hour or so. Regardless of the moisture content of the soil or the time of day, the thermometer will give an accurate reading.

Bush beans are an easy crop to overplant because they are so prolific. I plant in short rows, 10 feet or so long; I plant several varieties at once, each with a different maturation rate; and I plant successive crops every 10 days or so until August, which gives me a staggered but manageable harvest. I start the beans off just as I do the peas, by wetting them with water, then dusting them with a nitrogen inoculant that helps the plants take nitrogen directly from the air. (This inoculant is available from garden centers and through catalogues; I use it conservatively, so a single envelope lasts me an entire season.) I sow the seeds at 1-inch intervals across the bottom of a flat-bottomed trench that is 5 inches wide and 3 inches deep. This is a thicker sowing of beans than many experts recommend, but I'm convinced that it produces a much more impressive yield. In May, when the soil is still relatively cool and moist, I cover the beans with only 1 inch of soil. I firm the soil with the back of my hoe to get a firm contact between the seeds and the soil. In about 45 to 60 days, depending upon the variety, we begin to pick beans. After a 2-week harvest I pull the plants out and use the space for another crop.

Now, pole beans are another matter altogether. Once planted, they stay in the garden all summer long. For my bean comparison, I planted several varieties of pole beans — Kentucky Wonder, Kentucky Wonder Wax, Romano, Blue Lake, and Enorma, a scarlet runner. Since these beans need a place to climb, I constructed a sort of maypole affair for them. I bought 5 cedar posts, each 8 feet long and 5 inches in diameter, and buried them 2 feet into the ground on 6-foot centers. At the base of each pole I drove 6 short stakes into the ground, making a 3-foot circle of stakes around the base of the pole. Then I connected the stakes to the top of the pole with heavy garden twine, and planted 6 bean seeds around each stake, 1 inch deep, making a total of 36 seeds per pole. When they sprouted, I thinned them to the 3 strongest plants at each stake, so each pole supported 18 vines. As the plants grew they wound themselves around the twine, and after 8 or 9 weeks I had the first of the harvest.

Beets In May, when the April sowing of beet seeds has produced seedlings that are about 1 inch tall, I thin them to 1-inch intervals. Many gardeners don't know that beet seedlings take quite well to transplanting. Pulled seedlings can be used to fill in any skips in the rows or be transplanted elsewhere in the garden. The greens of later thinnings can be eaten, but the first ones are too tiny to bother with.

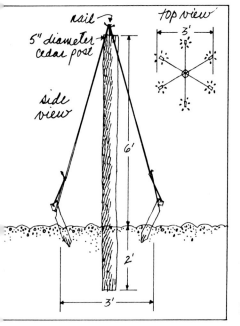

May is the beginning of the leaf miner season, bringing in a blizzard of questions from viewers who ask why their leaves develop dead, mushy, gray areas. There is no way to cure this leaf miner damage once it's happened, but preventive treatment can protect the plants from injury. Beginning in mid-May, I spray the plants with diazinon at 10-day intervals. One caution: diazinon stays on the leaves for about 14 days, during which time they should not be eaten, so I avoid spraying during the last two weeks before harvest. (For more on the leaf miner, see page 154.)

Broccoli One year we fell behind in our attention to the broccoli plants, and we paid dearly. We did give them an initial drenching with diazinon, but we neglected periodic applications through the growing season, and the root maggot took advantage of us. The problem became evident during a spell of warm, sunny weather late in May. The plants wilted despite repeated watering, and wilting in damp soil is always a sign of trouble. Digging around one of the plants, I found its roots riddled with tunnels in which ugly white maggots squirmed on exposure to the sunlight. The plants hardly seemed worth saving, but I soaked the soil with diazinon and mounded extra soil up around the plants' stems. Gradually they responded, but the crop was poor. So now we take care to treat all the cabbage-related plants with diazinon every 10 days, aiming the solution directly at the base of the plant so it seeps down to the roots, or we use root maggot mats (see pages 152–153).

To stay ahead of the imported cabbageworm caterpillar, I continue to apply *Bacillus thuringiensis* at 7- to 10-day intervals.

In May I sow a new crop of broccoli from seed for harvest in late summer. First I prepare the soil by adding 5-10-5 fertilizer (about 2 handfuls for a 6-foot row), and dig it into the top 4 or 5 inches of soil. There's already lime in the soil, of course, but I add more because a near-neutral or sweet soil is an unhappy environment for clubroot, a fatal cabbage-family disease that causes malformed roots. I sow the seeds in the furrow, half a dozen seeds in clusters every 2 feet. Later in the month, when the plants are about 1 inch tall, I thin to one plant every 2 feet. The plants will need diazinon for control of root maggots and *Bacillus thuringiensis* for the cabbageworm, but the cutworm collar won't be necessary, as cabbage-related plants grown directly from seed in the garden are rarely bothered by cutworms.

Cabbage As with the broccoli plants, one of the most important activities for cabbage in May, if root maggot discs are not used, is drenching the soil with a diazinon solution at 10-day intervals to combat this omnipresent pest. It's also important to spray with *Bacillus thuringiensis* at 7- to 10-day intervals to control the imported cabbageworm caterpillar.

Some years in the garden I have enough space to grow midsummer cabbages, which I start from seed sown in May. I prepare a short row, working in 2 handfuls of 10-10-10 fertilizer and twice that amount of ground limestone for a 6-foot row that will produce 4 huge plants. Although the soil already is reasonably sweet, this extra limestone helps to control the much-feared clubroot disease. I sow a cluster of 4 to 5 seeds at 2-foot intervals. (The later varieties produce larger heads than the earlier sowings, so are given an extra 6 inches of space.) When I sow the seeds I water the soil with a diazinon solution, which I'll repeat every 10 days or so through the summer; if I decide against diazinon, I slip a root maggot mat around each saved seedling when I thin the plants to 1 plant at each site later this month.

Carrots Our April sowing of carrots needs attention in May, about a month after planting, when the radishes used to mark the rows are ready for harvest and the carrot seedlings themselves need to be thinned to 1-inch intervals. This is a tedious job if the original sowing was heavy-handed, but it's worth the effort to give the plants plenty of room to grow. The pulled seedlings are too small to be useful in the kitchen; I usually throw them on the compost pile.

Late in May I sow another double row of carrots to back up the April crop. Sometimes our May soil conditions are a little soggy, making the process of covering the seeds evenly rather difficult. I solve this by filling the furrow with dry soilless mix, after which I moisten the furrow. It's much easier than trying to work with wet soil and tiny seeds. Besides, the soilless mix doesn't form a crust, so the seedlings emerge from it very easily. I'm sure it helps to produce a high percentage of germination.

Whenever I work with carrots, I lay a board down between the rows, and stand on it rather than on the soil itself. It's hard enough to grow straight long roots in my rocky soil; the least I can do is to distribute my weight so as not to compact the soil unduly. As an added bonus the boards help control weeds between the rows if they are left in place.

The best carrots are those that have grown with ample water and fertilizer, so I keep our crops well watered and feed them twice, once when they're about 3 inches tall and again when they're twice that size. I use a handful of 5-10-5 to a 5-foot row, scattering it in two 6-inch bands, one on either side of the row. Sometimes the very moist, well-fed conditions that produce the finest carrots will cause some of

Harvesting carrots using a board to avoid compacting the soil

the crop to split open. This can be discouraging to gardeners when they first run into it, but it's usually no more than 2 percent of the crop that splits, and although it's not particularly attractive, the split won't hurt the taste at all.

Cauliflower In our first season in the Victory Garden our production schedule forced us to buy our cauliflower seedlings from a local nursery. They eventually turned into beautiful plants with heads worthy of the county fair, but not before they all but perished from a generally fatal disease called, unattractively enough, clubroot. This disease is usually traced to plants that have grown in unsterile conditions, so I attribute our problems to infected seedlings, which is one of the hazards of buying them rather than starting them from seed. Unfortunately there is no way to identify the disease until it is well under way, but it will make itself known as soon as the hot weather comes. One blistering day in May we noticed that the plants were wilting even though the soil was damp (always a danger signal). I removed the cutworm collar, brushed the soil away from the plant, and noticed a tumor-like growth on the stem, just at the soil line. The prognosis was not good: ordinarily as this disease progresses, it decreases the plants' ability to tolerate hot midday temperatures, because it chokes off the water-carrying cells within the stems. Usually the plants die.

But we made an effort to save ours. We added two clubroot enemies to the soil: ground limestone and PCNB, a chemical sold under the name Terraclor. Then we hilled the soil up several inches around the plants in hopes of encouraging new roots to form higher up the stems. We were lucky. After two weeks the roots were developing and the plants were off the danger list, the intensive care program having proven a great success.

The treatment for clubroot won't immunize the plants from root maggots or the cabbageworm caterpillar, so I continue to apply diazinon at 10-day intervals and *Bacillus thuringiensis* at 7- to 10-day intervals.

I sow another crop of cauliflower in May, following the same procedures as I do for this month's sowing of broccoli and cabbage. The crop will be ready for harvest in late summer or early fall, depending on the variety.

Chrysanthemums For years to come the late summer and autumn Victory Garden will be ablaze with chrysanthemums, all the descendants of some beautiful plants we bought our first July to set in along the central path we call Main Street.

These plants flower from August to October. After the ground freezes we mulch them with a layer of leaves or salt

Chrysanthemum flanked by alyssum

marsh hay to protect them over winter. By early May each year the plants that bloomed the previous summer begin bright new growth and are ready for dividing. It may seem strange to you, but I dig up the plants and give away all but one. If the plants were left undisturbed, they would set small flower heads and make spindly growth because they would be overcrowded and would have used up the soil nutrients. I divide the one plant that I save into its single stems and roots and I plant each of these divisions separately in the rich Victory Garden soil at 18-inch intervals. Each division will, by late summer, be as large as the parent plant and covered with flowers. After planting them I pinch them back to about half their height to encourage them to make many branches. Then I give each a drink of transplant solution and they're off and growing.

Corn I'm a believer in the old farmers' adage, "Plant corn when oak leaves are as large as a squirrel's ear." So I usually plant the Victory Garden corn in late April, counting on mild weather in May. As a precaution against unpredictable chilly nights, though, I always keep a bit of salt marsh hay on hand and cover the seedlings if a frost is predicted. A frost wouldn't bother the seeds in the ground, but it would kill the seedlings. Salt marsh hay laid on the ground around the plants is also a good mulch in a dry May, as it conserves the moisture in the soil.

In May, when the seedlings are about 3 inches tall, we evaluate the corn plot and thin the seedlings to one strong plant for each location. With plants spaced about 12 inches apart we get strong growth and abundant harvests.

Cucumbers In addition to nutritious soil, cucumbers need hot, humid weather. In fact, the tenderest and most expensive greenhouse cucumbers are given 80-degree daytime temperatures throughout their growing period. I can't control the outdoor temperatures in the Victory Garden, of course, but with some careful work ahead of time, I can set the plants into the warmest and best-fed soil possible.

I begin in the middle of May, and fork a couple of bushels of well-rotted horse manure (2 quarts of dried cow manure, the kind usually sold in packages at garden centers, can be used instead) along a 15-foot row, even though the soil was limed and manured the previous fall. Then I add half a pound of slow-release fertilizer and dig it in, too, and rake the bed smooth. To warm the soil I cover it with a 30-inch-wide strip of black agricultural plastic mulch, available from any garden center, and bury the edges in the soil to prevent it from blowing away. Late this month, or early in June, the mulch will have warmed the soil to 85 degrees, so I can set in the cucumber seedlings that I started in April.

1. With a spade make a slit in the ground

2. Cut the plastic. Push the edges into the slit. Black agricultural plastic mulch

3. Peel back the top of the peat pot below the soil line.

4. Set in the plastic mulch and water with transplant solution.

To set the seedlings in, I use a trowel to make holes right through the plastic mulch. I train the Victory Garden cucumbers up a fence, so I set the plants out at 12-inch intervals. Just before setting the seedlings out, I peel the lip of the peat pots back to below the soil line to prevent the lip from drawing moisture from around the plants. Then I cut off the weaker of the two seedlings in each pot (I cut rather than pull, because the root systems of the two seedlings are usually intertwined, and cucumber plants resent root disturbance), set the plants in, and give each a drink of transplant solution.

Dahlias Dahlias are native to Mexico, so they are accustomed to warm weather and full sunshine. In May, when the Victory Garden weather has gotten warm, I set out into the open garden the young plants that I rooted in April. I set them at 2- or 3-foot intervals, depending on the expected size of the mature plants. Low-growing varieties are set closer together than tall ones.

If you plant dahlia tubers, do so about a week after the last frost can be expected. I set them in 4 or 5 inches deep, and 2 or 3 feet apart, depending on the ultimate size of the mature plants. The culture of the tuber-grown and cutting-grown plants is identical, and equally good results can be expected from either method.

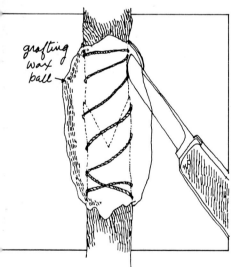

grafting
wax
ball

Fruit Trees One March in the Victory Garden I grafted a young apple tree with several fine varieties. By early May the grafts were about 6 weeks old, and it was time to see how well they were doing. The Golden Delicious graft had not yet produced leaves, though the buds were swelling. The McIntosh was in good shape, as were the old varieties known as Blue Pearmain and the Gravenstein; all were producing healthy new growth. But we lost a couple too, victims of a windy day when a cold frame cover blew over against them. May was too late to try additional grafts to make up for these losses because the operation must be done in the early spring, before the buds swell.

In May, when the grafts were about 2 months old, I cut the string under the grafting wax so that it would not constrict the expanding new growth. This is very easy to do, requiring only a very sharp knife and a steady hand. I cut the string against solid bark so as not to damage the tissues of the graft and I left the cut string and the wax on the tree to continue to provide support.

Garlic In most parts of the country garlic does best when it's planted in late fall for harvest the following summer. But in our first year we planted it in May and it did quite well, probably because the soil had been so well prepared. Garlic likes a well-drained sandy loam with an abundance of organic matter and lime.

Planting is simple. I bought my bulbs in a food market, separated each bulb into single cloves, and planted the cloves 4 or 5 inches apart, pushing them into the soil until the pointed tops were just barely covered. By early fall each clove produced a large bulb with no more help from me except to keep weeds under control.

Kohlrabi Live and learn: we gave ourselves an unforgettable lesson in kohlrabi-thinning one year, when through an oversight we neglected a final thinning. The plants were left at 3- to 4-inch intervals rather than the proper 6- to 8-inch spacing. The results were disappointing — weak spindly plants hardly worth harvesting. Since that time we've been careful to give the plants the wider 6- to 8-inch spacing they need in order to produce beautiful specimens.

Lettuce The first of our lettuce is ready for harvest in May. Here's a tip for keeping it fresh for several days: dig up the whole plant and put the roots into a plastic bag or flowerpot, then treat it as a houseplant. The plant will con-

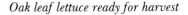
Oak leaf lettuce ready for harvest

tinue to grow if given bright light and you can harvest the leaves for salads as you need them.

I start other crops of lettuce in May, too, sowing a few seeds every week to insure a prolonged harvest in the summer. Because these May-sown plants will mature during hot weather, I plant varieties that are able to stand up to the summer sun, such as Slobolt, Oakleaf, and Matchless.

Melons I prepare the soil for the Victory Garden melons just as I do for the cucumbers, as both need warmth and food. And just as with the cucumbers, I grow the melons on a fence, which saves space, keeps the plants from roaming all over the garden, and keeps the fruit clean and free of slug or field mouse damage. Toward the middle of the month, I add about 2 bushels of well-rotted horse or cow manure to a 15-foot row, the soil having been limed and manured the previous fall too. Then I dig in half a pound of slow-release fertilizer, and rake the bed smooth. In order to prepare a warm spot for the seedlings that were started in April, I mulch the soil with a 30-inch-wide strip of black agricultural plastic, burying the edges against the wind. By late May or early June, the mulch will have warmed the soil to 85 degrees, which the melon seedlings will love.

I set the seedlings in by punching holes in the plastic with a trowel at intervals of about 4 to 6 feet. Before I set the plants in, I peel back the lip of the peat pot and cut off the weaker of the 2 seedlings. Once they're in, I water them well with transplant solution.

Parsley plants in the herb corner of the Victory Garden

New Zealand Spinach May can be an unhappy month for spinach lovers because, with the arrival of warm weather, there won't be another opportunity to sow spinach seeds until late in the summer. Luckily, though, New Zealand spinach provides a good summer substitute, so in May I set out the seedlings begun in April. I peel the edges of each pot down below the soil line to prevent them from acting as wicks and drawing the water from the soil. Then I plant the seedlings at 18-inch intervals, giving each a drink of a transplant solution to get them off and growing.

Parsley In May I set out the parsley seedlings that I began indoors in March. The only trick here is to plant them at the same depth at which they grew in the pot. Occasionally in the first week or so after transplanting, a few of the older leaves die, probably because their fragile connection to the stem was disturbed. This doesn't concern me, as new leaves will grow up from the center of each plant; parsley plants will continue to grow larger and larger, even though their leaves are harvested to lend color and flavor to the kitchen.

Petunias Petunias are probably the most popular of all the summer annuals. They'll bloom until freezing weather in the fall if the old blooms are picked off to prevent the formation of seeds.

In May, after I've moved the tulips from the bed alongside the Victory Garden's greenhouse, I set annuals, including petunias, in their place. I give my petunias a strong hold on life by starting them from seeds in December or January and growing them indoors until March, when they go into the cold frame to grow slowly in night temperatures barely above freezing. By May, when I set them into the garden at 12-inch intervals, these seedlings are short and bushy, with several stems and as much as a 6- to 8-inch spread of foliage. They are far superior to the lanky specimens available in cut-rate outlets, sporting a weak flower atop a single, skinny stem.

Potatoes In May the early potato varieties planted in April break through the soil, and when these young plants are 6 to 8 inches tall, they're ready for their first hilling-up. First I scatter 5-10-10 fertilizer on the ground on both sides of the potato row at the rate of 2 handfuls to a 10-foot row. Then

Hilling-up potatoes

I pull 3 or 4 inches of soil in from the sides of the trench to cover the stems of the plants, covering the fertilizer at the same time. This feeds the plants, keeps their roots deep in the cool soil, and kills weeds. It also eliminates any chance that the young potatoes forming on the roots will be exposed to light. Light causes the skins of potatoes to turn green, and these green skins are poisonous. (For more information about hilling-up, see the glossary entry on page 313.)

Early in May I plant another crop of potatoes, these of a late variety, by the traditional planting method described in April.

Radish harvest

Radishes There is no question in my mind that radishes grown in the early spring are the best tasting we get all year. If it were not for that fact I wouldn't bother with the early radishes because of the hateful root maggot. This pest can be controlled by diazinon applications directly on the seed row at planting time, and again 3 to 5 days after the tiny plants come out of the ground. That second application is the critical one. I remember one painful May day when I was harvesting radishes for the whole television world to see, and every one I found was heavily infested with maggots. I checked the records and discovered I had neglected the second application of diazinon.

In spite of the diminishing quality of the warm-weather radishes, I do continue with weekly plantings until about the first of June. Given rich, moist soil, the roots that mature in the summer even as late as early July are still not too hot-tasting.

Rhododendrons I really don't have room in the Victory Garden for rhododendrons, but one May I set in a plant, just for demonstration purposes. I bought a heavily budded rhododendron that was about 2 feet tall and just coming into flower. That's the wrong time to move most plants, but it's a perfect time to transplant rhododendrons: for one thing, it's easy to tell exactly what shade the blossoms are; for another, rhododendrons begin their strongest growth period immediately after blossoming, so by moving them at that stage of growth, the shock of transplanting is diminished.

I began by digging a hole about 6 inches deeper than the ball of earth around the plant's roots and 12 inches wider than the ball on all sides. This may seem large, but a rhododendron lasts a lifetime if planted properly. I set aside half of the excavated soil to use elsewhere in the garden. To the remaining half I added an equal quantity of sphagnum peat moss, and used part of this mixture to fill in the bottom 6 inches of the hole. Then I firmed it with my feet and set the plant in at the depth it grew in the nursery. The planting depth is so critical that I laid a stick across the sides of the hole and the top of the ball to make sure they were at the same level. After I put the plant in the hole I filled in around it with the balance of the peat moss/soil mixture, firmed the soil around the roots with my feet, made a shallow saucer of soil around the plant to hold water, and gave the plant a drink. Our plant was tied and wrapped in burlap to hold the root system intact, but the plant's roots soon forced their way through the burlap and expanded into the soil.

I had received a deluge of questions on the propagation of rhododendrons, so I propagated the plant by layering. I found a low branch on the plant, and just where it curved upward I removed a leaf or two and shaved off about ¼ inch of the outer bark from the underside of the curve. I touched a little rooting powder to this bare spot, gently bent the branch so this section rested on the soil, and then pinned the curve to the soil with two crossed sticks. I covered this pinned area with a few inches of moist soil, so the leafy end of the branch extended freely. The rhododendron branch rooted into the soil and was ready to be separated from the parent plant in about 12 months.

Roses If ever it was true that an ounce of prevention is worth a pound of cure, it is true of roses. If you wait until you can see trouble, it is most likely too late to stop it. Trouble, in the case of roses, comes in a big package. Everything that crawls and all disfiguring diseases seem to like roses. In May, the main threats are aphids and black spot. Aphids are insects that will, if allowed, cover the buds and suck nourishment from the plant's cells. The blossoms will be deformed, and there's a definite possibility that the aphids will spread viruses from plant to plant as they slurp their way across the rose garden. Black spot is just what its name suggests: a fungus disease that infects the plants' leaves, turning them yellow with ugly black blotches. When the leaves fall to the ground the spores are splashed back onto the plant with the next rain, infecting the plant over and over again.

Black spot is particularly virulent in the cool damp days of the spring, but aphids are problems all summer long. So in mid-May, just as the rose buds begin to swell, and religiously every week thereafter throughout the summer and fall, I spray my rose bushes. I use a prepackaged combination of four fungicides and insecticides that I buy at the garden center in dry, powder form. This mixture includes carbaryl, which controls Japanese and other beetles; malathion, a wide-spectrum insecticide that controls aphids and many other insects; dicofol, which controls the red spider mites that suck the plants' nourishment; and folpet, a fungicide specifically for the control of black spot. I mix according to the package directions, adding about ¼ teaspoon of liquid detergent to each gallon of water. The detergent helps the mixture stick to the foliage.

Shallot bulbs ready for planting

Shallots The shallot is an onion relative much loved by gourmets. It tastes like a very mild onion, with a touch of garlic's pungency. It's a hardy plant that will grow in any part of the country. According to an old saying, shallots should be planted on the shortest day and harvested on the longest day. In mild climates this saying holds true, but in the Victory Garden the shortest day of the year falls in our cold winters, so we plant shallots in the spring and/or fall.

Shallots like light, well-drained soil kept relatively dry all through the growing season. Unlike garlic, shallot bulbs are not enclosed within an all-encompassing outer skin, so I just separate the slender onion sections and plant each so their pointed tops are about ½ inch beneath the surface of the soil, with 6 to 8 inches between the sections. Each produces a cluster of bulbs.

Silver Fleece Vine This hardy twining vine, known botanically as *Polygonum aubertii*, is native to western China and will grow in almost any garden in the United States or southern Canada. By late summer or early fall it's at least 8 to 10 feet tall, and covered with a cloud of small, snowy white blossoms.

The vine I planted in the Victory Garden had 4 or 5 slender stems, some as tall as 30 inches, which is typical of container-grown plants sold by nurseries in the spring. (I had already prepared my garden soil so well that it needed no further work before I set the plant in, but if I'd been planting in unworked soil, I would have made a mixture of two parts soil to one part peat moss, added a slow-release fertilizer, and maybe a little compost.) I set the plant into its hole at the north end of the greenhouse, and made sure that it sat in the Victory Garden soil at the same depth it had in the nursery. To give the vine a head start, I twined the new growth around a string trellis that I had strung from the roof of the greenhouse down to ground level. All vines do best when given a support to climb on as soon as they're planted. Left to struggle along the ground, their growth is relatively poor.

Spinach May marks the arrival of the leaf miner, an insect that has a penchant for spinach. The first indication of the scourge is the appearance of tiny black flies that lay minuscule white eggs on the bottom sides of the leaves. Once the eggs have hatched into larvae and bored their way between the layers of the plants' leaves, they are all but impossible to control. So, beginning early in May, I spray the plants with a diazinon solution every 10 days, stopping about 2 weeks before harvest. Diazinon stays active on the leaves for 14 days, during which the leaves are inedible. Pyrethrum is a nonchemical alternative to diazinon treatments for leaf miner, but it isn't usually as effective.

Silver fleece vine in flower

May is the first harvest month for spinach. I pull the whole plant out of the ground, cut off the roots at the soil line, and prepare for a treat.

Squash Winter squashes are big, slow-growing plants that need warm weather. So I don't plant them until late May or early June. Some of the trailing vine types spread to 15 feet or more, and they can be in the ground as long as 110 days before harvest. With that kind of growing time, they need special soil attention. I start by digging a hole about the size of a bushel basket; I fill the hole half full of well-rotted horse manure or compost that's been thoroughly blended with about ½ cup of a slow-release fertilizer. Then I fill the rest of the hole with regular garden soil, until I've made a slight mound, about 4 inches high at the center. I don't add any more fertilizer at this point because the new roots of the squash are very susceptible to damage if they come into contact with the fertilizer granules.

I plant 6 winter squash seeds on the mound, spacing them in a circle so that all seeds are separated by 4 to 6 inches, and push them 1 inch into the soil with my finger. When they sprout, I save only the 2 strongest plants at each hill.

Strawberries About a month after having been planted in the garden, June-bearing strawberry plants begin to blossom and are anxious to set fruit, but I don't let that happen. I want them to have a full growing season to send out their runners and make a solid bed of plants; if they set fruit this early, their energy will be sapped, so I snip all the buds from the plants.

Early in the summer, I pluck the blossoms of first-year everbearing strawberries, too, which continue to produce fruit year after year. But along in August, I let the blossoms stay on the plants to produce a good harvest of fruit for the fall.

Sweet Potatoes The sweet potato, like the peanut, is usually considered a southern crop, but the growing season in the Victory Garden is more than the 120 days they need, and my crops do quite well. The sweet potato shares another quality with the peanut: it does not appreciate all the soil preparation I've done in the Victory Garden. It likes a poor, dry, slightly acidic soil with little fertilizer. It is subject to a scab disease similar to that which attacks the ordinary white potato if it's grown in sweet or alkaline soil.

Sweet potatoes are grown from sprouts. The sprouts, or slips, are easy to grow from the potatoes themselves — I sometimes bury the sweet potatoes in a hotbed in early April,

Sweet potato plant growing in a bushel basket

and have sprouts by May — or slips can be bought through southern seed houses. In May, when the soil is warm, I plant out slips that are about 6 inches tall.

In the open garden, the sprouts can be planted about 18 inches apart in a row that's been mounded to improve drainage, but these plants are such exuberant growers that I've chosen not to plant them in my small garden. I do sometimes plant a single sprout in a bushel basket filled with soil. Oddly enough, those grown in such confined quarters, or in poor soil, are rounder and meatier than those grown in the rich soil in the open garden, where they have a tendency to become long and spindly.

Tomatoes Toward the middle of this month, or 10 days before they are to go into the open ground, I put the tomato seedlings that have been enjoying the good warmth and light of the greenhouse into the slightly more hostile environment of the covered cold frame. On warm days I open the cover but at night I keep it closed and covered with a tarp if a frost is predicted. This controlled chill helps the plants harden off, so they can better tolerate field conditions.

Because tomatoes thrive in highly organic soils, I make sure that we plant ours in ground that is well prepared. Into soil that has been manured, limed, and fertilized with 5-10-5, I squander as much compost as I can find. In the Victory Garden's first year compost was scarce, and we were unable to add any significant amount to the tomato plantings. We had good tomatoes that year, but nothing compared to those we grew the next season when we had 9 cubic feet of brown gold to enrich our garden soil.

To set the plants into the garden I use my planting board to mark out the intervals in the rows and then set each plant slightly deeper into the soil than it was growing in the pot. If the plants are in peat pots, I make sure to peel away the top lip of the pot to prevent its acting like a wick, releasing soil moisture to the atmosphere. I also put a cutworm collar around each plant and drench each with the transplant solution.

Over the years, we've grown tomatoes in and up all sorts of contraptions and the spacing of the plants varies with these support devices. One year, we grew a whole line of plants on a trellis of strings and wires, as many commercial growers do. First we set in the plants at 18-inch intervals. Then with two stout 6-foot cedar posts set at either end of the row we connected a solid strand of wire at the top, and another length of wire 6 inches from the bottom. Then we connected the 2 wires with a length of string at each location, and trained the vines up the strings. (As the plants grew, we removed the suckers, or side branches, so each plant had only one strong stem.) This method has its advantages: the fruit is held up off the ground and the yield, while not particularly

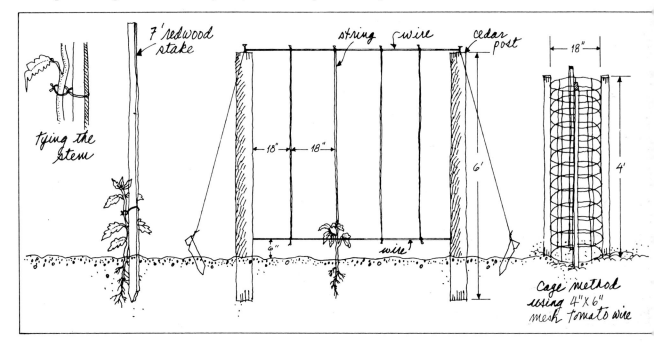

tying the stem

7' redwood stake

string   wire   cedar post

18"

18"   18"

6"

wire

6'

18"

4'

cage method using 4"x6" mesh tomato wire

heavy, is often earlier than with some other techniques. On the other hand, constant labor is needed to train the vines to cling to the string; there is inevitable damage when plants chafe at their moorings in windy weather; and keeping the cedar posts upright and the wires properly tensioned is difficult when the load of fruit becomes heavy as the season advances.

A simpler, more conventional method of training tomatoes is to plant at 18- to 24-inch intervals, place a stake at every plant, and train each plant to a single stem. (I use seven foot redwood stakes, which last for years). Training consists of simply tying each stem to a stake with garden twine and removing the suckers as they grow. The tying is a chore that must be done once a week as the plants increase in size but the rewards are early, clean fruit. (For an illustration of the tying technique, see page 91.)

Young tomato seedlings in a six-pack

Perhaps the easiest method of growing tomatoes is to plant at 3-foot intervals and let the plants sprawl on the ground with nothing more than a bed of hay mulch to keep the fruit relatively clean. I say relatively because some injury, especially from slugs and careless foot traffic, is inevitable. Another problem we've found with the sprawl method is inherent: they sprawl onto the pathways, into other crops — all over the garden if you let them. And because no pruning is done the crop matures later than with the single-stem methods. (Pruning encourages early ripening at the expense of heavy yield.)

If you press me, I might say I like the cage method of growing tomatoes the best. We have two types: one made from dog wire rolled into 4-foot-high cylinders, 18 inches in diameter, into which we cut several 4 × 6-inch openings. The other is a cage with the same dimensions except the wire we use is sold as tomato wire and already has the 4 × 6-inch openings in it. As you might suspect, cages made from tomato wire are a bit more expensive than dog-wire cages, but are much easier and faster to construct. And there are not as many sharp ends to scratch the hands when harvesting.

With both types of cages, I set the plants in at 3-foot intervals, put one end of the cage over the plant and tie the cage to four 4-foot stakes driven into the ground. Inside the cages, the tomato seedlings are not restrained in any way, so the yield is enormous. The harvest is a bit later than with single staking but sometimes a compromise is possible if some pruning is done in July to eliminate all growth that extends beyond the top of the cage.

Tulips In April, the Victory Garden's tulip bed comes into flower, the brilliant payoff to the bulb-planting of the previous fall. I plant several varieties, early-, mid-, and late-season, in different colors and heights, and the month-long flower display is dazzling. By early in May, though, it is pretty well over. The flowers are fading and the foliage is be-ginning to brown. This is an important stage for the plants because the nourishment from the foliage accumulates in the bulbs, strengthening them for another year, but it does give the tulip bed an untidy look. So I add some new color: a vivid red azalea; a group of petunia seedlings, not yet in flower, that will spread rapidly and soon produce bright pink blos-soms; some purple johnny-jump-ups, the plant from which pansies were bred; and several clumps of clear blue forget-me-nots in full flower.

By mid-May, the tulips have progressed from the merely scruffy stage to the downright ugly and more drastic measures are called for. It's at this point that I lift the entire plants (foliage, bulb, and all) and relocate them for growing on in a less conspicuous setting. I move the bulbs with their leaves still attached into a trench, label them, and cover the bulbs with about 4 inches of soil. The idea is to let the foliage ripen. When it has turned completely brown in early July I dig up the bulbs, divide and grade them, put them in paper bags and save them for replanting in the fall.

Turnips It's not unusual for the March planting of the humble turnip to be the most spectacular crop in the May garden. The seedlings double in size every week, making the thinning process even more critical than usual. During May I pull every other plant in the row, using the pulled seedlings for turnip greens, and leaving a final spacing of 4 to 6 inches between the plants.

May still being root-maggot season in the Victory Garden, I drench the soil in the turnip row with diazinon. I do this early in the month, so that when I thin the plants toward mid-month, the diazinon will have had two weeks to dissipate, and the pulled seedlings will be edible. Immediately after thinning, I give the remaining plants a final application of diazinon and the crop is ready for harvest by the end of May.

Q&A

Q: Last summer I had an infestation of slugs. I was told not to use metaldehyde. Beer didn't work and neither did salt, and now they're back this spring. Help!

A: Metaldehyde is the specific insecticide for slugs: it comes in both pellet and meal form. I don't favor the pellets because birds are apt to eat them, which would kill them. But I don't mind the meal because the particles are small enough to sink into the soil. I put it on late in the day when the soil is moist, so the particles settle more easily in among small crevices in the soil surface.

But there's another way of combating slugs, and snails too. Both are nocturnal creatures, eating at night and sleeping in the day in a dark place. So I lay down a few shingles or old cabbage leaves, and the slugs will crawl underneath for a snooze after their feeding period. In the morning they'll be under that shelter and I either step on them, or scoop them up. This is a safer approach and most of the slugs in the garden will fall for it. I sometimes need to repeat the procedure when a new generation of slugs comes along.

Q: How much sun should my fuchsia plant have? Does moving this plant cause the blossoms to fall off?

A: First of all, the plant needs partial sun. Moving the plant around will cost you a few of the old petals, but that's normal. After the petals fall off, only the seed pods are left: if you pick these pods off, your fuchsia will continue blossoming all summer long.

Q: Only two of our six dogwood trees bloomed. What should I do to make the other trees flower?

A: It might be that your trees are too young to flower. My hunch though is that the trees are too shaded. Dogwoods bloom best when they get plenty of sunshine.

Q: For the past three years my tomato, pepper, eggplant, and cabbage seedlings have grown 2 inches tall, then collapsed and died. Friends say they had damping-off disease. Are they right?

A: Yes. In the future make sure you use sterilized soil. Sow your seeds thinly so there's plenty of air space between the plants. And don't water the plants in late afternoon, so the soil's surface is dry at night, when damping-off is most active.

Q: Is there anything to be done with leggy tomato seedlings?

A: Yes. When you transplant them, set them in right down to their seed leaves. They will make new roots along the buried stems and grow rapidly.

SOME OF THE BASICS

Thinning If every seed sown in the garden were guaranteed to germinate, single seeds could be planted at predetermined intervals along a row and thinning wouldn't be necessary at all. But since no such guarantee exists, the solution is to sow many more seeds than needed and then thin the rows after germination, giving the strongest and best-situated

seedlings space to grow. Believe me, I know that yanking healthy seedlings out of the garden goes against a gardener's grain but it has to be done. Crowded seedlings grow into miserable, leggy, unproductive plants. Besides, seedlings pulled from the Victory Garden are never really lost. Some crops — spinach and beet greens for instance — are at their tenderest when they're young, so the thinning is actually a harvest. Some seedlings

can be transplanted to grow into full-size plants elsewhere in the garden. Even seedlings that can't be eaten or transplanted can be added to the composter and recycled. So there's no reason for gardeners to give in to the urge to leave dense rows of seedlings crowding each other for growing space.

For many crops, early cucumbers, melons, and summer squashes among them, I usually start seedlings indoors, 2 seeds to a pot, though only one of those seedlings is intended for transplant. I find that by the time thinning is needed the root systems of these plants are apt to be entangled; so rather than pull the extra seedling and risk losing both by mistake, I use scissors to clip off the extra one at the soil line. Where only a few pots of seedlings are concerned, this far safer approach isn't much trouble.

Clipping is far too labored a technique in a garden row, though, so I use one hand to anchor the good seedlings, and pull out the extras with the other hand. In the garden, I generally thin most crops twice: when their true leaves appear, I thin to half the final interval; then when the seedlings are about 2 inches tall, I thin them to the permanent spacing. This improves the margin of survival, should some disaster befall the crop in its early days.

I find that thinning is easiest after a rain when the soil is still moist, because the unwanted plants slip from the soil with a minimum of disturbance to those that remain. So if there hasn't been a recent rain, I water the garden well the day before I plan to thin my crops.

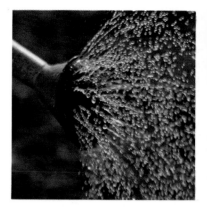

Watering Water is important all through a plant's life, but it never matters more than during its first days in the ground. Quite simply, if newly sown seeds dry out, they will not germinate; and if newly emerging plants, lacking the root structure to delve deeply for moisture, dry out, they die. So immediately after I sow a row of seeds, I water the row with a fine spray, gentle enough to leave the seeds moistened but undisturbed. I keep the surface of the soil moist during the days or weeks while the seeds are germinating, and as soon as growth is visible through the soil, I increase the watering vigilance. The tiny plants are easily washed out so I water them lightly but frequently, sometimes as often as twice daily.

Of course gardens need water throughout the entire season, and the Victory Garden with its raised beds needs water even more frequently than most. As a general guide, any garden needs at least 1 inch of water a week; I use a rain gauge to judge this, but an empty can in the garden would do the trick as well. If the heavens fail to provide the necessary moisture, some sort of mechanical watering gadget is a must. There are several of these on the market, some better than others. Here's a sampling:

Drip irrigators: There are several kinds of drip irrigation equipment, but at their simplest, they are nothing but lengths of hose through which water oozes into the soil. They're particularly good because the water can seep down without wetting the foliage and inviting leaf diseases. With this method of watering there's minimal water loss through evaporation. I use two basic kinds of hoses in the Victory Garden. One is a plastic hose with tiny holes all along its length. The other is a canvas hose that allows the water to escape from its entire surface.

Rotary sprinklers: Inexpensive and reasonably effective, rotary sprinklers have one disadvantage: they distribute the water so quickly that puddles form on the soil's surface unless the machine is turned off every 10 or 15 minutes to allow the moisture to soak in, and this is a bother. Most of these sprinklers also apply the water in a circular pattern, so the corners of rectangular gardens must be watered by hand.

Oscillating sprinklers: These are my favorite. They apply the water in a rectangular pattern, and the wand moves slowly enough to give the water a chance to soak in. The only problem with them is that there is quite a bit of evaporation and water loss on hot, windy days.

Impact sprinklers: Without doubt, these are the most sophisticated of the watering devices, and are the favorites of commercial growers with large and often oddly shaped plantings because the spray can be adjusted to any shape garden.

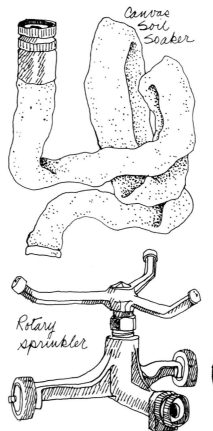

Canvas Soil Soaker

Rotary sprinkler

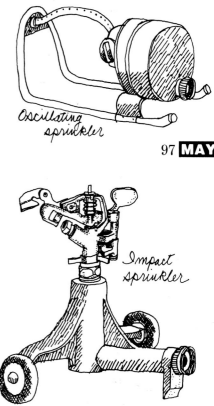

Oscillating sprinkler

Impact sprinkler

They're certainly effective, and while they're expensive and seemingly complicated, they last for many years with little maintenance.

The time-honored way to keep moisture in the soil as long as possible is mulch: an insulating layer between the soil and the hot sun. The simplest of these is a dust mulch, which is nothing more than a thin layer of soil loosened with a cultivator. The theory is that the act of loosening the surface soil breaks down the capillary link between the lower soil moisture and the air above ground. Some scientists reject this argument, but the fact remains that plants grow more easily in cultivated soil than hard soil. Besides, weeds have to be controlled, and cultivating accomplishes this, too.

In the Victory Garden, where the sandy soil dries out so quickly, organic mulches can be a godsend. (In heavier soil they can present some problems: they prevent the soil from warming in the spring, and they present a perfect haven for slugs.) There is quite a variety of organic mulches to choose from. Grass clippings are fine, as long as there's been no weed-killer used on the grass; I put only 2 inches of grass clippings on the soil at a time, as thicker layers rot into a slippery mess. Old or spoiled hay works too, as does straw, but old hay often leaves behind a blanket of weeds and grasses after it decays. Salt marsh hay is by far the best, but it's expensive and hard to find; on the other hand, since it originates in saline areas, any seeds it carries will die in normal garden soil. With any of these organic mulches I sprinkle a little nitrate of soda over the mulch. Otherwise, mulched crops are apt to turn yellow, suffering a temporary loss of nitrogen to the bacteria that decays the mulch.

Fertilizing All fertilizers have a three-number notation: it refers to the percentages of nitrogen, phosphorus, and potassium respectively in the fertilizer. For instance, 5-10-5 is 5 percent nitrogen, 10 percent phosphorus, and 5 percent potassium, also known as potash. The remaining 80 percent of the substance is filler. These three elements are the main nutrients that plants need. Nitrogen is responsible for rapid growth and dark green leaves; all plants need it, especially those whose foliage is the harvest, such as spinach, collards, and lettuce. Phosphorus is important for the root growth of every plant in the garden; it helps plants develop sturdiness and aids in the production and maturation of flowers and fruit. Potassium provides the balance between the growth factor of nitrogen and the ripening influence of phosphorus; it's necessary for new cell growth, especially in the roots and buds, so it's important for root crops such as beets and potatoes.

We use a variety of fertilizers in the Victory Garden, each to meet different needs. When the soil is prepared for planting we use either 5-10-5 or 10-10-10, both commercial granular fertilizers; in this granular form, some of the nutrients are released to the crops immediately, and the rest are released over a period of a few weeks.

You may find that garden centers stock fertilizer formulas different from the ones that I use. The reason is that fertilizer manufacturers supply specific mixtures to fit local soil conditions. I suggest that you use these fertilizers according to the instructions on the labels rather than try to find the exact type that I use.

Slow-release fertilizers are chemically identical to the granular fertilizers, but they are coated with a water-permeable material so the nutrients are released to the soil much more slowly over many months. I use the slow-release fertilizers for slow-maturing crops such as melons and squash and for plants that are in the ground for several years, such as rhubarb, asparagus, and raspberries.

Foliar fertilizers are meant to be mixed with water; they are available either as crystalline or liquid concentrates. The one I use most frequently has a 23-19-17 formula. I add it to water to make the transplant solution that I give to all seedlings at the time of transplanting. I also use foliar fertilizers on plants that appear, from their yellowing foliage or uneven growth, to need a helping hand.

As a general rule I apply all fertilizers sparingly rather than generously. It is possible to overfertilize plants, in which case the leafy growth will be lush, at the expense of poor fruit production. In acute cases of overfeeding, plant roots can actually be burned and the plants will die.

Bone meal is another fertilizer used in the Victory Garden, though less frequently. This fertilizer, nothing but powdered animal bones, contains 23 percent phosphorus in a slowly available form. It helps in the development of strong root systems, so I use it on thick-rooted crops that last for years, such as peonies and bulb plants. It's a fine fertilizer for perennials.

If possible, I like to add 2 or 3 inches of manure to a garden every fall and dig it into the soil. Cow manure's the best bet but it's not easy to find, so horse manure is the second choice. We use fresh manures: they break down through the winter, improving the soil's texture and adding trace elements such as iron, sulfur, magnesium, copper, and boron, which are needed in small amounts and may not be available in commercial fertilizers. Manures can't, however, function as complete fertilizers. They do not contain enough nitrogen, phosphorus, or potassium to keep the crops well fed. In fact, manures are so low in these critical nutrients that one would need to add 20 pounds of cow manure to do the job of 1 pound of 5-10-5 commercial fertilizer.

I don't advise gardeners to leave the manuring until the spring. Fresh manures are too harsh to use so close to planting time, and the well-rotted manures that would be gentle enough to use in the spring are almost impossible to find. Used according to the instructions, the packaged, dehydrated manures available in garden centers and department stores are handy if expensive alternatives. As concentrates they contain the percentages of nitrogen, phosphorus, and potassium that plants need, so they're popular with gardeners who would rather avoid the commercial fertilizers. They have two negative qualities: for one, the nutrients are released to the soil only as the material decays, so the spring crops have less to feed on than the summer crops; for another, the bulk of these manures has been altered in the dehydration process, so they do not effectively improve the texture of the soil as other organic materials do.

Cultivating There are two goals in cultivating: to loosen the soil, easing the way

for air and moisture to circulate around a crop's roots, and to control weeds. As far as I'm concerned the way to take the drudgery and grumbling out of this task is to cultivate as frequently as once a week. It's

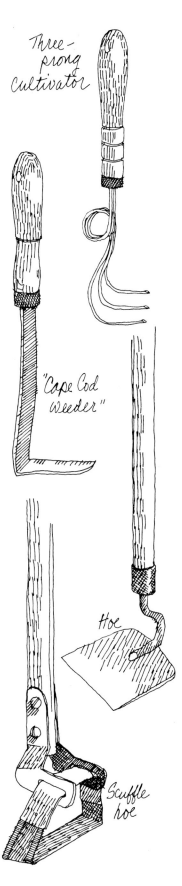

Three-prong cultivator

"Cape Cod Weeder"

Hoe

Scuffle hoe

best to cultivate lightly, loosening only the top ½ inch of soil; this is plenty deep enough to slice off the weeds without damaging the roots of the crops.

In the Victory Garden I use four different tools in cultivating, each with its strong points.

"Cape Cod Weeder": This L-shaped hand cultivator has a sharp edge and a point, so it can be used to weed close to and under the foliage of small plants which the other tools cannot reach easily.

Three-prong cultivator: This hand tool is an old-time favorite. It can't slice off weeds but if used diligently to loosen the soil it will prevent the weeds from growing.

Hoe: The hoe is certainly known to all gardeners and is among the easiest of the cultivating tools to use. Pulled through the soil, the hoe will slide under the weeds and cut them off below the soil level. It's also a helpful tool for hilling-up. But it can't be moved in close to the rows, so the weeds that grow among the crops have to be pulled by hand. (A helpful tip here: always sharpen your hoe before you go to the garden. Don't let the expression "dull as a hoe" have special meaning for you!)

Scuffle hoe: This long-handled tool has the advantage of working in both stroke directions, back and forth. It does essentially the same job as a regular hoe, but it generally requires less effort to operate.

Snap beans

JUN

Plant
Beans
Beets
Carrots
Pumpkins
Squash

Thin
Basil
Beets
Carrots
Parsnips
Pumpkins

Start Seedlings
Brussels Sprouts
Cabbage
Cauliflower
Corn
Cyclamen
Primroses

Transplant
Cabbage
Cauliflower
Celery
Eggplants
Okra
Peppers
Squash

Harvest
Beans
Beets
Broccoli
Cabbage
Carrots
Kohlrabi
New Zealand Spinach
Parsley
Peas
Potatoes
Swiss Chard

Special Events
Chrysanthemums
Endive
Evergreens
Irises
Leeks
Onions
Rosemary
Tomatoes

JUNE

In June, summer arrives in the Victory Garden. The rainy spring weather lets up and the night temperatures usually stay above 55 degrees even early in the month. It's warm enough for the potted herbs to be put outside and for the seedlings of the warm-weather crops to be transplanted to the open garden. Because the sun can be quite strong, I usually sow the seeds of late June plantings deeper than the early spring crops, putting the seeds in twice as deep as I do in April and May.

Thanks to this warm weather, June is the month I can begin to start seedlings in the Victory Garden's nursery bed rather than in the greenhouse. I use the uncovered cold frame for the nursery; it gives the plants fresh air, sunshine, and protection too. The nursery bed is one of the great economies of gardening because the seeds can be sown much closer together than they can in the open garden, since this is not their permanent location. I often start lettuce, broccoli, brussels sprouts, cabbage, and cauliflower in the nursery bed in June. As a vacancy turns up in the garden, I transplant a seedling to fill it. I sow the seeds of perennials and biennials in the nursery bed too; they can be moved later in the fall or left there through the winter and transplanted in the spring.

Speaking of perennials and biennials, June is the perfect month to order seeds for next year. Sown in July, the plants have ample growing time during the rest of the season to make sturdy specimens that will blossom the following year. In June the perennial border is a riot of color as sky blue flax, golden yarrow, stately delphinium and flower-laden bee balm, multicolor irises and roses, and snowy Madonna lilies open their blossoms in response to the pleasant weather.

Most gardeners set out their annual plants in the spring, when the garden centers carry the best of their selection. By the time the summer arrives the only seedlings still on the market are the dregs of the spring offerings, and they're usually too leggy and woody ever to recover in the garden. So this month I plant a few annual seeds to guarantee fresh, healthy young seedlings for setting into the garden in July. They'll grow quickly at this time of the year — dwarf marigold seeds can be sown even as late as July. There's no garden anywhere that doesn't have blank spots now and again and it's a joy to have vigorous young seedlings to pop into the vacancies.

Basil By June, the basil plants begun in May are ready for thinning to one plant every 12 inches. With this generous spacing the plants will grow to 18 inches tall. I sometimes transplant the pulled seedlings or I use them in the kitchen, as they have their full flavor even at this young age.

Basil is a cut-and-come-again herb, but only if its inclination to produce seeds is thwarted. I do this by pinching off the ends of the stems, removing the entire clusters of flower buds. The plants redirect their energy toward forming new tender, leafy shoots.

Beans In June some of the bush beans planted in May are ready for harvest. I pick them when they're at their best, before the swelling of the seeds is visible through the pods. Bush beans usually produce one large harvest and a series of smaller ones over about a two-week period, and I find that the yield is best if I pick early and often. One thing to remember when picking beans is to do so only when the foliage is dry. Leaf diseases are spread if the plants are picked when they are wet with dew or rain.

When the harvest of the first crop is over, I pull the plants out and sow another crop of bush beans just as I did in May, with one exception: the hotter weather dries the soil quickly at this time of year, so I put the seeds 2 inches deep in the soil, rather than 1 inch. In the warm June weather, the seedlings are often out of the ground within a week.

In the Victory Garden, June is the first month warm enough to plant lima beans, which need soil warmed to at least 65 degrees. As with all other legumes, I moisten the seeds and treat them with a nitrogen inoculant before planting, but there the similarity between the lima bean and its relatives ends. I plant limas 6 inches apart, in contrast to the close spacing of the other bush beans. I set them in the bottom of a flat-bottomed trench 6 to 8 inches wide, spacing the seeds in two staggered rows, then pull 2 inches of soil over them. In a week they're usually showing their first growth.

One year we had a disaster with our lima bean crop. We were a little late with our planting of a short demonstration row, and after two weeks in the ground only three seedlings had managed to struggle up. As I began to look for reasons, I remembered that the seeds themselves were only marginally acceptable: we'd bought them from a seed rack late in the spring, though we buy nearly all our seeds from mail-order seed houses. The seeds had been dry and cracked and, incidentally, hadn't been treated with captan to prevent rotting, an oversight I did not correct. My other crops of limas have done well, so I'm inclined to blame the seeds. This is a good lesson for gardeners: buy your seeds directly from a

Bush beans ready for picking

seedsman if possible. They will have been properly stored to retain their viability, which is not done with seed-rack packages.

Beets The first of the Victory Garden beets, begun in February and set into the garden in April, are ready for harvest in June. These beets could be left in the ground for quite a while yet before harvesting, but they're at their tenderest and tastiest when they're about 2 inches in diameter, so I usually pull most of my crop this month.

By early in June, the seeds planted in the open ground in April have become 4-inch seedlings and are ready for thinning to 2- or 3-inch intervals. To ward off the late-June leaf miner surge, any beets in the ground in June will receive fortnightly diazinon applications through the month, though due to the two-week life of diazinon, none of these plants are harvested within 14 days of treatment.

Beets are good root-cellar plants, so I sow another crop in June for harvest in the fall. I sow two rows, 4 to 6 inches apart, and sprinkle the seeds in at 1-inch intervals just as I did in April. The hot June weather has the potential to bake the life out of these seeds, so the watering routine is especially diligent.

Broccoli Aside from periodic treatments with *Bacillus thuringiensis* and diazinon, the May planting of broccoli needs no attention in June. The seedlings set out in April, though, are ready for harvest. I cut them just below the bud clusters while the buds are still tightly compressed and blue-green in color and before the buds start producing tiny light yellow flowers. I use a sharp knife to sever the main broccoli head from the main stem, leaving the rest of the plant in the

Broccoli plant with main head and side shoots

soil. Within a week or so secondary shoots will grow from the main stem: they aren't as large as the first harvest, but they're just as tasty. By the way, don't worry if your broccoli harvest is a little bigger than you can manage, for this is one vegetable that freezes beautifully: just blanch it in hot water, seal it in a plastic bag, and put it into the freezer.

Brussels Sprouts In the last week of June I plant brussels sprouts in the nursery bed, where they'll be protected but out in the fresh air and sunshine. I sow the seeds about 1 inch apart, so they won't be crowded if they have to wait an extra week or so before I put them into the garden proper next month.

Cabbages

Cabbage Cabbages have a rather odd, nonconformist trait. Even when seedlings are treated identically, they mature differently and can vary in harvest time by as much as three or four weeks: the harvest of the seedlings I set into the Victory Garden in April usually begins in early June and continues through the month. This variability works to the home gardener's advantage, as several heads of cabbage at one time would present quite a challenge to the cook. In fact, to help gardeners stretch out the harvest season, some seed houses sell mixtures of early-, mid-, and late-season varieties.

I've received a number of questions from viewers who have one of the more common problems with cabbages: as the heads mature, they often split open if there's too much water in the soil or if the plants are growing too rapidly. There's an easy way to prevent this: cut along one side of each plant with a spade, lift it partially out of the soil, then let it settle back. The plant's abbreviated root system won't be able to draw in enough moisture to split the head, but the plant will continue to develop. When the heads are firm and solid, I harvest them by cutting them just below their heads.

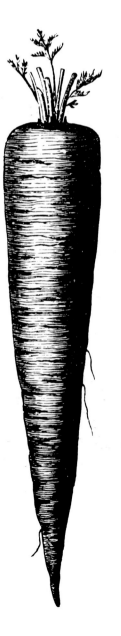

I also start the seeds of mid- and late-season cabbages in June, planting them about ½ inch deep and 1 inch apart in a nursery row. That sowing is a little thinner than is normal because I sometimes find that I have to leave the seedlings in the nursery row longer than I might wish while waiting for a garden row to become available, and this generous spacing will give the plants room to grow without crowding. After the seeds are sown in the furrow I cover them with plain dry sand, which will help deter the damping-off fungus that attacks seedlings and give the tiny plants an easier surface to push through. Of course I water the soil after planting and keep it moist at all times.

Late in June, when there's a row open, I transplant these seedlings into soil that's been prepared as for the April sowing. I set them in deeply enough so the seed leaves are just about at soil level, spacing the seedlings at 24-inch intervals, rather than 18-inch, because mid- and late-season cabbages produce larger plants than do the early varieties. At this point I have a choice of using a root maggot mat around each plant stem or putting a cutworm collar around each plant, and making a saucer of soil to funnel liquids to the roots. If the latter method is used, I give each plant a drink of diazinon to control root maggots. And I continue spraying with *Bacillus thuringiensis* at 7- to 10-day intervals to combat the cabbageworm. All newly transplanted seedlings get a drink of water fortified with a water-soluble fertilizer.

Carrots The Victory Garden has its first carrot harvest in June, when the April sowing is young and tender and ready for harvest. If you've been of the opinion that storage, shipping, and aging have no adverse effect on carrots, an early harvest from your own garden will show you the error of your ways, for the taste of these new carrots is superb.

The May sowing needs thinning in June, when they are about ¾ inch tall. This can be an exasperating task, but the seedlings should stand 1 inch apart in order to grow well.

The seedlings slip out more easily (as do the weeds) if the soil is moistened before the thinning operation begins. Of course, I always stand on a board, not directly on the soil, when I work with carrots because compacted soil will produce gnarled roots.

I sow a third crop of carrots early in June, sprinkling the seeds into two furrows 5 or 6 inches apart and ½ inch deep. I use potting soil, sand, or a soilless mixture to cover the seeds because these materials stay soft and give the seedlings an easier exit. We can have an occasional blistering day in June so I sometimes need to moisten the seed rows twice a day, because if the seeds dry out, even once, most of the young seedlings will never see the light of day.

Cauliflower The head, or edible portion, of a cauliflower plant is actually a cluster of undeveloped flower buds. If allowed to go their natural way, these buds open into small yellow flowers. The gardener's goal is to prevent this, to let the head grow to its maximum size while staying frosty white.

By early in June, the flower clusters in the cauliflower plants transplanted to the Victory Garden in April grow to about the size of teacups and are ready for the blanching treatment that will produce the biggest, whitest heads. Blanching shields the bud cluster from light, which prevents the buds from flowering and keeps them tender and snowy white. There are a couple of ways to blanch cauliflower. I either break a few leaves over the little head to block out the light or I pull the long outer leaves up around the head and secure them with a plastic bag tie or a rubber band so each plant wears a topknot of leaves. I always do this operation on a dry, sunny day so moisture won't be trapped around the buds and cause them to rot. I leave the heads covered until harvest.

The cabbageworm will plague cauliflower all season long, so I continue applications of *Bacillus thuringiensis* at 7- to 10-day intervals.

Frankly, I consider purple-headed cauliflower to be the royal line among the many varieties of this vegetable. The heads are large and tender, the flavor subtle, and it's much less trouble than white cauliflower because it needs no blanching. Actually purple-headed cauliflower is a cross between broccoli and cauliflower, and seed catalogues sometimes list it as both. When cooked, the color lightens to a pale green.

As is the case with all cauliflower, the purple-headed variations need to mature during the cool weather. Because the growing season is so long, from 80 to 115 days depending on the variety, there is time for only one crop in the Victory Garden's growing season, planted early in June for harvest in

Cauliflower leaves tied around the head for blanching

Purple-headed cauliflower

October. I sow the seeds in a nursery row, ½ inch deep and 1 inch apart, and cover them with dry sand to protect the emerging seedlings from damping-off fungus. Purple cauliflower plants grow to be about 3 feet tall and they belong in a section of the garden where they won't shade shorter and less vigorous plants. So when an appropriate spot opens up in the garden, I prepare the soil as for all the cabbage-related plants (see April), and transplant the seedlings to 24-inch intervals.

Celery At long last, the celery seedlings sown in February are ready for the open ground early in June, when there is no longer any threat of night temperatures below 55 degrees. If the celery is set in when the nights are too chilly, the plants will go to seed instead of making succulent stalks.

Celery needs moisture, organic matter, and fertilizer: plants grown without this helpful trio are apt to be tough and stringy. Since there is already peat moss and lime in the soil, the only additive needed is 10-10-10 fertilizer (about 1½ pounds to 100 square feet) dug into the soil. Once this is done, I set the plants in at 8- to 10-inch intervals and water them with transplant solution to get them off to a fast start.

Through the growing season I use rotenone to ward off aphids and Maneb to protect the plants from leaf blight. And because celery needs an ample diet, I side-dress the rows a couple of times during the growing season with 5-10-5, once in mid-July and again in mid-August.

Chrysanthemums By mid-month, the single-stem chrysanthemum divisions set out in May and pinched back to encourage branching have developed several stems. When each of these stems has made 4 to 6 inches of new growth I pinch off the top ½ inch so the plants will continue to branch and develop bushy growth. By the time the plants are ready to blossom they will be grand and full, with a dozen or more stems each.

Corn There is an old saying in New England that corn should be knee-high by the fourth of July. But in the deep compost here in the Victory Garden even the slowest of my corn has that old saying bettered before the end of June.

Corn silk, the female flower of the corn

Sowing a second crop of corn in six-packs

This makes me all the more anxious to protect the crop from the ravages of the European corn borer, an insect that invaded this country around 1900, ending centuries of untroubled corn agriculture. In the years since its arrival it has spread and multiplied and is now the number one problem for corn growers in many parts of the country. Despite its name, the corn borer does not limit its diet to corn: it attacks at least two hundred other kinds of plants. (The experience with the corn borer is one of the reasons that customs officials are so careful with plant material brought into this country. It doesn't take much of a start or very many years to produce an enormous population of troublesome insects.)

The corn borer hatching time varies in different parts of the country. (A county agricultural agent can give you exact information for your area.) In Boston the first brood appears around June 10, so that's when we mount our attack with an insecticide called carbaryl, sold under the name Sevin. I spray the plants in the evening after bees have returned to their hives for the night, because this material is toxic to bees as well as to corn borers. Or I spray in the morning before there's any breeze to speak of so the insecticide will stay put on the corn and not blow around the garden. To help the carbaryl adhere to the glossy corn leaves, I add ¼ teaspoon of detergent to every gallon of spray. I aim the spray directly down in every center, or whorl, of leaves and I repeat this spraying every 4 or 5 days until the crop is ready to pick.

I am frequently asked at this time of year if the suckers, or side shoots, growing around the base of the corn stalks are sapping the plants' strength. No, they're not. In fact, they're giving the plants strength. If they were removed the plants would suffer.

The earliest of my corn crop will be ready for harvest by early July, so about 10 days before, in the latter part of June, I sow another crop in six-packs, 1 kernel per compartment. Ordinarily corn isn't a vegetable that's transplanted, but it can be done easily if the plants are grown in containers so the root balls are undisturbed. I put these plants into the section of the corn bed that's vacated by harvest. By saving growing time I'll be able to grow two crops from the same stretch of garden.

Cyclamen Cyclamen plants teach a gardener to be patient: a seed needs 15 to 18 months of good care to coax it into flower. But once it blooms it's a splendid houseplant with few rivals. It begins to blossom in October or November and continues to bloom until April, repeating this performance year after year.

Cyclamens can be planted in any season, but I usually

start some seeds in June to begin to blossom two autumns hence. The seeds are about 1/16 inch in diameter and easy to plant individually. I have good luck sowing them in peat pellets, pushing one seed ¼ inch down into the top of each pellet, but they can also be planted in ordinary potting soil. In either case, cyclamen seeds germinate quickest in darkness, so I put them in total darkness for 40 days and 40 nights, after which the first of them will start to sprout. As they germinate, I shift them into bright light, but not full sun.

Eggplants Eggplants like moisture, heat, and food, so I wait until early June to set out the seedlings sown in April. By this time of year there's not much danger of the night temperatures dropping below 55 degrees.

Although the Victory Garden soil is fertile, I dig 5-10-5 fertilizer into the soil (4 or 5 pounds to 100 square feet) before setting the plants in at 2-foot intervals. Eggplants are on the cutworms' list of delicacies, so I slip a cutworm collar over each plant. Then I shower them with transplant solution to get them off to a fast start.

Another method for blanching endive is to lay a board over the row

Endive Early in June, before the sizzling weather arrives in the Victory Garden, I blanch the endive by pulling the outer leaves of each plant together with a string or rubber band to form topknots on each plant. The goal is to keep the inside growth protected from the light, which will cause the inner leaves to turn pale green and become free of the bitterness often associated with endive.

Evergreens The art of evergreen pruning is a little like the art of barbering. The best pruning job, like the best haircut, is the one that doesn't look recently done. The goal in pruning is to follow the plant's natural shape. For instance, if an evergreen that is naturally columnar is pruned to any other shape, it will shoot straight up again along its characteristic line of growth. So it's important to know a plant's natural shape before the pruning operation begins.

I rarely take hedge clippers to evergreens. Clipping might, to some eyes, make a bush look neat and orderly, but it couldn't possibly make it look natural. Instead, I evaluate the bush, single out any branches that defy the plant's basic shape, and cut them off within the bulk of the plant so the cut stems don't show.

Irises By early June the last of the Victory Garden's bearded, sometimes called German, irises will have finished flowering. For the young clumps I do nothing more than remove the old flower stalks so the plants don't waste their energy producing seeds. But clumps older than 3 or 4 years have grown crowded and have exhausted the nutrients in the soil, so their blossom production will begin to lessen unless they're divided. This is the best time of the year to divide bearded irises because the plants enter semidormancy after blooming; their plump feeding roots die back to the thick rhizomes that rest near the top of the soil. By digging and dividing now, the plants suffer almost no transplanting shock.

Bearded irises grow outward from the center of the plant, so the youngest and healthiest roots are at the outer fringes of the clumps. When dividing the plants, I choose growth with a double fan of leaves and a Y-shaped root. (I discard or give away the others.) I prepare the soil with peat moss, compost or other organic material, and bone meal. Then I set three of these divisions in a triangle so the fans point outward and I position the rhizomes, the thick fleshy roots, so their tops show at the surface of the soil (this will help produce abundant flowers in future springs). This gives the Victory Garden a perfect beginning for a handsome clump of irises that can grow undisturbed for three or four years.

Kohlrabi A good kohlrabi harvest is only possible with plenty of nourishment, so early in June I side-dress the rows with 5-10-5 fertilizer (5 or 6 ounces to a 10-foot row). I

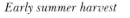

Early summer harvest

scratch the fertilizer into the soil with a cultivator, and then hill this soil up against the base of the plants, just below the swellings. The fertilizer will feed the plants and the soil will add support and keep them from toppling over.

The kohlrabi is ready for harvest by the end of June, when the swollen part of the stem is about the size of a tennis ball. I cut the plant with shears below the swelling, then cut off all the leaves and peel it before cooking.

Leeks The leek seedlings set into the garden in April looked like nothing more than thin wisps of grass, but by June they have grown to be robust plants. I fill in the trench as the plants grow, so by June the ground is level and 6 inches of the leeks' succulent stems are underground blanching to a creamy whiteness. (If by chance you did not plant your leeks in a trench, June is the month to begin hilling soil around the plants, right to the base of the leaves, to tenderize the lower portion of the stems. Scatter 5-10-5 fertilizer, about 5 ounces to a 10-foot row, before each hilling.)

New Zealand Spinach After about a month in the ground, the New Zealand spinach seedlings set into the garden in May have grown to be about 18 inches tall, with dark green succulent leaves. At this point I snip off the top 3 inches of each branch, which encourages the plants to become compact rather than rangy. The leaves of these snipped tips are the first of the harvest, but they are hardly the last: the plants will continue to bear leaves throughout the summer and into midautumn.

Unlike true spinach, in which the entire plant is harvested, only the leaves of the New Zealand spinach are picked. Once the plants have developed into thick, bushy beauties, I pick only the mature leaves and let the stem tips continue to grow. After a while the plants look a little like half-plucked chickens, but it's the foliage in the kitchen, not the appearance in the garden, that counts.

Okra The okra seedlings begun in peat pots in April are ready for the open garden in June when the warmer weather arrives. After thinning to 1 plant per pot, I set them out at 18-inch intervals and give them a drink of transplant solution to get them off to a good start. The okra harvest will begin next month and last until frost.

Onions Onions are relatively trouble-free crops for home gardeners, but problems do occasionally develop, the worst being onion maggots and onion thrips. The maggots are most prevalent in late May and June; they're not much to worry about in dry areas or during dry summers, but if the

weather's moist they can be devastating. I control the maggots by spraying the plants with diazinon or malathion at 7- to 10-day intervals for three weeks, beginning when the flies are first noticed.

Onion thrips are tiny rasping insects that injure the foliage of onions and other plants. The injury, white blotches on the leaves, first appears in June; if left unchecked, the entire crop will be lost. To control the thrips, I use diazinon or malathion at 7- to 10-day intervals for a total of 3 applications. If by some catastrophe I'm struck with both maggots and thrips, the 7- to 10-day applications of diazinon or malathion will take care of both.

Parsley By June our parsley plants have grown to a size where they can tolerate regular picking without damage. I always harvest the older foliage so the tender growth from the center of the plants has a chance to mature. Sometimes parsley plants seem to stop growing, in which case I scratch in a bit of 5-10-5 fertilizer around them, and then give them a good drink of water so the fertilizer is carried to the roots and assimilated by the plants.

Parsnips After two months in the soil the parsnips planted in April have grown large enough to begin crowding each other, so the time for thinning is at hand. I leave only the strongest plant at each location. Then, because parsnips like plenty of fertilizer and moisture, I scratch a teaspoonful of 5-10-5 around each plant, keeping it well away from the crown, and give the plants a good drink of water.

Peas June is pea-picking time in the Victory Garden and both the March planting of green peas and the April planting of edible pea pods are ready. One of the dividends of home gardening is that vegetables can be harvested while they're still tiny and tender, and then cooked right away. Because we've sown the pea seeds so heavily, we have an abundant harvest of one of the sweetest vegetables going.

Peas and pea pods need a two-handed harvest: I hold the stem in one hand and pull the pod loose with the other. If I were to yank at the pods without anchoring them with one hand, I'd be very apt to pull the entire plant out of the ground, and as long as the plants are producing, I certainly don't want to do that.

When the harvest is finished, though, the plants should be pulled up and added to the compost bin. They're a

Little Marvel peas ready for harvest

plus for the compost pile because they are so nitrogen-rich and will nourish the compost.

Peppers   Pepper plants thrive on warm weather and rich soil, so I add cow manure and compost, along with 5-10-5 (about 5 pounds to 100 square feet), to the planting row, which is about as much as I can do for any plant. When I'm sure the night temperatures won't drop below 55 degrees, I thin to 1 plant per pot, set the plants in at 18-inch intervals, give each a cutworm collar, and water them with transplant solution.

Occasionally we have a cool June and I dare not set my pepper plants outdoors. If the peat pots are filled with roots when this happens, I shift the plants into individual 5-inch plastic pots, because the last thing I want to do is to stunt the plants' growth. By giving them more root room, I can afford to wait until the weather warms up, even if it means a week or two. The plants will be growing the whole time.

Potatoes   The late varieties of potatoes planted in May are about 8 or 10 inches tall by June, so they're ready for hilling-up, just as the earlier varieties were last month.

The early varieties, planted in April, show the first signs of yellowing leaves in late June, and that's an indication that the harvest is on the way. When all the leaves have yellowed and the foliage is withered and dry, the potatoes will be ready for harvest. Luckily, though, it's possible to steal a small harvest before the potatoes are fully matured. In fact, these stolen new potatoes are just delicious. About 2 weeks after the potato blossoms appear, there will be a crop of small potatoes underground. All I do is scratch away at the soil with my hands until I find the potatoes and pull them out. They range from kumquat-sized to lemon-sized, and they have a tender skin and a sweet flavor. By the way, if during the digging I accidentally scratch the skin of a potato, I make sure to harvest it right then. Left in the ground, that scratch would develop into a rough scab.

Primroses   Thanks to Shakespeare, primroses are unshakably associated with the lining of paths to disaster, but that's only because they are so irresistibly tempting. It's a temptation to which I willingly succumb, so in June, I start the seeds of both indoor primroses, which will bloom in the winter, and outdoor primroses, which will blossom next spring. The planting medium is pure compost, sifted through a ¼-inch mesh of hardware cloth. Any particles that are too large to sift through I put in the bottom of a 4-inch plastic pot to provide drainage. Then I add the sifted compost right up to the top of the pot. (If you have no compost of your own, this

Pepper seedlings protected by cutworm collar

Opposite: Harvesting new potatoes

is one instance in which peat moss is not an acceptable substitute: instead, find the richest topsoil you can, such as that under a bush or leaves, and sift it just as you would the compost.) Over the compost I sprinkle about ⅛ inch of milled sphagnum moss to help prevent damping-off and then I drop a couple of pinches of seeds into the moss (2 pinches will produce dozens of plants). The seeds are so small they're nearly invisible, and if buried at all, they'd never see the light of day, so I just leave the seeds resting on the moss, and bottom-water the pot until the moss feels moist. Then I enclose the pots in plastic bags to help keep the humidity high and to prevent the seeds from drying out.

Pumpkins Pumpkins, like winter squashes, need a big supply of food to last them during their long growing season. I begin by digging a hole about 2 feet across and 18 inches deep for each hill of pumpkins. I fill the hole with equal parts of compost or manure and soil, to which I add a handful of slow-release fertilizer. This well-prepared soil will insure the plants a steady supply of nutrients over their 4-month growing span. As I refill the hole, I mound the soil mixture into a hill about 4 inches high in the center, with the hills about 10 feet apart to allow for the plants' long vines.

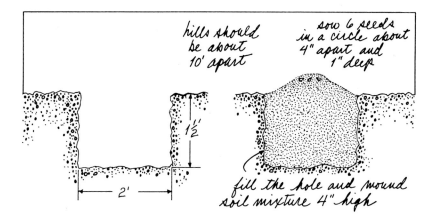

hills should be about 10' apart

sow 6 seeds in a circle about 4" apart and 1" deep

1½"

2'

fill the hole and mound soil mixture 4" high

I sow 6 seeds in a circle on each hill, about 4 to 6 inches between them, and push each seed into the soil about 1 inch deep. In a week or so most of the seeds have germinated, but some are weaker than others, so I save only the two best and discard the others (they don't take well to transplanting). If I were to neglect this thinning process, I'd have 6 plants' worth of foliage all summer long, and not a glimpse of a pumpkin in the fall.

Rosemary Rosemary is a popular herb grown for its aromatic needlelike leaves, which are useful in cooking and in making a potpourri. In order to concentrate the essence of its

fragrance it needs to be grown in relatively dry, well-drained soil. It is hardy in open gardens only in the South and South-west. Gardeners in other parts of the country do best by growing it as a pot plant both summer and winter.

Plants can be started easily at any time of the year by taking cuttings from the stems. We frequently have a small supply of young plants in the Victory Garden to give to visitors: sharing plants is one of the joys of gardening.

Squash By June the Victory Garden is warm enough to receive the summer squash seedlings planted indoors in late April. Before I put them in I prepare the soil with 1 or 2 shovelfuls of compost at 4- or 5-foot intervals. Because the mature plants will form circles of foliage 4 feet in diameter, I set single plants into these deposits of rich, soft soil, then give each a drink of transplant solution to get them on their way.

If I haven't planted my winter squash seeds in late May, I do so early in June. I prepare the soil and plant the seeds just as I do for pumpkins.

Strawberries I've planted the Victory Garden's June-bearing strawberries in a matted-row system to give them as much growing room as possible. Still, if these runners were given uncontrolled rein of the row, they would probably grow so thickly that the yield would actually be diminished. So I train the runners, putting them where I want them and anchoring each with a small stone so the plants will root with 8-inch intervals between them. Fourteen months after planting, when the strawberries begin to bear fruit, the yield will be huge because each plant will have had sufficient growing space to develop its full potential.

Swiss Chard Usually the April sowing of Swiss chard is large enough to begin to harvest in June. This plant will continue producing foliage until the fall, so I harvest by picking only the outer leaves. If the foliage looks a little weak, I scratch 10-10-10 fertilizer around the plants to revive them.

Tomatoes During June, I begin to receive questions about a tomato problem known as blossom-end rot. This is a physiological disturbance in the plant that results in fruit with a black, watery depression on the bottom. There is no spray that works for this problem, but there are some ways to prevent it.

The first prevention is soil with an ample supply of calcium, an element found in ground limestone. I frequently find that the repeated watering of the garden has washed out so much of the earlier applications of ground limestone that by June the pH has dropped to a point where blossom-end rot is a real possibility. If a soil test shows the need for more calcium I spread some limestone throughout the entire area of the tomato patch, and then water it in. There is enough calcium in the soil if the pH reads between 6.8 and 7.0.

The second way to prevent blossom-end rot is to give the plants an even supply of moisture in the soil. I have abandoned mulching for most of the garden because it attracts slugs, but with tomatoes it's a must. I mulch around the plants with salt marsh hay, grass clippings, or leaves to a depth of 3 to 6 inches (a thicker layer for the lighter materials). If it settles down to almost nothing, I add a little more during the summer.

Parent strawberry plant with runners

Blossom end rot

Q&A

Q: My ten-year-old wisteria vine has never bloomed. Why? My soil is sandy, but that hasn't prevented my fruit trees from bearing or my dogwoods from blossoming.

A: Your wisteria is probably so happy with the fertilizer and moisture it's getting that it has no inclination to blossom. What you should do is check the new growth as it comes from the stem, by cutting each new stem back to two leaves. You should have blossoms next year. If that doesn't work, cut around the plant with a sharp spade, severing some of the roots. (Stay at least 3 feet from the trunk.) This often shocks a wisteria into blooming.

Q: Two years ago I transplanted some peonies into my garden but they haven't flowered yet. What's wrong?

A: If your peonies are getting enough sunshine, then the problem is most likely that you planted them too deeply in the soil. Peonies should be planted in the fall, usually in September. Even at that time of the year there'll be 2-inch buds for next year growing from the roots. This September, dig your plants up and reset them so those buds are no more than 2 inches deep, and give each peony a big handful of bone meal.

Q: What's the best way to cover dwarf cherry trees and blueberry bushes to protect them from the birds?

A: I use black plastic mesh from the garden center. I've had mine for ten years and it's still perfectly fine. The birds scold me for it, but I get to eat the fruit rather than watch them indulge themselves at my expense.

Q: My geraniums are leafy but they have no blooms.

A: I think the difficulty is probably too much water and, possibly, not enough sunshine. Grow them in pots, keep the soil dry, and avoid overfeeding them.

Q: What's all this about suckers? Why are they harmful to some plants and not to others?

A: Sorry, but there's no hard and fast rule about leaving or taking off suckers. We leave them on corn to help build strength in the plants. With tomatoes grown on stakes, we remove them to restrict all growth to single stems and get early fruit. On the other hand, with tomatoes grown in cages, we leave the suckers. It just depends!

CONTAINER-GROWN VEGETABLES

I've received dozens of questions at the Victory Garden about the possibilities of growing vegetables in containers on patios and balconies, to which I respond that if ground space is unavailable, container-grown vegetables have quite a bit to recommend them. For one thing, they're portable and can be turned to face the sun, brought indoors when storms threaten, or even taken along on the family vacation. They're handsome, even the most ordinary of them. And while pot-grown vegetables are a little more space-hungry than houseplants, any size patio — even a wide windowsill — is large enough for some sort of arrangement.

Which is not to say that container-grown vegetables don't have their problems. Most notably, they dry out in a wink because their root systems are confined to such a limited amount of soil. They sometimes need water more than once a day, and this repeated watering will both compact the soil, damaging its structure, and wash nutrients away, robbing the plants of the food they need. All things considered, though, container-grown vegetables are well worth the effort, as long as some forethought goes into selecting the plants and pots, and the maintenance is unfailing.

As to the plants themselves, almost anything, even sweet corn, can be grown in containers if there's a watchful eye nearby. I've had the most success with those that have modest root systems, such as eggplants, peppers, cherry tomatoes, lettuce, onions, carrots, and herbs. I've even grown cucumbers and sweet potatoes successfully; they don't have small root systems, but do fairly well in large containers. There's no difference between the timing of ground-planted crops and those grown in pots, so the information given in the alphabetical entries applies to container gardening as well.

There are some special things to consider in container gardening, particularly the pots themselves and their relation to the plants to be grown in them. Unlike house plants, which will drown if the container is too large for the plant, pot-grown vegetables kept outdoors drain so quickly that the larger pot is an advantage. I've used nearly every kind of container I could find: pots; tin cans; wooden, plastic, and clay tubs; jardinieres; window boxes; bowls and buckets. I've been pleased with the results from all of them, with the sorry exception of clay pots. Handsome as they are, it's hard for me to love clay pots for outdoor container gardening: they're heavy, which is an advantage in the wind, but if they tip over they're apt to shatter; more significantly, they breathe moisture through their porous sides, making watering a constant chore. Plastic and metal pots are less beautiful but they don't dry out as quickly. Although the major worry for container vegetables is drying out, they do need modest drainage. The stones or crockery needed for houseplants aren't necessary, but I do provide drainage holes in all these containers to carry off excess

Wooden container

#10 can

Plastic Pot

Pail

moisture in the event of a heavy rainfall.

Given the speed with which containers surrender their moisture, pot-grown vegetables demand super soil. I sometimes use a packaged soilless mix of half vermiculite and half peat moss with some nutrients added, though there are several other excellent soilless mixtures, the products of experimental research at state universities. All these mixes are free of disease, their soil structure is ideal, and they're easy to

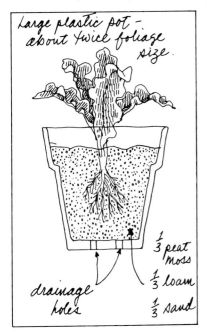

use and find. But they are expensive, and in container gardening expense is a significant issue because the soil is so exhausted after the growth of a single crop that it can't be used again. So I sometimes use my own medium of one part peat moss, one part garden loam, and one part sand (not beach sand, which is salty) and a slow-release fertilizer (14-14-14). Ordinarily I use the packaged mix for the small containers and my home-mixed soil for the large ones.

One problem common to all container-grown plants is this: when the pots sit in the midsummer sun, the soil becomes too hot for healthy plants. I counteract this by grouping my plants together so the foliage will shade the pots, then I either plunge the pots in peat moss or sand to hold moisture or I toss some mulch over the pots to further shade the roots from the sun.

Maintaining the container garden requires a constant eye but not much in the way of effort. Watering is obviously the critical element. I water whenever the soil is dry, and I test for dryness by grabbing a handful of the surface soil. If it feels dry, I water. And sometimes I find that I'm watering more than once a day, especially when the sun or wind is strong. Fertilizing is the only other chore. In addition to the slow-release fertilizer in the soil, I fertilize the plants every week with a water-soluble fertilizer (23-19-17).

Above: Potted pepper plant

Below: Mint confined to a pot

Zucchini plant

JUL

Plant
Beans
Beets
Chinese Cabbage
Cineraria
Collards
Cucumbers
Delphiniums
English Daisies
Forget-Me-Nots
Kale
Lettuce
Pansies
Radishes
Rutabagas
Sweet William

Special Events
Dill
Lawn Care
Lilacs
Petunias
Poinsettias
Roses
Silver Fleece Vine
Tulips

Transplant
Brussels Sprouts
Chrysanthemums
Corn
Cyclamens
Delphiniums

Thin
Chinese Cabbage
Rutabagas

Fertilize
Asparagus
Eggplants
Melons
Parsnips
Rutabagas

Harvest
Beans
Beets
Broccoli
Corn
Cucumbers
Eggplants
Leeks
Lettuce
Okra
Onions
Peppers
Squash
Tomatoes

JULY

By the time July arrives in the Victory Garden, the soil has been hard at work for four months and it may begin to show some signs of wear. So before I put in any additional crops to fill the vacancies left by harvests, I add nutrients and, if a soil test indicates the need, ground limestone. This is the only way to keep the soil in condition for the intensive production I ask of the Victory Garden. I view the garden soil as a savings bank: it needs periodic feedings in order to keep producing.

July is usually the hottest month in the Victory Garden, which makes this the watershed month in the planting of cool-weather vegetables that would go to seed if subjected to July's baking sun. Rutabagas and Chinese cabbages sown this month will be safe in the soil through these hot days, and will mature during the cooler weather of August and September. Of course there's still time this month for more sowings of the main-season crops that form the backbone of the Victory Garden — if I have the space I can even put in a late crop of corn for harvest in the fall.

The perennial border is, I proudly admit, always spectacular, but in this month's scorching weather it is an absolute showpiece. The hollyhocks are in bloom, along with the phlox, baby's breath, blue flax, western bleeding heart, coreopsis, Shasta daisies, delphiniums, geums, and those marvelous hybrid lilies. The foxglove will breathe its last this month, so after I pull it out and compost it I fill in the vacancy with some of the chrysanthemum plants I divided in May. These will begin to blossom in September and continue until late in the fall.

Asparagus In appreciation of the thick layer of compost beneath its roots, the Victory Garden asparagus has made strong growth in the ten short weeks after planting in May, and produces the filmy green foliage that is the manufacturing element of the plant. Whenever the sun shines on a plant's leaves, nature's marvelous alchemy goes to work combining elements from the soil and atmosphere to strengthen growth. Much of this vigor is being stored underground, building strong roots for next year's crop.

To further help these plants grow sturdily, I side dress the rows in July. The roots of asparagus grow at least 2 feet in all directions, so I scatter a dusting of 5-10-5 or 10-10-10 fertilizer in 2-foot paths down both sides of the trench, taking care to keep the fertilizer itself away from

direct contact with the plants' stems. Then I pull another 2 inches of soil in around the bases of the plants, leaving the trench 4 inches deep, and the roots further buried in cool, nourishing soil. Eventually the asparagus trench will be filled in and the roots will then be safe from inadvertent damage by cultivation.

I'd also advise side dressing established beds of asparagus at this time of the year. It'll help them rebuild their roots and produce a large crop the following spring.

Beans Young beans are worlds better than old ones, so we continue this month to pick our bush beans every two or three days, depriving them of the opportunity to age and toughen. The only caution about the bean harvest is to make sure that there's no moisture on the plants, as there's a good chance of spreading a bean disease known as anthracnose from damp plant to damp plant.

Bush beans seem to be at their most tender late in the season, so I always plant a crop in July that will be ready for harvest in September. I use the same planting procedure I use in May, but because July is our hottest month in the Victory Garden I protect the seeds from the baking sun by covering them with 2 full inches of soil.

Beets Like most vegetables, beets are at their best when they're small and young. So I usually finish off the harvest of our April crop in July and follow along with the seeds of another crop that we'll harvest in the fall.

Beets are for the most part a trouble-free crop, but sometimes they are plagued by leaf miners. July isn't the worst of the Victory Garden's leaf miner season, but they're lurking close at hand, so I continue diazinon treatments to stay ahead of the problem. As we get within a couple weeks of the harvest I switch to malathion, which has a shorter active life than diazinon, or stop treatments altogether.

Broccoli Broccoli produces bonus crops, small but tasty side shoots that grow from the main stems of the plant. We harvest the first of these dividends in July, following our June picking of the plants' massive central heads. The plants will keep producing these bonus shoots until we're hit with freezing weather in the fall, so long as the shoots are never cut back to the main stem. I leave the base of the shoots and a couple of leaves on each stem so new stems can grow from these leaf junctures.

All summer long I keep an eye on the Victory Garden soil, adding nutrients as they're needed. Cabbage-family plants are finicky about the acidity of the soil — they do best at 6.5 to 7.5 — so before I sow another crop I usually find that I have to add more limestone to sweeten the soil. I also add 10-10-10 fertilizer and about 2 inches of compost, and dig them into the soil to the depth of the spading fork. Then this revitalized soil is ready to receive another sowing of broccoli seeds, a pinch at 24 to 30-inch intervals. The seedlings will be ready for thinning next month, but in the meantime there's plenty of room for a crop of lettuce transplants to mature between the broccoli plantings.

Brussels Sprouts Toward the middle of this month, I transplant the brussels sprouts seedlings that have been growing in the nursery row and move them to larger quarters in the garden proper. These plants will grow to a good 2½ or 3 feet, so after I prepare the soil as I do for this month's sowing of broccoli I set the seedlings in at 18-inch intervals in rows 3 feet apart. Eventually the plants will need every bit of this space, but for now there's room to interplant a few seedlings of bolt-resistant lettuce in the rows.

As a member of the cabbage family, brussels sprouts are set upon by a variety of pests and plagues, so when I set the seedlings in I give each a cutworm collar and a drink of transplant solution boosted with diazinon to control the root maggots (or I use a maggot mat in place of the collar and the diazinon). The imported cabbageworm caterpillar is a threat

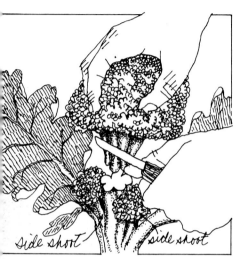

side shoot   side shoot

too, so I spray the foliage with *Bacillus thuringiensis* at 7- to 10-day intervals. Time-consuming as these precautions may be, they are worth it, and the plants will begin their long harvest season in September.

Chinese Cabbage These succulent football-shaped vegetables are not among the most well known of the Victory Garden crops, but they're a nice variation on the cabbage theme and deserve more attention. They taste something like lettuce, so they're usually grown to be eaten raw rather than cooked. There's nothing much to planting Chinese cabbage as long as they're not sown too early in the summer; if they mature during the hot summer weather they go to seed rather than make a head. I put our crops in anytime from the middle of July to the middle of August, and they're ready for harvest through the fall.

As with all the cabbage-family plants, the success of the crop hangs on the soil preparation. These vegetables need rich, moist soil that's high in organic matter and nearly neutral, so I dig in at least 2 inches of compost and a dusting of ground limestone, and drop a pinch of seeds at 1-foot intervals along the row, thinning later to the strongest plant at each

Chinese cabbages (front) alongside a row of collards

interval. (I just compost these pulled seedlings because they produce flower spikes, rather than heads, if they're transplanted.) Every 2 or 3 weeks I side dress the rows with a handful of 10-10-10 for every 5-foot section of the rows. And to ward off the cabbageworm caterpillar I treat the plants with *Bacillus thuringiensis* at 7 to 10-day intervals through the growing season.

Chrysanthemums All through the spring I nurse my chrysanthemum plants along in a reserve bed in the garden; I keep the growth pinched back so that by this month, although there are no flower buds showing, the plants are green and full and ready to be moved into the other locations in the garden. I usually set some of these plants into the perennial border to fill vacancies left by the foxglove and Canterbury bells, both biennials that finish blossoming in midsummer. Chrysanthemums are sturdy plants that will hardly know they've been moved as long as they're kept moist in their new spot. They'll wilt a little if they dry out, so I wait for a cloudy day before I move them around, and spare them the full heat of the sun.

Healthy collection of cineraria plants

Cineraria The velvety, daisylike blossoms of this choice houseplant come in a dozen variations of reds and blues, from pink to deep red and from lavender to rich purple. Seeds sown this month will be flowering plants by the next winter and spring.

Like most amateur gardeners, I want no more than two dozen plants, some for myself and others to share with friends. I begin with a 4-inch plastic pot filled with potting soil, and add a ⅛-inch layer of milled sphagnum moss over the soil. Then I sift the seeds as evenly as I can over the surface. The seeds are so tiny — they're all but invisible — that they will fall down within the moss, which is all the covering they need. I bottom-water the pot so as not to wash away the seeds and then set the pot inside a clear plastic bag and put it in a warm, bright but sunless spot. The plants will break through the surface in about 10 days and be ready for transplanting next month.

Collards Until relatively recently collards were a curiosity crop outside the Deep South, but they're tasty and high in vitamins, and as northern gardeners have discovered these admirable qualities, they've gained quite a following here too. They need a long growing season, and they're tastiest after they've been treated to a frost, so southern gardeners do best to wait until the late summer or early fall to sow the seeds, giving them a harvest during the winter and spring. I usually put the Victory Garden crop in during July,

Collard greens

so they'll be ready in the fall after the frost has killed off most of the rest of our leafy vegetables.

Early in the month I sprinkle a few seeds into a seed bed and give them about 2 weeks of growth before I scoop out the seedlings with my trowel. After I prepare a garden row as I do for broccoli, I set out the individual 2-inch seedlings at 3-inch intervals and water them with transplant solution. This is rather close spacing for such potentially large plants, but in August when they're ready to be thinned to 6-inch intervals the pulled plants will make a fine fresh salad. They'll need thinning again late in August to their permanent spacing of 18 to 24 inches, and these pulled plants will make another fine young harvest. When I thin the plants I scatter a light dusting of 10-10-10 to encourage rapid growth, and I also treat the plants through their growing season with *Bacillus thuringiensis* to combat the imported cabbageworm caterpillar.

Corn Undoubtedly the major problem for corn growers everywhere is pests. I can take care of the birds and squirrels by putting a paper bag over each ear of corn in the garden, but the raccoons are another problem entirely. (An electric fence, carrying a very mild current, is very effective, but poses a potential hazard for wearers of heart devices such as pacemakers. Once their toes are tingled raccoons look elsewhere for their corn. Electric fence kits are available through the mail and from some garden centers.) I've also heard that planting squash and pumpkins around the corn bed helps — apparently the prickly stems are more than raccoons can put up with. This is an old Indian trick; I've never tried it, but it sounds intriguing. My own solution has been to set cage traps (fried chicken is the best bait) that catch the animals without hurting them. In the morning I put the cage into my car, drive the raccoon far out into the country, and let it go

Bird- and squirrel-proofed corn

One corn crop growing to back up another

According to the seed catalogue, the early corn varieties that I plant in April are due for my table in 58 days, but they hardly ever arrive on schedule. I do have corn in July, though, which is very early in this area. Judging from my mail, gardeners have trouble knowing when their corn is ripe, so I'll pass along some tips. First of all, the corn silk itself should be completely brown all the way through. And the ear should feel firm; if it feels soft and a little hollow, the kernels haven't filled in the ear yet. Of course if all else fails, there's always peeking to see if the ear is completely filled in and the kernels are full size, though peeking will sacrifice the section of the ear that's exposed.

Once the harvest is over, I pull up the old corn plants and shred them into my composter. This leaves a vacancy in the corn bed, which I fill with the corn seedlings sown in six-packs in June. First, though, I replace some of the nutrients the first crop of corn exhausted by adding horse manure and 5-10-5 fertilizer to the soil. Then I set the plants out at 12-inch intervals with 12 inches between the rows, and I'll have corn in September and October, long after most gardeners have forgotten this vegetable altogether.

Cucumbers Why are some cucumbers bitter? There are several reasons. For one, some varieties are more bitter than others. Recent research shows that the bitterness factor may be genetic, at least in part. Some varieties, under all test conditions, remained sweet while others displayed varying degrees of bitterness. (Two of my favorites in the Victory Garden are Saticoy and Burpless Hybrid, varieties that never get bitter, regardless of how large they grow.) Growing conditions also affect bitterness: cucumbers given plenty of moisture, fertilizer, and warm temperatures are rarely bitter. Or bitterness can be a function of age: many cucumbers turn bitter toward the end of their fruiting season, after about 2 months of harvest, as the vines get old and the nourishment in the soil becomes depleted.

July is the beginning of the harvest for the Victory Garden cucumbers. I harvest the pickling varieties when the fruit is 1½ to 3 inches long, the slicing cucumbers when they're about 8 inches long, and the Burpless Hybrid when the fruit is 12 to 20 inches long. The abundant harvest will last only through the end of August, so I always begin a new crop of cucumbers in July to come into its fruiting season in the fall. If the garden is full, I start 2 seeds in peat pots filled with pure sifted compost. When the seedlings appear, I set them out just as I did the first crop in May, except that the weather is warm enough to do without the plastic mulch. If there is room to plant the seeds directly into the garden, I do so, saving a step and any possible transplanting setbacks. One

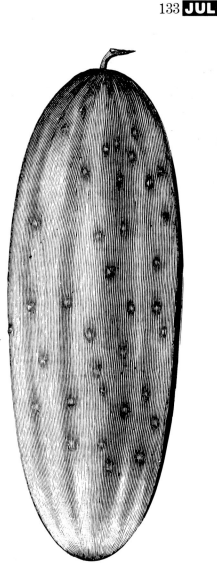

year I planted a second crop of Burpless Hybrid cucumbers from seeds, at the base of the compost pile. I began by working some of the compost into the soil and adding a bit of 5-10-5 fertilizer. Then I dropped the seeds at 3-inch intervals, covered them with about ½ inch of soil, and kept them moist. I put a trellis up against the compost bin; when the seedlings came up, I thinned the plants to the strongest one at approximately 12-inch intervals and trained them up the trellis. They grew to be about 7 feet tall and bore handsome fruit through September and October.

Cyclamens Cyclamens make some of the most beautiful and longest lasting of the pot plants for the home or greenhouse. They usually require about 15 months or more to produce their first flower, but once they become mature, they blossom from October until April year after year. Colors range from snowy white through many shades of pink to dark red and lavender shades. There are single, double, miniature, and sweet-scented varieties.

Cyclamens make tiny bulbs beneath the soil before they send up their first tentative leaf. There's no predicting the exact time of germination — they sprout on their own individual timing — which is why I only put one seed to each peat pellet when I planted them in June. But sometime in July, around 40 days after planting, the seeds will show some top growth. I check the seedlings daily to make sure they're moist, and as they begin to send roots out through the sides of the peat pellets I pot them into individual 3-inch pots and regular potting soil. It's important at this point not to set the cyclamens in any deeper than they grew previously: eventually the bulbs will stand about one-third to one-half out of the soil.

Delphiniums In severe winters, the mortality rate among delphiniums can be discouragingly high, so I usually start new plants from seed in midsummer to guarantee a supply of healthy plants for the next year. Delphinium seeds germinate fastest when they're very fresh. So while they can be bought from garden centers at this time of year, the better idea is to gather seeds from existing plants. This has to be done in July, when the seed pods have turned from green to brown; I just peel the pods open, gather the brown-black seeds, and plant them this month to give them the longest possible growing season to build strength for next year's flowers.

I start the seeds off in the garden, sowing them at 1-inch intervals about ¼ inch deep and covering them with a soilless mix that's soft and easy to keep moist. After about 2 months, when the seedlings develop their first true leaves, I

Delphinium

transplant them to separate containers and winter them in a cold frame. It's possible simply to transplant the seedlings to a wider spacing in a garden row and then set them directly into the perennial border in the fall, but in the cold parts of the country it's safer to put the plants out in the early spring and spare them the harsh winter outside.

Dill Even if dill were utterly useless in the kitchen, I would grow this plant just for its looks. Luckily it's a far cry from useless, as good cooks know. Its foliage can be picked anytime, and it's delicious with potatoes and cucumbers, as well as in soups, stews, and meat and egg dishes; its green seeds are the essence in dill pickles. Plants from the April sowing are full grown in July and seed heads are ready to collect. When the seeds begin to turn brown, I cut the heads off, dropping each one into an open paper bag. After a few days in a warm room, all of the seeds will have dropped out of the seed heads so I seal them in a jar with a tight-fitting top and use them during the winter when fresh dill leaves are unavailable. Dill seeds that fall to the ground will germinate either right away or the following spring, and it's a good idea to allow this to happen because there will always be plants

Dill

sprouting at random around the garden. Strangely enough, these self-sown plants are usually more robust than those that gardeners plant themselves.

Eggplants A good gardener is constantly on the alert for signs of distress so problems can be solved before they turn into catastrophes. I keep an eye on our eggplants this month because they sometimes develop pale foliage early in July, a sign that they need a boost with 5-10-5 fertilizer. I scatter a small handful on the ground around each plant, covering an area about 2 feet in diameter. Eggplants have very shallow root systems, so when I scratch the fertilizer in I don't dig any deeper than ½ inch. By late in the month these eggplants will be ready to pick, when their outer skin is still shiny but before they grow any larger than an orange. This is only half the size of the eggplants sold in supermarkets, and at this tender age they're far superior.

Sometimes the gardener's watchful eye will turn up a simple problem, and sometimes it won't. The Victory Garden was only three months old when I first noticed that the eggplant foliage was turning yellow and brown, sign of a disease known as verticillium wilt. It's often fatal to tomatoes and peppers, its favorite victims, and it cuts down severely on the production of eggplants. Its most insidious property is its long life; it stays active in the soil for at least fifteen years. There's not much that can be done about it, other than to rotate the susceptible crops. (Professional growers spend the time and money to fumigate the soil every season, but that's way beyond the capacity of the Victory Garden's and most home gardens' budget.)

If you have only a small garden that you use year after year, you may find that the easiest way to grow eggplants is to sow the seeds in a sterile potting soil and transfer the seedlings into large containers filled with the same potting soil, where they'll live the rest of their days. The disease probably won't get to your plants that first year and you'll be surprised how well eggplants do when grown this way. Some tomato varieties are resistant to verticillium wilt, but only a few of the eggplant varieties have had this factor bred into them. I've never grown them but I understand that the varieties Black Jack and Superhybrid are partially tolerant to verticillium wilt and are worth trying.

Eggplant at the perfect harvest size

English Daisies In San Francisco's Golden Gate Park, and in other areas along the cool West Coast, English daisies bloom continually through the grass even though they're regularly cut off by lawn mowers. This is the true daisy, from which all other daisies take their name. They're 6 or 8 inches tall at maturity, bearing single or double white,

English daisies

pink, rose, or red flowers from early spring through the mid-summer. Technically they're perennials but most gardeners treat them as biennials or, in the South, as annuals.

Here in the north I sow seeds of the English daisy in July so I'll be sure to have robust plants for the following spring. The seeds are minute but they germinate readily; some will even begin to blossom in the fall. I sow them in a nursery row outdoors or in a flowerpot indoors, barely covering the seeds. When the potted seedlings develop their first true leaves I transplant them to a nursery row and let them grow there for the rest of the season. In the spring I shift them to their permanent locations in the garden.

Forget-Me-Nots   One of the earliest flowers to bloom in the spring is the delightful blue, pink, or white forget-me-not, an old-fashioned flower that deserves more attention than today's gardeners afford it. It's usually treated as a biennial, although some of the plants live for several years. July is the best time to sow the seeds because it gives the plants several months to make sturdy clumps of foliage before the cold weather arrives. I sow the seeds in shallow drills in full sun, covering them with no more than about ¼ inch of soil. I try to sow sparingly so the seedlings don't crowd one another and make the September transplanting job more difficult.

Kale In its planting, care, and rich nutritional value, kale is quite a bit like collards. Both are cabbage-family crops that produce loose, leafy growth rather than heads. They also fall prey to the problems shared by other members of the family, so they do best when grown in cool weather. Kale can be sown in the spring, but it improves after a frost, so I usually sow our crop in midsummer, using the same procedures I use for collards, and harvest it in the fall.

There are two common kinds of kale. Siberian kale has very curly gray-green foliage, while Scotch kale is a bluish-green and a little less curly. Occasionally seed catalogues will advertise a plant known as flowering cabbage, but it's actually a specialized form of kale. Its "flowers" are only pink, red, yellow, or purplish leaves arranged in tight rosettes.

Lawn Care Some gardeners labor under the myth that laying sod produces an instant lawn. In a very real sense it does, but just as much soil preparation is needed to prepare the ground for sod in July as is needed for the grass seed planted in September. For that reason it's sometimes best to lay the sod in small manageable sections, rather than all at once. (If you do this, store any extra sod on plastic or on a driveway, as its inclination to grow is strong, and it'll root into soil wherever it has a chance.)

To prepare ground for laying sod, I spread 2 or 3 inches of peat moss, a dusting of ground limestone, and a special high-nitrogen lawn fertilizer over the soil. Then I dig all these additives into the top 6 inches of soil, so everything is thoroughly mixed, and firm the soil with a roller (or with my feet if the area is small). The firming gives the grass roots a

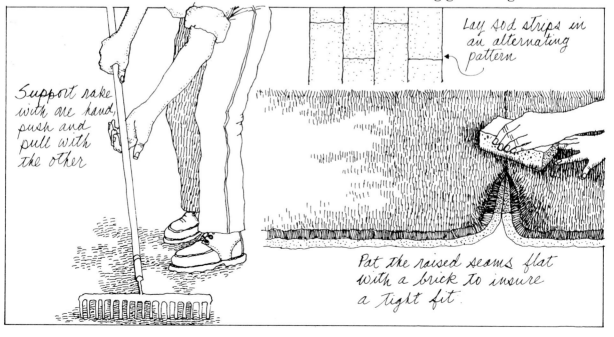

Support rake with one hand, push and pull with the other

Lay sod strips in an alternating pattern

Pat the raised seams flat with a brick to insure a tight fit.

solid surface that will not sink later on. Once the soil is firmed, I use an iron rake to level the surface. Raking is a two-handed operation, as the illustration shows. If I were to lazily pull the rake over the soil with one hand, the only effect would be to glide over high spots and dig into low spots.

Now for the sod itself. Although this is not instant gratification, it certainly is a quick and painless way to a handsome lawn. There are no weeds; it produces a lawn in an afternoon that would be two years growing from seed; the thickness of the roots prevents washouts and erosion; and when all the time and labor are figured, the cost is probably worth it.

Sod is grown in special sod nurseries and is prepared for sale by being cut by a machine that slices through the soil about 1 inch beneath the grass. Then this 1-inch-thick strip of sod is rolled into a jelly roll, which is the way it's sold in garden centers. The only job left is to unroll the sod like a carpet. While doing this, I lay boards over the newly laid sod and stand on the boards, not on the firmed soil, as my footprints would make the surface of the soil uneven.

In order to camouflage the seams of the sod strips as much as possible, I lay the strips out in such a way that the ends of the strips do not line up, much the way that a mason constructs a brick wall. To make sure the seams of the strips are as snug as they can be, I line up the thicknesses of the two pieces, actually crowding them against each other so they raise off the soil slightly, and then pat the seam down with a brick. This makes the seam as tight as it can be, and so less obvious.

Within 24 hours the grass roots begin to grow into the new soil, and after a couple of weeks, with a little moisture, there'll be a firm lawn to be proud of.

Leeks The leek seedlings I set into the Victory Garden in April do not reach their full maturity until late in the fall, their stems long and white from growing in the trench. Though they're at their biggest in the autumn, they are edible throughout their growth, so in fact the harvest can begin as early as June or July. I usually harvest a few through the season as I need them, and leave the rest to grow to full size. This is a luxury the commercial growers can't afford; they are forced to harvest the entire leek crop in a single operation in order to turn over their acreage to another planting. Once again, the home gardener wins out.

Lettuce My tip for growing lettuce in July is a simple one: plant varieties that the catalog says are suitable for hot weather. I find that Slobolt, Matchless, and Summer Bibb are good summer varieties. During hot weather lettuce will

do best if given a little shade. Plant it on the north side of the corn patch, for example, or some area where the hot midday sun will not hit it.

Lilacs Lilacs, in fact most flowering shrub plants, are several years in growing, so nurseries rightfully demand some very high prices for those large enough to go into the garden. With a little effort and a lot of patience, though, these young plants can be had for almost nothing. Flowering shrubs that do not produce suckers can't be divided, but many can be propagated easily from stem cuttings. I've grown rose, lilac, forsythia, hibiscus, hydrangea, and other bushes in the Victory Garden. I particularly enjoy taking cuttings from a friend or relative's shrub; the plants become living emotional links between people. My 30-year-old rosebush is one that my uncle started for me when my wife and I moved into our new house many years ago. Each time I see the plant I remember him.

The ideal cutting is taken from the current season's growth of a healthy plant; it should be neither the strongest nor the weakest growth on the plant, but simply an average stem. I like the cuttings to be about 4 or 5 inches long with no flower buds and about 3 to 4 mature leaves. For instance, in the case of the rose cutting that I showed in a demonstration session, I removed the tip of the cutting and with it the seed pod that would have drained the plant's strength. Then I removed the leaves that would have been buried in the rooting medium and cut the bottom of the stem about ¼ inch below a leaf joint. (Because of its larger leaves I took a slightly different tack with a lilac cutting: I removed all but about 4 leaves from the stem and then sliced off the top half of each leaf, reducing the amount of greenery that the stem had to supply with moisture.)

Moisture is the key ingredient from here on, so after I dipped the bottom inch of each cutting into rooting powder and set 2 or 3 of the cuttings from one plant together in a pot filled with builders' sand, I set the pots into an orange crate with about 2 inches of damp peat moss in the bottom. The orange crate is an ideal container for this because there's plenty of space for air to circulate through the slats of wood. A thin sheet of rigid plastic over the crate helps maintain the humidity level.

Then I set the whole crate out underneath the crab apple trees, where it would be shaded, kept the cuttings watered, and waited for them to root. The rooting time varies with the different shrubs. Forsythia can root in 2 or 3 weeks, while lilacs may creep along for 6 months or more before rooting. But when new leaf growth signaled the development of roots, I gently transplanted the cuttings to individual pots filled with potting soil and set the pots into the cold frame for the fall and winter. As soon as the warm weather arrived in the spring, I set the plants out into the garden.

Melons Melon plants seem to double in size every week during the hot July weather. Occasionally this speedy growth will leave the foliage a little pale, so I spray the leaves with a water-soluble fertilizer. It's too late in the season to add fertilizer to the soil but this foliar feeding will give the plants a quick and needed boost.

I'm often asked why there are so many flowers and so little fruit on melons. Although there are sometimes villains to be blamed for a low yield, the answer is usually much simpler. Most melon plants, unless very amply fed, rarely produce more than three or four good melons. The reason is that a large proportion of the blossoms are male and cannot produce fruit; only the female blossoms carry tiny melons behind their yellow flowers.

Okra I've heard it said that a person has to have been born in the South to like okra. I beg to differ with that idea, as so many other gardeners do who have tried this delicious vegetable. I'll confess that I was gardening in Texas when I first learned to like okra, but I've never had a garden since without it. For the uninitiated, the "gumbo" in those mouth-watering Creole dishes is none other than our friend okra. It is a type of hibiscus and is related to hollyhocks and marsh mallows. The edible portion is the immature seed pod.

In the Victory Garden, and in other areas in the North, okra grown from seed planted in April reaches a height of 3 to 4 feet by July and the first harvest is ready. As is so often the case, the youngest vegetable is by far the best; okra pods are at their peak when they're only half grown or no more than 2 inches or so long. So I begin the harvest in July, and harvest every day or two to prevent the pods from growing large and woody. If the harvest isn't kept up, the plants will stop producing.

Onions The collapse of the onion foliage is the first sign that the harvest is near at hand. When the tops lose their green color and flop down onto the ground, the onion bulbs are reaching maturity and will soon be ready for pulling. (If

Onions nearly ready for pulling

you want all of your onions to mature at one time, the maturation process can be speeded up by knocking any still-green foliage over to the ground.) When the foliage has completely browned and withered, the onions are ready to pull. The first of the Victory Garden onions to reach this stage are those planted from sets in March. They're ready for harvest by late this month.

The closer to autumn an onion matures, the better its chance of keeping through the winter months. For that reason, I don't use set-grown onions for storage, waiting instead for seed-grown bulbs.

July brings in the first of our true scallion harvest too, the products of bunching onion seeds sown outdoors in April. These do not form bulbs, only slightly swollen bases, and are very tender and delicious in salads. They're ready for harvest when the foliage grows to about 6 to 8 inches tall, but they're edible at every stage and may be eaten when much smaller.

Pansies Every spring, predictable as the rain, letters flood into the Victory Garden from viewers who bemoan their negligence in not following along with my pansy culture. The seedlings are expensive, and in quantities large enough to make an impact on the garden, the expense can be prohibitive. So every spring my response is the same: plant seeds in July, and you'll have hundreds of plants next summer for no more than the price of the seed package and your labor.

A harvest of scallions

Pansies are treated as biennials, although they sometimes survive more than two years. Planted one year, they usually bloom and die the next, being perfectly hardy through the intervening winter. So in July, I start with a flat of potting soil and make tiny furrows about 1½ inches apart and ¼ inch deep. Then I sprinkle the seeds thinly in the furrow at intervals of about ¼ inch, and cover them with about ¼ inch of milled sphagnum moss. I always label the rows as I do this so I know what I've got when the foliage comes up; otherwise there isn't a clue to what color bloom the plants will have. These seedlings are ready for transplanting in August.

Parsnips Parsnips are rather a luxury crop in the Victory Garden because they occupy a piece of ground continuously from early spring until late fall, or even until the following spring. But there's nothing quite like the flavor of a fresh parsnip after it's been touched by frost in the fall or frozen in the ground over winter.

Occasionally the growth of the parsnip plants slows down a bit during the summer and the plants develop yellowish foliage. I solve this with a quick shot of foliar fertilizer mixed with water, sprayed right onto the plants' leaves. Within a week, the plants will be a rich, dark green again.

Sweet peppers, ready to pick

Peppers Our pepper harvest begins in July, with the earliest of the peppers — big, rich beauties thanks to our compost. Of course, peppers have the same flavor at all stages of their growth, so they can be harvested at any time. Once picked, though, they don't store too well and are apt to turn mushy, while those left on the plant will stay crisp and fresh and turn a dazzling red in the bargain. So I usually harvest some while they're young and leave the others on the plant for a later picking.

Petunias Petunias have a habit of becoming a little straggly by late midsummer. The blossoms are perfectly fine, but they appear only on the tips of the plants. When this happens in the Victory Garden, I cut the flowers back to about 2 inches from the ground so the plants will be able to produce new foliage and flowers that will last the rest of the season. A good feeding of liquid fertilizer helps them along in the process. (If you have continued to make small sowings of annuals through late May, you now have on hand a nice supply of young plants that can be used to replace those that look a bit moth-eaten.)

Poinsettias Every summer without fail, I have on my hands a number of poinsettias that are overgrown and unkempt. If the plants are to be compact and bushy and filled with flowers in December, they have to be cut back in July. So I take the potted plants that blossomed indoors last winter and cut all the branches back to about 2 inches from the soil. I know this seems a drastic measure, but in a month's time the plants will be revived and ready for the next stage in their reclamation process.

The cut stems are well worth saving as they will make handsome new plants too. I dip them in rooting powder and set them into plastic pots filled with coarse moist sand or perlite. Poinsettia cuttings wilt severely unless a very humid atmosphere is maintained around them, so I build a little plastic greenhouse over the cuttings, using an inverted plastic cup or a plastic bag. The pots then go into a lighted, but not sunny location. If they show signs of wilting, I remove the mini-greenhouse and mist the tops with tepid water.

Radishes The Victory Garden's midsummer mail always brings in dozens of radish problems. "My radishes are all tops and no bottoms. What's up?" The problem there is too much shade, or crowding, or too much nitrogen. "I can't talk for a week after eating my radishes. Why are they so hot?" Well, summer radishes are usually hotter than spring radishes, but they'll be hotter still if they grow slowly in dry soil. I've had the best luck by giving them plenty of fertilizer and moisture; they grow so fast they don't have time to get hot.

In mid-July, I sow a crop of winter radishes. I've grown Black Spanish, which becomes about 4 or 5 inches in diameter at harvest, and White Chinese, which produces a root about 6 inches long. I add lime to the soil if a soil test indicates the need, along with some compost and a handful of 10-10-10. I also mix diazinon powder into the soil to prevent damage by root maggots. I sow the seeds in a ½-inch furrow, about 2 inches apart. They'll be ready for harvest in November, but they'll keep way beyond Christmas if I store them in wet sand.

Roses The secret to continuing summertime blossoms from hybrid tea, floribunda, and grandiflora roses is pruning to prevent the plants from setting seeds. When a

Peace, a classic hybrid tea rose

Cut about ¼" above the first 5 leaf grouping

blossom begins to fade, I cut it off the plant. The important thing here is to look down the stem for the first leaf with 5 leaflets on it, and cut about a ¼ inch above that leaf. If the stem is cut closer to the tip, it will still make another blossom but it will be meager and weak stemmed.

Rutabagas A viewer wrote me once complaining that his rutabagas were nearly too bitter to eat. Problem was, he'd planted his crop in the spring, so it had matured during the summer weather. These plants just can't take those hot days and summertime droughts. To be tender and sweet they should be planted in midsummer to mature in cool fall weather.

I prepare the soil for the rutabagas, also called winter or yellow turnips, with compost and 5-10-5 fertilizer (about 5 pounds to 100 square feet). Then I sow the seeds at 2-inch intervals along a ½-inch furrow, cover them, and water the row. Late in the month, or early in August, I feed them again with 5-10-5, and thin the seedlings to stand 6 or 8 inches apart. Even at this seemingly generous spacing, the plants will be crowding one another by harvesttime in October.

Silver Fleece Vine It started out in May as a slender vine less than 2 feet tall, but by July the silver fleece vine showed every sign of climbing up and over the top of the greenhouse. This vine flowers in September, so to shape the plant around the back door of the greenhouse and to stimulate it to produce blossoms, I pruned it in July. I cut off any stems that straggled over the path, so that all the growth was relatively close to the vine's main branches. With each cut I made sure that 3 or 4 leaves were left on the remaining portion of the stem; this encourages more side growth, and the more side growth, the greater the floral display in the fall.

This plant is so spectacular that it's brought dozens of questions from viewers interested in propagating it. Professional nurserymen grow them from softwood cuttings taken early in the summer, a very difficult and demanding procedure. The plants are inexpensive, so I'd advise buying an initial plant. Then if the urge strikes, you can propagate them by layering them as you would a rhododendron (see page 85).

Squash As vegetables go, squash is relatively unbothered by insects and disease, but there is one danger that lurks through the summer: the squash vine borer. It appears in early July in northern gardens, and bores into the vine, causing it to wilt and eventually die unless corrective action is taken quickly. I spray the vines with a plant-derived insecticide called rotenone, beginning when the squash runners are 1 foot long, usually about the first week of July. I spray the

The silver fleece vine climbing up and over the greenhouse

Zucchini blossoms

base of the plant and the runners about once a week for the rest of the month. This usually prevents the problem before it happens.

If a borer sneaks by me, the wilting vine will announce its presence. The entry hole will be quite obvious because of a mass of "sawdust" beneath the hole. The borer in all likelihood will not be far along in its journey to the end of the vine. So I dig it out of the vine with my knife and cover the wounded area and several feet of vine with 2 inches of moist soil. (One of the reasons I'm so partial to the Waltham Butternut squash is that it's bred for resistance to these beasts.)

Blossom-end rot is another of the tribulations of squash plants (particularly summer squashes and zucchinis). It shows up as rotten fruit, the first indication being the blossom end that often fails to develop fully. Evidence seems to show that this is a physiological disease similar to the one that causes blossom-end rot in tomatoes. The cure is a preventive: allow the plants plenty of ground space so they do not touch one another. Keep the soil sweet by using enough limestone to maintain 6.5 to 7.0 pH. Keep the phosphorus level in the soil high by using a fertilizer with a high phosphorus level and relatively low levels of nitrogen and potash: 5-10-5 is satisfactory. Finally, make sure that the soil moisture level stays relatively stable. Mulch around the plants if necessary to keep soil moisture from fluctuating. When you cultivate, do so very lightly so as not to disturb feeding roots close to the surface.

A word about squash blossoms. There are both male and female blossoms on squash plants. They are quite distinguishable: the male flower's stem is slim and straight; the female stem has a bulbous growth just below the flower, which eventually becomes the squash fruit. Usually, squash plants produce a number of male flowers before the females appear. There are always more male flowers than female.

The summer squash transplanted into the garden in May are usually ready for their first harvest in July. I pick them when they're small — no more than 6 or 8 inches long — so they're tender enough to eat raw. The larger squashes just don't hold a candle to the tiny ones. During a good season summer squashes grow so rapidly that it is necessary to pick them every day or, at most, every other day. Production slows down if fruit is allowed to mature.

Sweet William I know these midsummer weeks are busy ones, but given the price of sweet William seedlings and the ease of sowing the seeds, it's certainly worth the time it takes to grow a tiny forest of these handsome plants to set out in a nursery bed in July, thence into the perennial garden in the fall or spring. The sweet William, in case you don't know, is an easy-to-grow biennial with flat 4 to 6-inch flower heads composed of hundreds of white, pink, dark red, or multicolored blossoms that appear in late May or June.

To get plants for another year, I begin in late June or early July by sifting a mixture of equal parts of compost, sand, and garden soil through a ¼-inch-mesh hardware cloth, saving both the fine sifted material and the coarser material that will not sift. I put some of the coarse material into the bottom of a flowerpot, where it will provide drainage, and then fill the pot with the fine mix.

Sweet William seeds are black and about $\frac{1}{16}$ inch in diameter, which is rather large as flower seeds go. I sprinkle the seeds sparingly across the top of the soil, trying not to overdo the sowing, as almost all of them will come up. Then I add a thin layer of milled sphagnum moss to prevent the seedlings from damping off, and bottom-water the pot. Given full sun or light shade and moist soil the seedlings will emerge within a week.

When their first true leaf develops between the seed leaves, they will be ready for moving to the outdoor nursery bed. I transplant them into a bed, spaced 8 inches apart in both directions — a homemade multidibble (see page 304) is a handy tool for this job. The seedlings are still very small at this transplanting stage but by fall the foliage will have filled in the entire bed. In November or December after the ground freezes, I mulch them with pine needles to protect them from freezing and thawing during the winter. They'll blossom the following May or June.

Tomatoes July is the month to observe the progress of the tomatoes we've planted in the Victory Garden. First of all let's consider the blemishes, minor though they are. Occasionally there is some yellowing or curling of the lower foliage, but that's not anything to be concerned about. Sometimes the ripe fruit will crack open, usually a function of a rainfall followed by sunshine. It sometimes happens on staked plants whose fruit is exposed, but rarely on cage-grown plants whose canopy of foliage shades the fruit. When I grow tomatoes on stakes, I keep the soil evenly moist, with a mulch if need be, and the cracking problem is minor.

By September the average home gardener is surfeited with tomatoes, but in July when the first ones ripen, it is a time for celebration. The later tomatoes, and those grown in cages, will need another month before they're ripe. Some-

A cage full of cherry tomatoes

times the vines of caged tomatoes will grow right up over the top of the cages in July, which means that too much of the plants' energy is going into the foliage and not enough into the fruit. I follow the lead of the commercial growers and cut back any of the tall stems that overstep the bounds of the cage.

Tulips It's time to dig the tulip bulbs out of their ripening row in the garden and put them into storage for a couple of months. After a tulip blossoms its bulb divides into two or more smaller bulbs. As I dig them I separate these bulbs according to variety and color and store them in paper bags until September, when they'll go back into the Victory Garden for blossoming in the spring.

Opposite: Balloonflower, a July bloomer in the perennial border

Q&A

Q: There's a foaming substance in the crotches of my plants and in the nearby fields of goldenrod. It looks like insect eggs. Anything to worry about?
A: What you've got is something known as spittlebug or froghopper. There's an insect within the foam that attacks about 400 different kinds of plants, especially strawberries. Methoxychlor is a specific control applied in early spring to catch young nymphs and in the fall to kill egg-laying adults.

Q: Do you have burlap on your wire fencing to shield the cukes and melons from the sun?
A: No. Our problem is high winds, which the burlap helps to control.

Q: My garden has recently become home to a huge colony of ants. What shall I do?
A: If you have ants, you probably also have aphids. Ants go after the sweet honeydew that the aphids secrete. If you take care of the aphids with a contact insecticide, the ants will find a new home.

PESTS & PLAGUES

Pests know a good thing when they see it. The Victory Garden, certainly the lushest garden I've ever grown, is the best thing the pests have seen in quite a while, too, and they've marched in by the battalion. My response to this is the judicious use of whatever defenses are indicated. If I can possibly do without chemical pesticides, I don't use them. I abide by the theory that a few bugs won't eat everything in sight, but if it's the garden or the bugs, I'm on the side of the garden. The use of pesticides is another case where more isn't necessarily better; I follow the label instructions to the letter, and concentrate sprays on the undersides of the leaves where most pests lurk.

Here's our most-unwanted list, along with the weapons we've used against them.

Aphids Sometimes called plant lice, aphids are an inevitable part of gardening. They come in a multitude of colors, but with one goal in life: to suck nourishment out of tender plant cells. Their life cycle is complicated in that aphids, hatched from wintering-over eggs, develop into females that give birth to generation after generation of living young, all females, until late summer.

Then some of the young appear as males. These mate with females, who lay eggs that live over the winter. Aphids may or may not have wings and they usually congregate on the most

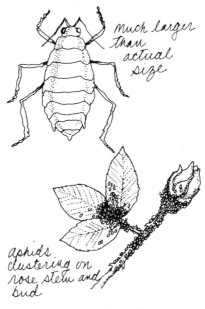

much larger than actual size

aphids clustering on rose stem and bud

tender part of a plant, the new growth at the tip or the underside of young leaves. Usually they appear in great numbers, sucking strength from plants and also acting as agents for the spread of diseases, especially viruses that further debilitate the plants. What's more, aphids secrete a sweet, sticky substance called honeydew, which attracts ants. If that were not enough trouble, black sooty fungus grows in the honeydew, shading the chlorophyll in the leaves from the sun, weakening plants, and making them sickly and unable to produce normal crops. Although tiny individually, aphids are a serious threat to gardens and should be dealt with early in the season before they multiply.

The old solution for aphid problems was nicotine sulphate, a derivative of tobacco. In the Victory Garden we use a rotenone-pyrethrum spray of very low toxicity to mammals.

Cabbage Maggots Victory Garden Enemy Number One. Left unchallenged, cabbage maggots, usually called root maggots, could easily make off with up to 80 percent of the root crops in the garden. They're ¼-inch-long white worms that hatch from tiny eggs laid by ¼-inch black flies. The flies lay the eggs at the base of a plant or in the soil close to the plant's stem. When the maggots hatch, they burrow into the lower stem and roots. The first sign of trouble is usually wilting and yellow foliage, but at that point it's too late to think of cures; plants will have been damaged beyond recall. Any control must be applied before injury has been done. Periodic diazinon treatments will take care of root maggots, but I was reminded by a British friend of a nonchemical treatment that was used years ago: essentially, a maggot mat is a physical barrier that prevents the flies from laying their eggs

Cabbage maggots are about ¼" long white worms

close to plants — no eggs, no maggots. In England it's common practice to construct root maggot mats out of 12-inch squares of carpeting material. One summer we tried this method successfully, but you might substitute squares of tar paper for the carpet. In the center, cut a tiny hole no bigger than the plant's stem. Then slice the tar paper from the hole to one edge so it can be slipped around the plant's stem. Once the mat is in place, tape the cut together with waterproof tape. As the stem grows it will expand the hole in the tar paper so the mat can be left on until harvest. This will protect the plants from the cutworms as well as the maggots. Use mats on broccoli and cauliflower as well as cabbage. Use diazinon to protect radish and turnip roots.

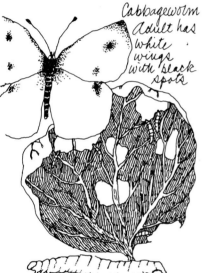

Cabbageworm adult has white wings with black spots

Larvae grow to be about an inch long and are green

Cabbageworm Caterpillars

About 1 inch long when full grown, these pests are the offspring of a white butterfly with black spots on the wings. A century ago the best weapon against them was an army of ten-year-olds armed with nets to snare the butterflies before the eggs were deposited. Now this army has been replaced by *Bacillus thuringiensis*, a nontoxic, nonchemical pesticide sprayed at 7- to 10-day intervals.

Cutworms may be gray, brown, black, striped or spotted.

shown larger than life size

Cutworms

There are many kinds of cutworms. Some climb trees, some work underground, but the ones that harass the Victory Garden are smooth, fat caterpillars that move along the surface of the soil at night attacking the tender stems of young seedlings, especially those newly transplanted to the garden. There are commercial insecticides available, but I prefer a safer approach: a cutworm collar that presents a physical barrier around my plants. I make these collars from 2 × 14–inch strips of lightweight cardboard or tar

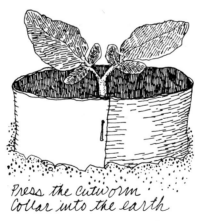

Press the cutworm collar into the earth

paper, stapled into a band. I slip a collar over each seedling after transplanting it to the garden, and press it down into the soil about ½ inch deep. No cutworm has the gumption or brains to crawl over. By the time the collar decays after a few weeks, the plants' stems are too strong for the cutworm to penetrate.

Japanese Beetles

The Japanese beetle is thought to have been brought to this country in soil around the roots of some plant that was imported from Japan shortly before World War I. Nowadays the practice of bringing soil into this country is prohibited because we surely don't want another pest as bad as the Japanese beetle. From that innocent-appearing beginning has developed a population of Japanese beetles in many parts of this country capable of destroying many kinds of ornamental and food crops. In the Victory Garden, adult Japanese beetles concentrate on our asparagus, corn, and rhubarb. The most effective control I know for adult Japanese beetles is carbaryl. In lawns, it's the grubs that cause the most trouble. They are gray-brown with brown heads, nearly 1 inch long, and usually curved. They eat the roots of grass, killing the plants. Most suggested controls during the grub stage have turned out to be relatively ineffective because mature beetles fly from garden to garden, eating as they go.

adult Japanese Beetles are green and copper. shown about twice life size.

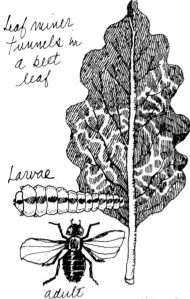

Leaf miner tunnels in a beet leaf

Larvae

adult

both shown over life size

Mexican Bean Beetles These are the black sheep of the normally harmless ladybeetle family. They look like ladybugs, but unlike ladybugs, they have 16 black spots on their backs. They're about ⅓ inch long and copper colored. They are most dangerous at their larvae stage, when they crawl along, rasping holes in and skeletonizing the leaves, working from underneath, where they're hardest to see. Their diet includes all kinds of beans except soybeans; they dote on lima beans. They're tenacious creatures, but they can be controlled with carbaryl, rotenone, malathion, or diazinon.

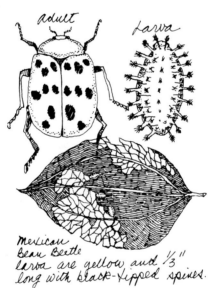

adult   larva

Mexican Bean Beetle larva are yellow and ⅓" long with black-tipped spines.

Leaf Miners Along with the root maggots these creatures cause most of our insect problems in the Victory Garden. There's a miner for almost every plant in the garden: one reference book lists 52 different leaf miners. Here, they are particularly attracted to our leafy vegetables, including spinach, beet greens, and Swiss chard; they arrive in surges in mid-May, late June, and mid-August, but are troublesome all season long. They live protected between the layers of leaves, eventually tunneling through the entire leafy growth of the plants, leaving them not only inedible but quite ugly. The only sure defense is periodic applications with pyrethrum, diazinon, or malathion to kill the grublike miners when they emerge from eggs and before they burrow into the leaves. Leaf miners also live on weeds, one more reason to keep weeds under control. We pick off and burn any foliage infested with leaf miners; otherwise they will pupate and become flies that will lay more eggs and repeat the deadly cycle.

Red Spider Mites Although they are technically known as two-spotted spider mites, these insects live up to their common name on all counts. They're red, they're spiders, and they're so tiny they're all but invisible. They prey on almost all plants, making their tiny cobwebs on the

Red Spider Mites are pin-head size or smaller. They are bright red in color

undersides of leaves and sucking nourishment from the foliage. They love hot weather, and multiply prodigiously in the midsummer heat. I keep my eye out for signs of their presence, and put any infested plants under a forceful spray of cold water to wash the mites from the foliage. If this does not work well enough to suit me, I use a miticide such as dicofol.

Slugs Probably the most repulsive of the garden invaders, slugs congregate on the soil wherever there's some damp, shady protection. We've even stopped general mulching in the garden because they became

Spotted Garden Slug

Slugs can be from ¼" to 4" long and are yellow-white, brown or black.

such a problem. There are dozens of old-time cures, most of which don't work. In the Victory Garden we corral them by laying down a cabbage leaf, or a half grapefruit rind, or a sheet of plastic. The night-feeding slugs congregate under these items just before dawn, so the next day we can scoop them up and get rid of them. Metaldehyde meal will kill them too; I don't use the pellet form, as birds or animals are apt to eat them and be poisoned. Read the metaldehyde label carefully and keep the material away from vegetables.

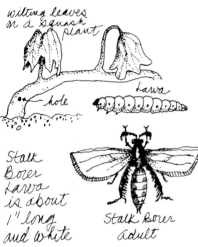

wilting leaves on a squash plant

hole

Larva

Stalk Borer Larva is about 1" long and white

Stalk Borer adult

Stalk Borers If ever there was an insect with an indiscriminate appetite, it is the stalk borer. Although stalk borers eat almost any kind of plant, they always work in the same manner. They burrow a hole in plants' stems and then eat their way along the inside. The first indication of trouble is a wilting stalk on a sunny day. Their entry holes are visible on stems, so when I notice one I slice upward from the hole toward the tip of the stem, prying it apart gently to locate the

borer and dispose of it. Sometimes a plant stem is so weakened by the borer's attack that it cannot be saved, but often the plant will make a surprising comeback once the borer is removed. The best control for stalk borers is weed control in the vicinity of a garden, because weed patches provide breeding grounds for these omnivorous pests.

Tomato Hornworms
The best thing about hornworms is their size. At 3 or 4 inches long, they can easily be spotted on the tomato leaves they feed on. I usually just pick off any that I see, but a spray with *Bacillus thuringiensis* will take care of them. Sometimes I find hornworms with small white eggs stuck to their skins. I allow these hornworms to live because a parasitic wasp has laid her eggs. Her young will kill the hornworm and when they are mature they will fly away to kill others too.

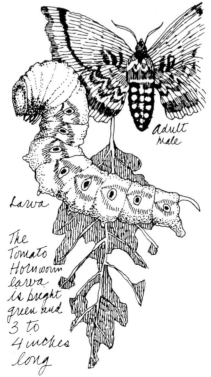

adult male

Larva

The Tomato Hornworm larva is bright green and 3 to 4 inches long

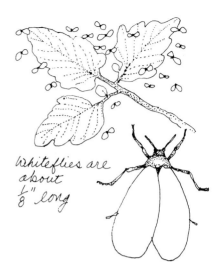

whiteflies are about ⅛" long

Whiteflies When a gardener, touching a plant, sets off a cloud of ⅛-inch whiteflies, he or she is in serious trouble. In their juvenile stages they suck juices from the undersides of leaves, leaving the foliage pale and mottled. They attack many kinds of plants, such as tomatoes, eggplants, squashes, beans, and even lettuce. I hit them hard early in the season as soon as I discover them. They can be controlled with a rotenone-pyrethrum spray, but only if the spray is applied every 4 to 5 days for 2 or 3 weeks, because these insects are invulnerable in certain stages of their life cycle.

Verticillium wilt in an eggplant

blight is the scourge of many of our flowers, geraniums and petunias especially; we control it by giving plants wide spacing so there is good air circulation, and by keeping the foliage dry.

Botrytis Blight on a geranium leaf

DEFENSES

Diseases In comparison to insects, plant diseases aren't much of a problem in the Victory Garden, but we don't escape scot-free. Our eggplants are sometimes hit with verticillium wilt, but plant breeders are working on varieties bred for resistance to this and other diseases. Black spot can attack our roses in the cool, damp weather of the spring and fall; I keep the roses and the surrounding area free of spotted leaves and I spray with an all-purpose spray weekly, starting as early in the season as there's new growth in sight. Botrytis

Benemyl is a satisfactory botrytis preventative. Damping-off disease, which is a fungus though it sounds like a functional disorder, attacks young seedlings; we've all but eliminated this problem by using milled sphagnum moss when we sow our seeds.

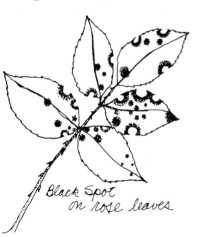

Damping-off Disease in a bean seedling

Black Spot on rose leaves

Pesticides are not items to be taken lightly. They are very serious business. They should be used sparingly and carefully to control specific insects and diseases that are present or due to arrive. Pesticides can be used to eradicate insects and diseases, but by that time the damage may have already been done. It is a wise gardener who learns the life cycle of each major insect and disease and strikes it early, when it is most vulnerable, with the least-toxic material that will insure protection. Follow the instructions given on the label: use the smallest dosage recommended and honor the spraying-to-harvest deadlines. Above all, keep them under lock and key and out of the reach of children.

Ordinarily in this book I've referred to the Victory Garden insecticides by their generic names but they are sometimes difficult to find unless the brand names are known too, so here follows a list of the generic and common names. Keep in mind, though, that new pesticides — and fungicides too — appear on the market all the time, so it's wise to consult with a garden center about the most recent products that have appeared.

All-Purpose Spray This four-way combination of fungicides and insecticides, including carbaryl, malathion, dicofol, and folpet, is sometimes sold as rose spray or general garden spray. Our early and periodic use of this combination is the reason our perennial border — our roses especially — is such a smashing success.

Compressed air sprayer

Bacillus thuringiensis This safe, nonchemical pesticide is sold as Thuricide, Dipel, or Biotrol. There's almost nothing negative to be said about it: it's effective, easy to use, nonpoisonous, and safe even for organic gardens.

Carbaryl This is sold as Sevin, and we use this pesticide to control Japanese beetles and corn borers. It's toxic to bees, but that's easily solved by spraying on a windless day late in the afternoon when the bees are in the hive. To lessen the danger to bees, I direct the spray into the center of each whorl of corn leaves, not on the general foliage or tassels.

Diazinon This is the broadest-spectrum, and probably the most potent, insecticide we use in the Victory Garden. Sold under many trade names, it has a residual toxicity of 14 days, which means that crops on which it has been used cannot be eaten within 2 weeks of spraying. We use the 4 percent strength powder when preparing soil, and the concentrated 18 percent liquid as a soil drench and foliar spray.

Dicofol This is the most effective low toxicity insecticide meant specifically for mites. It's sold as Kelthane.

Malathion A broad-spectrum insecticide sold under its generic name, malathion has a residual toxicity of only 7 days, during which time treated crops cannot be eaten. For this reason, we sometimes use malathion as an alternative to diazinon close to the harvest.

Rotenone-Pyrethrum These two insecticides are often paired and sold under several names, including Red Arrow and DX. We like this combination because both ingredients are botanical, that is, derived from plants, so they can be used indoors.

Rechargeable cordless electric sprayer

Fungicides are used to prevent diseases, not cure them, so they have to be used while the plants are still healthy. Many gardeners find it difficult to go to the bother of treating a healthy plant, but that's the secret to success. We rely on four fungicides in the Victory Garden.

Benemyl Sold as Benlate, this fungicide is the most expensive of the group, but also the best. We use it to control mildew and fungus diseases on our flowers.

Captan Sold as Captan 50W, Orthocide 50, and Orthocide 75, we use this fungicide as a seed coating to prevent rot, and in wintering-over our gladiolus corms.

Maneb Available as Manzate, Dithane M-22, or Ortho Maneb, this is effective against rust disease on bean plants.

Folpet Marketed as Phaltan, we use this fungicide primarily in the all-purpose spray that keeps our perennials and roses in such superb shape all season long.

A final word on this subject: these pesticides and fungicides are effective outdoors or in the greenhouse, but they are not all suitable for use indoors, where ventilation is a problem and food surfaces are close by. For indoor plants, my suggestion is that you keep them washed and check them frequently — get up close to them so you'll be able to spot even the tiniest creatures before they get out of hand. If you discover an infestation, try to identify the pest and check with a garden center for a specific, safe treatment. If you've got a serious infestation, protect your other plants by throwing the damaged one as far away as you can.

Main crop tomato

AUG

Plant
Beans
Endive
Peas
Spinach

Transplant
Cineraria
Pansies
Poinsettias
Primroses

Thin
Beets
Broccoli
Collards (see July)
Radishes
Spinach

Fertilize
Broccoli
Radishes

Harvest
Beans
Beets
Corn
Garlic
Melons
Onions
Potatoes
Shallots
Squash
Tomatoes

Special Events
Basil
Chrysanthemums
Corn
Geraniums
Roses
Strawberries

AUG

It's a beautiful, lush month in the garden. The hollyhocks, phlox, bee balm, lilies, gaillardias, coreopsis, and veronica are in full bloom in the perennial border. The delphiniums we cut back after their early summer flowering begin to reward us with more spikes of handsome blue and purple blossoms. As some of the annual plants in the perennial border begin to feel the effects of their age and the weather, we pull them and move chrysanthemums from their nursery rows to fill in the vacancies.

There's no greater truth in gardening than that gardeners must plant far in advance if crops are to mature at the right time. In the Victory Garden greenhouse there are always seedlings growing, some for later transplant to the garden proper and others as houseplants. One August, for instance, the cyclamen seeds we'd planted in June were up and growing and ready for individual pots, though it would be another 14 months before they would blossom. Our coffee plants, sown many months earlier, relished the warm August weather and grew continuously, sending out shiny bronze-green leaves that turned to dark green when they reached full size. And some cactus seeds we'd planted the winter before had become a bewildering variety of plants with an amazing diversity of shape and spine arrangement.

As I see it, there's no reason to grow a vegetable garden unless the vegetables are harvested when they're young and tender, long before they reach the age at which they're usually sold in supermarkets. August is the cornucopia month of the year, so picking those young vegetables means a daily trip through the garden, basket in hand. Along the way, I usually pick a few herbs for drying and freezing, and move some of the still-growing herbs into pots and onto a kitchen windowsill, so the fragrance will drift in with the breezes. And of course to keep the garden producing for as long as I can, I take advantage of these harvested areas to plant some of the cool-weather crops that will mature during the fall.

So, August is a rewarding month, a payoff month. But not a month for resting on laurels.

Basil Fresh basil is one of the staples of any herb garden. The leaves are delicious with fresh tomatoes, or in pesto sauces. But the plants are so prolific, especially if the seed pods are kept pinched back as they should be, that there

A cluster of basil plants

is no way that most gardeners can manage to stay up with the plants' production. They can give some away to friends and still have plenty left to preserve for the winter. I think basil takes best to freezing in airtight bags, but it can also be dried, in which case I wait for a sunny day to give the dew a chance to dry from the plants, cut a few stems with a knife or shears, wrap a rubber band around this bouquet, and hang it upside down in a cool, dry, shady place. (I use a rubber band rather than string because it contracts as the stems shrivel, preventing them from falling loose.) After a few days, when it's perfectly dry, I crumble the foliage and store it in a jar for use all winter long.

Beans The year that we did the pole bean demonstration crops I found myself in a bucket of hot water at harvesttime. I had mentioned that while I thought the scarlet

A bush bean

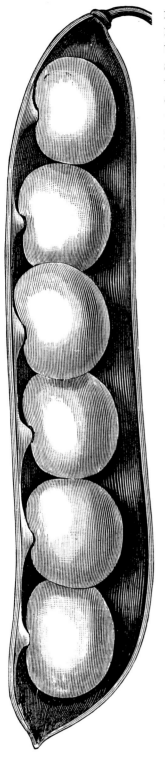

runner flowers were quite good looking and that the luxuriant foliage was handsome, I couldn't say much for the beans themselves, finding them too tough for my taste. The entire scarlet runner bean lobby, if there is one, must have been watching that show, because letters came from all over the country to challenge my unfriendly remarks. One British viewer wrote in to say that in her home country the scarlet runner bean was a great favorite. She thought my mistake was in leaving the beans on the vine too long, and suggested that I pick the pods before the beans inside have developed too far, and then slice the beans french style for cooking. If the beans are left on the vine too long, she went on, just remove the seeds inside and cook them as any other shell beans. It's advice worth trying.

On the assumption that September will be warm and sunny, we plant our last crop of bush beans in the Victory Garden in early August. We can't plant this crop any later than the middle of the month or we'll never have weather warm enough for them to mature.

August is a bean harvest month, too, as bush and pole beans continue to bear heavily. And in August the limas planted in June are ready for picking. In my opinion canned or dried lima beans are hardly worth the eating, but the Victory Garden's harvest is another story entirely. I pick them when the pods are about 3 inches long and the beans inside are small, sweet, and succulent. Happily, the lima harvest is a long one; it continues right up until the first frost. (As with all the bean crops, I harvest limas when the weather is dry to avoid spreading anthracnose, a fungus disease, from wet plant to wet plant.)

Beets Mid-August usually brings another invasion (gratefully the last) of leaf miners to the Victory Garden, and they head right for the beets and Swiss chard. If we've been anything less than diligent with our treatments, they will lay their eggs on the undersides of the leaves, and the first sign of trouble will be the resulting colony of tiny white dots. Once the eggs are spotted, there's an uphill battle at controlling the beasts, so those preventive doses of pyrethrum, diazinon, or malathion are really a must.

There are several successive crops of beets in the Victory Garden through the summer, and each crop needs to be attended to in turn. Not only do all the beets need periodic diazinon or malathion to control leaf miners, but they need thinning too. When the plants are about 1 inch tall, I thin the rows to 1-inch intervals, and as the seedlings reach a height of 2 or 3 inches, I thin them to approximately 3-inch spacing, transplanting the extra seedlings if I've got the room in another section of the garden.

Broccoli By August the July sowing of broccoli needs thinning to one healthy seedling at each interval. If I have the room I carefully lift the extra seedlings and transplant them to other spots in the garden. (One year I even moved one plant to a large pot, where it did beautifully.) If the garden is a little tight for space, I don't bother pulling the extra seedlings; I just clip them off at the soil level with my thumbnail. This is not only the easier thinning approach, it's safer for the remaining plants. After the extras have been removed I give the remaining plant at each spot about ½ teaspoon of 5-10-5 fertilizer — no more for a plant this age — being especially careful not to let the fertilizer touch the stems of the plants. After scratching the fertilizer into the soil very lightly, I give the plants a drink of water, not only to dissolve some of the fertilizer so the plants can use it, but to consolidate any soil I may have loosened around the plants.

Chrysanthemums Chrysanthemums vary considerably in their hardiness or tolerance of cold weather. Most so-called garden chrysanthemums are able to survive outdoors when temperatures fall to zero degrees Fahrenheit, provided they are given a light mulch after the ground freezes. Others are strictly indoor plants suited for greenhouses or windowsills. But all chrysanthemums are sensitive to day length. Normally they blossom in the fall when

Chrysanthemum divisions coming into bloom

days become short, but florists nowadays bring them into bloom at all seasons by manipulating the day length.

One year we had a nonhardy plant that bloomed indoors in November. When it stopped flowering, we cut the stems back to the soil and kept the plant alive in a cool, brightly lighted location. In the spring it began to grow rapidly, but with only a few stalks. To make the plant bushy, we cut off the tips of the stems, then saved them to make more plants. They rooted easily in damp sand and were then potted into 6-inch pots filled with soilless mix. By late fall we not only had the original plant, but we had several offspring made from the cuttings.

Cineraria Transplanting cineraria seedlings is no job for the impatient. After a month, the seeds sown in July produce tiny seedlings with their first true leaves. And I do mean tiny. The entire seedling is no more than ⅛ inch tall. But, because cinerarias are so susceptible to damping-off disease, I give them added growing room with good air circulation as soon as possible. To handle these miniature plants I whittle a wooden plant label into a slender, flat stick about 4 inches long and use it to prick the seedlings up out of the soil. When I carry them, I hold them by the leaves themselves, not by the stems, because the stems are so fragile that even the gentlest pressure of my fingers could squeeze the life out. I move the seedlings into six-packs filled with soilless mix and set them in at the same level they grew in the pot.

Corn One of the lessons I've learned in my years of gardening is that innovation and faith are good friends in the face of the unexpected calamity. One August we suffered a freak hurricane in the Victory Garden, a very uncommon problem in this area of the country, and our tall late-season corn plants weren't quite able to stand up to it. When the rains finally stopped and the winds died down the cornstalks were listing badly to the side. Unwilling to give them up, I straightened and staked them and pulled soil in around the roots. After a couple of weeks the ears were ready to harvest; the stalks never did regain their posture, but they did the most important thing — they matured the corn I thought I was going to lose.

Cornstalks are particularly rich material for the compost bin, a result of the nutritious soil they grow in. So after the crops are harvested I pull the stalks up and chop them into the composter — a shredding machine is the simpler but noisier alternative — to decompose and enrich my supply of brown gold. Sometimes, if the compost bin is full, I use hedge shears to chop the stalks into 6-inch pieces, then bury them as I spade the ground over for another crop.

Endive For all its simple appearance, endive is not the easiest plant to grow because it must have cool weather or it will send up tall seed stalks, destroying its usefulness in salads. I usually hazard a crop in early spring, hoping it will be large enough to blanch and use before hot weather arrives. Sometimes I win, sometimes I lose. However, if I plant endive in August to mature in the cool fall, I almost never fail. When planting the second crop of endive, I drop 3 or 4 seeds at 12-inch intervals along a row. Because the seeds are light-sensitive I don't cover them with soil. I just press them down a bit and give them a drink of water. These seeds, exposed as they are to the summer sun day after day, are more in need of moisture than most seeds, so the watering care has to be especially alert. They usually germinate within 10 days, often to the surprise of gardeners who are conditioned to believe that all seeds must be covered with soil before they will sprout.

Geranium cutting dusted with rooting powder

Garlic Garlic is one of the most carefree crops in the Victory Garden. So while it's inexpensive to buy, it's still worth the few minutes it takes to plant. I usually plant a crop in October; it winters-over in the soil and begins its growth as soon as the soil warms in the spring. I plant a second crop in May, too. Both plantings mature in August but, logically enough, the bulbs from the fall planting are larger as a result of their earlier start.

When the stems lose all trace of green and the tops bend over, the garlic is ready to be harvested. I use a fork to ease the plants out of the ground, dry the cloves for a couple of days, outdoors if the weather is dry or under cover if it's not, and then hang them in a mesh bag so the air can circulate around them.

Geraniums There's a common autumnal syndrome among gardeners, brought on by the first frost. In an effort to save their geranium plants from this killing blast of cold, they run out into the garden, jam big plants into small pots, and run back into the heated house, plants in hand. Three weeks later the plants have lost most of their leaves and the gardeners wonder why.

I avoid this disappointment in the Victory Garden by taking cuttings in August of the healthiest geraniums in the garden, to guarantee a generation of thriving young plants through the winter. I begin by snapping off stems about 3 inches long; I never use a knife to do this as it's likely to spread diseases from plant to plant. Then I strip each stem of all but 3 or 4 of the top leaves and leave the stems exposed to the air for a day to dry the end of the stems and keep them from rotting.

When the stems are cured I moisten each end slightly and dip it into rooting powder. These cuttings would probably root without the powder, but I take the extra precaution anyway. Then I set each stem into a pot of coarse builders' sand. I sometimes advise individual plastic bag greenhouses for rooting plants, but this isn't a good idea with geraniums as the leaves are particularly prone to decay. Uncovered they may wilt a bit but they perk up with a light sprinkling of water once every 2 or 3 days. In about 3 weeks the roots are ½ inch long, so I repot them into regular potting soil. I always make a point of transplanting rooted cuttings when the roots are no more than 1 inch long; if they are any longer than that they are easily broken in transplanting.

Melons The Victory Garden is a study in gardening efficiency. Our space is so limited, and our ambitions so great, that we've had to take every possible step to make the most of the space we have. Which is why we've grown our can-

A melon supported by netting

taloupes along a fence, a solution that has the added benefit of good air circulation and sunshine, early ripening, and reduced pest and disease problems. The only problem with this vertical melon garden is that the fruit is usually too heavy for the foliage to support, so the gardener has to lend a helping hand. When the melons grow to about the size of grapefruit, I bag each individual fruit with some mesh material that will support the melons as they continue to grow. I use either an old nylon stocking or an onion bag or plastic netting, tying it with twine to the fence. The melons can continue to grow without bearing the full burden of their own weight.

Our cantaloupes begin to ripen in August, when the skin is textured with a network of tan ridges all around the fruit and the melon's background color has changed from green to beige. I'm often asked for indications of melon ripeness. One sure method is what I call the "slip test." If you look carefully at the stem end of a melon, you will find a disk

A sure indication of melon ripeness

of fibrous tissue at the point where the stem joins the melon. When a melon is fully ripe, the disk separates from the melon just as a leaf falls from a tree in the autumn, leaving a scar, but without costing the fruit so much as a drop of it's sap. If a melon disk slips off the fruit with the slightest pressure of your thumb, you know that the melon is ripe and that you are in for a real taste treat.

Of course the real ripeness giveaway is that wonderful melon aroma all through the garden. One year this aroma caught the fascination and the noses of some neighborhood youngsters who managed to invade the garden and make off with every melon but one. When we passed the story along to a friend of ours, an eminent plant breeder, he was sympathetic but not encouraging. "Finger blight," he said. "Very serious. No cure."

Onions Our onion harvest continues in August, when the spring plantings of sets and seedlings are mature. I cure them after pulling, letting them dry in the sun for 2 or 3 days, and then moving them to a dry, warm place for 4 to 6 weeks until the skins are completely dry and the tops withered. Then I store them in a cool, airy spot for use through the fall and winter.

As you pull your onions, you will probably observe that the stalks of some are much thicker than others. Sometimes they are called "thick-necked" or "bull-necked." These onions will not store as well as do those whose stalks shrivel away completely, so I advise using these first. If you want to store your onions in an open mesh bag, cut the stalks off about an inch or two above the bulbs when you pull them. If you want to braid them so as to hang the bulbs in an airy place, do the braiding soon after digging because the stalks will still be relatively pliant. Above all, don't pile freshly

picked onions more than two deep; without air circulation, they're apt to start new root growth in the dampness, or worse yet, to rot.

A storage basket of onions

A pansy grown from seed

An edible podded pea

Pansies By August, the pansy seedlings sown in flats in the greenhouse in July have developed their first true leaves and are ready to be introduced to the great outdoors. When room opens in the garden, I use a multidibble (see February feature, p. 304) to set the little plants into the garden at 4-inch intervals, making sure to cluster like plants together and transferring the labels. After they're mulched in November, they're ready for their winter outdoors.

Peas If I had the power to shake one gardening myth, it would be that peas are strictly a springtime crop in northern gardens. I never let a year go by without planting a crop of peas in August to pick in October. The procedure is the same as for the spring crop, but the harvest is often tastier and crisper because the pods mature in cool rather than warm weather. There's just no reason to miss this fall treat.

Poinsettias By August the poinsettia cuttings taken in July have developed roots that are about 1 inch long, so they're ready for moving to 3-inch pots filled with potting soil. I take them out of the plastic bag greenhouses and put them in bright sun so that they can develop sturdy growth. During especially hot days, if wilting occurs, I mist the foliage with tepid water, but I am very careful that the leaves are dry before nightfall to avoid setting up conditions that might encourage leaf diseases.

Late in August the plants will have made enough growth to be shifted into the pots in which they will remain through their blossoming period. Some plants I transfer to 4- or 5-inch pots and grow as single plants; others I shift to 6-inch pots, setting three plants to a pot. These make a handsome and colorful display beginning about the middle of December, continuing for many months thereafter.

Potatoes The first of our early varieties of potatoes are ready for digging in August when the foliage has died down entirely. The first step is to pull out the withered vines and put them on the compost pile. Potatoes don't necessarily grow directly beneath the vines; instead they grow on underground stems called stolons that may reach as far as 10 inches out from the center of the row. Rather than take a chance of stabbing a potato, I begin digging about 1 foot out on either side of the center of the row, using a 4-tined spading fork. This digging operation requires a light touch because any potato that is damaged in digging is likely to rot. Early potatoes are not as long-lasting in storage as are late varieties; for that reason I usually dig only enough for a few days' use in the kitchen unless I want to use the potato row for another crop.

After digging them, I leave the potatoes sitting on top of the soil for 2 or 3 hours to dry thoroughly. Then I put them in burlap or mesh bags and store them in a dark, cool place. If

Digging potatoes

they're left in the light, even for a few days, they'll turn green, and green potato skins are inedible.·

(One viewer wrote in to say that her potatoes, still a few weeks from harvest, were too near the surface and were turning green. Would mulch help, she wondered? It would, but I suggested that she hill some soil up around the plants, covering the potatoes. After 2 or 3 weeks the green potato skins would turn brown and be ready for harvest. After all, hilling-up is standard practice in potato culture because it keeps the tubers deep under ground where they are protected from the light.)

Primroses Primroses are great flowering plants for the winter months, but they require many weeks of careful culture before they begin to make flower buds. I usually grow three kinds of primroses. The polyanthus is hardy outdoors, but will blossom indoors as well; its blossoms may be creamy white, yellow, pink, red, lavender, or purple. The fairy primrose, an indoor type in most parts of the country, has slender 10-inch stems bearing small pink or white flowers arranged in tiers. The obconica primrose is a coarser-leaved form with white, pink, or lavender flowers; some people don't like to

A primrose plant

grow the obconica primrose because the hairs on the bottoms of the leaves sometimes cause a skin rash.

I sow primroses in June, using pure compost. They start from dustlike seeds and though they grow quite rapidly, they are still tiny in August when they are ready to be transplanted to individual containers. I fill six-packs with compost or potting soil and transfer the seedlings from the seed pot to the packs on the tip of my knife. They are usually only about ⅛ inch across at that time, just sending out their first true leaves. As the weather becomes cooler toward the end of the month, they respond with strong growth, for they need cool temperatures, moist soil, and partial shade to do their best.

Radishes Most gardeners are familiar with ordinary radishes, but few have grown the larger, milder-flavored winter radishes that can be stored for use long after the ground freezes. Compared with their summer counterparts, winter radishes are giants. They can grow to be about 6 inches long and 3 or 4 inches across, so it's important to give these whopping plants plenty of room and plenty of food as well. In August I thin the July sowing to 4- or 5-inch intervals and then side dress the rows with 5-10-5 fertilizer. The row looks a trifle sparse after this thinning, but the radishes grow fast and furiously after this and the foliage fills in the row in no time.

Winter radish

Although winter radishes don't look like ordinary ones, their appearance doesn't fool the root maggots, so I treat these seedlings with diazinon at regular intervals, every 10 days until harvest.

Roses Many gardeners in northern parts of the country nearly despair about growing roses. They plant them in the spring, enjoy their lovely flowers during the summer, and then find their plants dead the following spring. To understand the problem, consider the ancestors of modern roses. Most of them came from southern China, a part of the world where the plants could grow more or less continuously throughout the year. This wanting-to-grow is a trait that is both good and bad: it gives us rose flowers all summer long, instead of only in June; but the bushes resist dormancy in the fall. They want to keep growing, and they do so until stopped by freezing weather. So the succulent growth, unprepared for winter, suffers badly when subzero temperatures arrive.

There are some steps that northern gardeners can take, though, to help their plants through the winter. The first is to stop feeding the plants after the middle of August. The second is to refrain from fall pruning, as this encourages new growth to emerge and it would only be killed by the cold weather. The third is to allow the rose flowers to mature into seed pods called hips. This seed-making process seems to satisfy some of the roses' urge to keep growing and helps them slow down in the fall. In November I'll cover the last of these protective measures, mulching around the base of the plant.

Shallots Shallot culture matches garlic culture, so the May and October plantings of shallots are ready for pulling this month too, when the leaves wither. I cure them just as I do the garlic, allowing the bulbs to dry thoroughly before storing them in mesh bags in a cool, dark place. To prepare these onion-related crops for long-term storage I cure them for 4 to 6 weeks in a warm, dry, shady location where there is very good air circulation; the bulbs must not be piled more than two or three deep. Many growers dry their bulbs in shallow flats fitted with wire mesh bottoms. The object is to toughen the outside skin and drive out all moisture that may be lurking beneath the outer scales so that loss from decay during storage is negligible. Both shallots and garlic last many months, even up to a year, if given a cool, dry, well-ventilated spot after the curing process is completed.

Spinach At long last, August brings the promise of weather cool enough for a fall planting of spinach. So, late in the month, I prepare the soil with well-rotted manure or compost supplemented with 10-10-10 fertilizer. Extra organic material and high-nitrogen fertilizer are especially critical at this time of the year because the spring and summer crops will have exhausted most of the soil's nutrients. I sow spinach in double rows, 8 inches apart, and space the seeds about 1 inch apart in a furrow ½ inch deep. In 7 to 10 days, when the seedlings come up, I thin them to 3-inch intervals. In September, when the seedlings are 2 or 3 inches tall, I'll thin them to their permanent spacing of 6 inches, using the plants I remove as the first taste of fall spinach, especially tender because it grows during cool weather.

Squash I was sent an interesting question once by a viewer, concerning squashes: "Does squash cross-pollinate, and if so, can I save the seeds for planting next year?" The answer is that many squashes do cross-pollinate; in fact, most summer squashes, winter squashes, pumpkins, and even gourds are as promiscuous as alley cats, and will cross with each other. The fruit that results from the initial crosses looks and tastes exactly like the variety that you plant, but there the resemblance ceases. The *seeds* of these crosses carry the genes of their licentious parents; when they are planted, there's no telling what kind of a squash-pumpkin or gourd-squash mongrel will result. It would take a braver soul than I to donate valuable garden space to this haphazard genetic experiment, so I buy new seeds of known varieties every year and am sure of what awaits me at the harvest.

Speaking of harvest, the summer squash are fruiting constantly in August. We pick them when they're no more than 5 or 6 inches long and just at their peak. These plants produce at a terrific clip, so it's important to pick them every 2 days so they won't become too large.

Strawberries One August day I was surveying the garden and I noticed a problem in the strawberry patch. Most of the plants were green and healthy, but one of them was in trouble: many of its leaves were brown and withered and what green growth it did have was way too small. I didn't know for sure what was wrong with it, but the plant was obviously afflicted with some disease and had to be pulled from the garden before I had an epidemic on my hands. Digging

Everbearing strawberries growing in a barrel

diseased plants out of the garden is an age-old remedy, an especially helpful one as far as strawberry plants are concerned, because they spread disease quickly from runner to runner.

The diseased plant was one of those that I had set out in April, but luckily the runners growing from this plant were in fine shape. So I cut the runners, removed the sick plant and a good portion of the soil around it, and discarded the whole diseased mess with the trash. Then I filled the hole with new soil and reset the plants disturbed by the removal process. I wasn't bothered with this disease again. This pragmatic approach to disease control is as old as gardening itself. Whenever you see a plant in trouble, take immediate action: get rid of it and the soil in which its roots grow. It's far better never to know the name of the disease than it is to lose an entire crop and know the name of the infection that caused the trouble.

Tomatoes In the last century tomatoes were considered an unworthy and even dangerous food, and gardeners didn't waste time on them except as ornamentals; they called them "love apples." How things do change. In the past few decades they've become the most popular vegetable that home gardeners grow, renowned for their delectable taste and high vitamin content.

Because they're so popular, and because August is the peak of the harvest, tomatoes make up the bulk of the questions to the Victory Garden this month. This one, for instance: "I have to plant my tomatoes in the same spot year after year. What should I do to the soil to compensate for this fact?" The answer is not in the soil: it needs only the standard preparation that you give it every year. Instead, you should take extra care selecting your varieties. When you read the seed catalogues, look for tomatoes that are marked VF or VFN: VF means these varieties are resistant to verticillium and fusarium wilt; VFN means that they are also resistant to nematodes. The wilt diseases and the nematodes live in the soil for years, and there's no getting around them except by choosing the right varieties.

I have a few problems myself with some Victory Garden tomatoes. One is sunscald on the fruit, which is analogous to sunburn on human skin. It occurs chiefly on tomatoes that are trained to stakes. Often there just isn't enough foliage on staked plants to give the fruit complete sun protection. Tomatoes grown in cages are usually free of this damage thanks to the thick foliage cover that protects the fruit from the sun. There is a trade-off, of course; you'll get earlier fruit if you train your plants to stakes; you'll get more perfect, but later, fruit if you grow the plants in cages. I suggest that you

Caged tomato plants

grow some plants each way so that you have the best of both worlds.

Another frequent question is in regard to yellowing of interior foliage on tomato plants. This comes about from the shading of old leaves by new growth higher up on the plants. It is not a cause for alarm; it's normal on most plants, even trees. Without full sunshine, leaves fail to function and the plant discards them.

Q: My asparagus bed is in its third year, and it is congested with weeds. Must I weed now or can I wait until fall?

A: You should weed now because the weeds are giving the asparagus too much competition. You'll have fine stalks next year if you weed now and also scatter some 5-10-5 fertilizer on the soil to build up strength for another season.

Q: We decided to experiment this year with a few rows of beans for drying. Should we pick our bountiful kidney bean crop while they're green, or let them dry on the vine?

A: Leave them on the vine until the pods have turned completely brown, then pull up the entire plants and store them in a dry place. When the pods are crisp, lay them on a tarpaulin and hit them with a stick to crack the pods and release the beans. Then rake off as many of the stems and empty pods as possible and put the beans and stray pods in a container. Next, choose a windy day and pour the mixture of beans and chaff from the container down onto a clean tarpaulin. The beans will fall straight down, but the chaff will blow away; this process is called winnowing.

Q: I have a 4-year-old pear tree that hasn't blossomed yet. What's wrong?

A: It's not surprising that the tree hasn't bloomed, as ordinary standard or full-sized pear trees are slow to come into blossom. They can grow for 5 years or longer before setting their first flower buds. Dwarf trees, however, begin to bear the second or third year after planting. You'll help things along if you tie the erect-growing branches to the main trunk of the tree in such a way as to get the branches as horizontal as possible. Fruit-bearing buds usually appear within a year or two of this treatment.

Q: We have just been given two horse chestnut trees, each about 6 feet tall. We've planted them about 15 feet apart. Do you have any tips for us on ways to insure their good growth?

A: Yes. Run out immediately and move one of them. These trees will grow to be 50 feet tall at the very least, and with only 15 feet between them, they'll form one great big tree. They should be at least 40 feet apart, and even then the branches will intermingle when the trees reach maturity.

Q: I have a very old Queen Anne cherry tree. Every spring it's loaded with blossoms but they fall off within a month, and then I get no fruit. What should I do?

A: Within 100 feet of your tree plant another variety of sweet cherry such as Black Tartarian or Bing. With the two sweet cherry varieties I'm sure you'll have fruit on both trees.

Q: I've got about 25 Chinese lantern plants in my garden, the offsprings of 2 plants I set out last year. When's the best time to harvest them?

A: When the little globes turn orange; if you pick them while they're still green, they won't turn that brilliant orange. By the way, I hope you've planted these in a corner of your garden that you can devote entirely to Chinese lanterns; these plants can develop into a terrible weed patch, as you can no doubt tell from the speed with which your plants have already spread.

THE COMPOSTER, OR THE BROWN GOLD CADILLAC

August is a month of ample harvests that leave behind bare stalks, old leaves, and discarded tops, so this is a good month to put a compost bin into use. There's just nothing like compost for plants; if there's a magic elixir for the garden, compost is it. I use a sturdy 3-bin composter in the Victory Garden, and I've included instructions so you can build one of your own. You'll never regret it.

Compost, as far as I'm concerned, is the gardener's best friend. It enriches the soil as it lightens it, and at the same time it increases the soil's ability to hold moisture. It's made from decaying plants, so it contains not only the major elements for healthy plant growth, but many of the vital trace elements as well. Which is why I call compost brown gold, and my fancy but simply constructed composter the Cadillac of composters.

Compost is made from a series of layers, like a rich Italian cake, but neither the sequence nor the proportions of the layers is strict. I start my compost with a layer of leaves, grass, weeds, straw, or some other organic material, spreading it over the bottom of the bin 5 to 10 inches deep. (I never use grass clippings from a lawn that's had weed killer used on it because the weed killer may stay active during the composting period and remain potent even after the compost is put on the garden, at which time it will kill the crops.) Over this organic layer I scatter a couple of handfuls of 10-10-10 fertilizer or a shovelful of horse manure to speed up the decaying process.

The real substance of compost is the organic refuse that comes from the garden or kitchen: faded flowers, banana peels, cornstalks, weeds, grapefruit rinds, old plants and

Wet the pile with a hose as you add new layers and water every few days when the weather is dry

make sure the pile is concave in the center to prevent water run-off.

1 to 2" of soil

dusting of ground limestone

5 to 10" of organic material

10-10-10 fertilizer or horse manure

5 to 10" of leaves, grass or other organic material

leaves. I don't add either meat or bones, as they won't decay with the other materials and they'll give off a powerful odor, attracting a menagerie of undesirable animals. When the layer of refuse is another 5 or 10 inches deep I dust it with ground limestone, and then add an inch or two of soil to prevent the compost from smelling like a garbage heap. Water is critical to the decay process so I always make sure that the growing compost heap is concave in the center to prevent run-off. I wet the pile with a hose as I add the layers, and I water it every few days if the weather is dry. I also continue to supplement the mixture with ground limestone, fertilizer, and soil. (It's possible to buy various materials that claim to speed up the composting process, but I consider them unnecessary because there's plenty of decay bacteria already in the natural ingredients.)

Air circulation is another must for a compost pile; the decay process is boosted by turning the pile so that the outer edges, which tend to dry out quickly, are turned inward toward the center of the pile.

This is where the 3-bin arrangement comes in handy. When the pile has decayed to a uniform yellow-brown and the individual elements have lost most of their original structure, I turn the entire pile into another bin, which buries the outer material on the bottom where it continues to decay. Then I begin a second generation of compost in the first bin. When the contents of the second bin finish decaying, I fork the compost over to the third

Ready to use, fully reduced compost

turn into middle bin so that newest material is on bottom

new material

Pasteurizing compost

bin for storage until I want to use it in the garden. In the harvest months of August and September, when the amount of garden refuse is staggering, the composter's 3-bin setup provides some much-needed storage room.

The compost is ready to use when it is crumbly and dark brown. Its texture is relatively uniform but there is always a discernible leaf or piece of stalk. The speed with which the material decays depends to a large extent on heat. During hot summer months the entire process can be over in 6 weeks; in the winter, very little decay occurs. So while it's a good idea to add kitchen waste to the composter during the cold months, nothing much will happen to it until the spring.

Compost is a treat for outdoor gardens and for indoor plants as well, but it needs to be pasteurized before it can be brought indoors in order to cleanse it of the assortment of bugs, weed seeds, and other undesirable elements that no indoor gardener wants introduced to houseplants. Pasteurization is a heating process, and it smells to high heaven. (One gardener, who tried to pasteurize his compost in the kitchen, claims that he and his family considered moving to a motel for a week.) To avoid the worst of the smell, I pasteurize outside in the garden. I light a charcoal barbecue grill and set an old shallow pan filled with compost over the fire. I let the whole mixture cook at 180 degrees for 30 minutes, using a meat thermometer to judge the temperature. I do three or four batches and then store the cooled compost in a plastic trash bag for the winter.

Building the Composter

1. Lay the bottom members on a flat section of ground: put two 9-foot lengths of 2" × 4" lumber 33 inches apart from outer edge to outer edge.

2. Cut 4 of the 12-foot lengths of lumber into 4 pieces each. Two of the pieces should be 32 inches long to form the sides of each of the bin dividers. The other two pieces should be 36 inches long, for the top and bottom of each divider. (Assembled in this way, the joints are protected from the elements.)

3. Staple a 3-foot square of wire fencing to one side of each divider. Drill and bolt the dividers to the bottom members, making sure that the wire on the end dividers faces outward.

4. Brace the back of the composter with a 9-foot strip of 2" × 4" lumber across the top of the dividers.

5. Cut a 9-foot length of wire and fasten it to the back of the composter with galvanized poultry-wire staples.

6. The front end of each bin is closed off as the bins are filled. We use 6 1" × 6" boards for each bin, with staples or nails partially driven into the long edges to allow for ventilation space. The boards slide into position along grooved strips nailed to the front of each divider. The two outside strips are L-shaped, and the inside strips are T-shaped; both are cut on a table saw from 2" × 4" lumber.

Materials

2" × 4" framing lumber, treated with a good wood preservative (do not use creosote)	3 9-foot lengths (for bottom members and top brace) 5 12-foot lengths (for dividers and grooved strips)
1" × 6" common pine	18 3-foot lengths (for front slats)
2" × 2" welded, galvanized 36" dog-wire or wire fencing	21-foot length (for dividers and back section)
⅝" galvanized carriage bolts, 4 inches long	12 (to secure dividers to bottom members and top brace)
16-penny galvanized spikes	5 pounds (to fasten the sides of the dividers)
Galvanized poultry-wire staples	250 (to secure wire fencing to dividers and back section)

Post Details

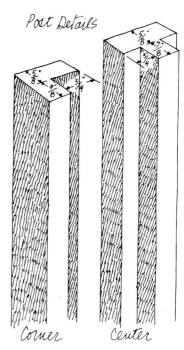

Corner   Center

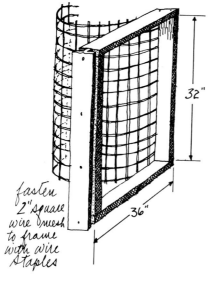

fasten 2" square wire mesh to frame with wire staples

32"

36"

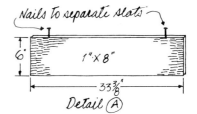

Nails to separate slats

6"   1" × 8"

33⅜"

Detail Ⓐ

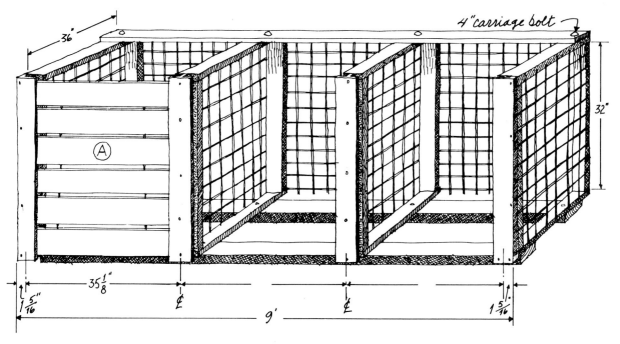

36"   4" carriage bolt   32"

Ⓐ

35⅛"   ℄   ℄   1 5/16"

1 5/16"   9'

The annuals of Main Street

SEP

Plant
Lettuce
Narcissus
Radishes
Tulips

Transplant
Delphiniums
Forget-Me-Not
Primroses

Harvest
Brussels Sprouts
Collards
Kale
Peppers
Pumpkins
Squash

Special Events
Celery
Lawn Care
Poinsettias

Divide
Daylilies
Peonies
Phlox

Take Cuttings
Impatiens
Phlox
Rosemary

SEPT

September is a good time to record the year's successes and failures. In the Victory Garden, where we grow several different varieties of the same plant and experiment with various growing procedures and planting times, there's just no way I could keep our track record straight without careful labeling in the garden, along with a yearly log. I keep a record not only of the big winners and losers but of the also-rans.

Our harvest continues through September, with the arrival of the traditional fall crops of squash and pumpkins to supplement the ongoing production of corn and tomatoes and beans and other main-season crops. Planting continues this month too, but at a slower pace: my garden isn't quite through for the season — I can still plant such cool-weather crops as spinach, lettuce, and radishes — but I admit that September is the time I begin to envy gardeners in warmer parts of the country. Fall is here, and winter's on the way. As a rule we don't have a frost in the Victory Garden until the middle of October, but we keep our ear to the weather forecasts through September, just to be on the safe side. Sometimes we'll have a freak frost, followed by another week or two of Indian summer, so it pays to bring whatever plants we can through that first nip. If I have pumpkins or squashes outside, I cover them with a tarp. If a hard frost is predicted, I pick all the green tomatoes and ripen them inside, and I harvest whatever melons, beans, or cucumbers are ready, leaving the immature vegetables on the vine and covering the foliage with several layers of newspapers. Eggplant is fairly tolerant of light frost, and some crops, including all the root crops and most of the cabbage family, are actually improved by the arrival of cool weather.

Brussels Sprouts Sprouts are sweetest after a good stiff frost, so although the first of our crop is ready for picking late this month, I usually harvest only a few, cutting the larger bottom sprouts from the stem for a modest taste of these little cabbages. I leave most of the sprouts on the plant through the frosty fall weather, harvesting them until the ground freezes.

Occasionally brussels sprout plants are late producing; the foliage is abundant, but the sprouts themselves are no bigger than small marbles. If the sprouts don't begin to grow by the middle of September, I pinch out the tip of the plant, which stops the plant's vertical growth and encourages the energy to go laterally and produce fat sprouts along the stem.

Brussels sprouts

Above: Blanching celery

Below: Mature celery plants

Celery Because moisture is the key to tender celery, commercial growers plant their crop in what's known as muck soil, which is wet, highly organic, and usually derived from an area that was once a peat bog. In the Victory Garden our soil is light and dries out quickly, and these conditions produce celery that looks great but is too stringy to eat. So we keep our crop well fed and watered through the growing season, and like the commercial growers we blanch the celery to tenderize the stalks.

In blanching, light is excluded so that chlorophyll is driven out of the cells, which leaves the stalks pale and tender. There are a number of ways to blanch a crop. With celery I stake two boards up against the sides of the plants in a 4-foot section of the row, leaving only the top leaves exposed to the light. Most families can't use enormous quantities of celery, and blanching in manageable 4-foot sections produces a series of small harvests. The celery is completely blanched after about a month. Through germination and early life celery plants are very sensitive to cool weather, but now that they're mature they can tolerate even a frost — in fact the stalks are crisper in the cool weather — so I can continue blanching these rows, 4 feet at a time, until the snow falls.

Collards Unlike so many other vegetables, the collard harvest lasts for months because only some of the tender, half-grown leaves are picked at any one time. After a while, the plants can begin to look a little moth-eaten, having lost a good portion of their leaves, but they keep producing their succulent greens for the kitchen, moth-eaten or not. There's no secret to the continuing harvest as long as the central bud at the tip of the plant's stem is undisturbed during picking, as this bud is the source of the plant's new leaves.

Daylilies Daylilies operate on a planting cycle that's about five years long. As they approach the end of that cycle, they produce a mass of foliage but very few blooms because the roots have extracted most of the available nourishment from the soil. So every five years, I dig up daylily plants in the fall and divide them.

Dividing daylilies is no job for the timid, as the roots are tough as nails. I sometimes use a spade and chop the root system with one good thrust, but a slightly less barbarous

Dividing daylilies

approach is to pry the roots apart with 2 spading forks driven in the root mass back to back. The idea is to divide the root clump into sections that are about the size of a head of cauliflower, and then replant the divisions into fresh soil (see April for more).

In the first year after division, the plants will produce a little growth and a few flowers. But after that they'll grow to beat the band until they're ready for division again in five years.

Delphiniums After a couple of months of growing time, the delphiniums I sowed in July will have become large enough to have developed 2 or 3 true leaves, so I prepare a slightly raised, well-drained garden row that can serve either as a nursery row or as a permanent location. First I dig 2 or 3 inches of compost into the soil, and then set the seedlings in at 6-inch intervals. Some years I decide against this, and just transfer the seedlings to separate containers and let them spend the winter in the cold frame, setting them into the perennial border in the spring. It's the safer way to handle relatively young plants.

Forget-Me-Not By early in September, the forget-me-not seedlings sown in July are usually showing their first true leaves, so I can transplant them into a nursery bed, setting the plants in with 6-inch spacing all around. The plants are very tiny at this stage but they grow rapidly as the cool weather approaches. In November, I give them a light mulch of pine needles, let them winter-over, and then move them into the perennial border in March.

Impatiens There are in fact some genuine mysteries in gardening. One of them is that this plant is known both as impatiens and as Patient Lucy, with never an explanation of how one plant can be both patient and impatient at once. It's also known as Busy Lizzie, which doesn't help matters. But, however it's known, this is a great plant. It's one of the few annuals that actually likes shade. It blossoms continuously and profusely: planted in the garden, it will flower from spring until the first frost; as a houseplant, it will flower all year long.

Impatiens is a difficult plant to start from seed because the seeds germinate slowly and irregularly. And, due to their susceptibility to frost, there's no way to save plants in the garden. So, this month, as the cold weather approaches, I take cuttings from the best of my garden plants for growing indoors. The cuttings root with no trouble at all: I just set them into damp sand. In 2 weeks there is a fine young root system started, at which time I pot the cuttings into commer-

An impatiens plant grown from a cutting

cial potting soil. When the plants get to be about 5 inches tall, I pinch back the top growth to encourage branching, so I'll have full, bushy, free-flowering plants all winter. When there's no more danger of frost in the spring, I move the plants into the garden for the summer.

Kale Like collards, kale is at its best after it's been through a freeze, so while our midsummer crop is ready for an initial harvest in September, I pick only a few of the leaves and let the others go through a frost. The plant will continue to produce through the fall and early winter as long as the central bud at the tip of the stem isn't disturbed during the harvest.

Kale is an all but unknown vegetable these days, so let me do my part to publicize its cause by passing along the bare outlines of a delicious recipe for Portuguese kale soup. There are dozens of variations of this recipe, but my favorite includes kale (or collards), garlic-seasoned smoked pork sausage, chopped onions and garlic, potatoes, tomatoes, and freshly cooked kidney beans in a chicken stock. Short of making the soup for you myself, I can do no more.

Winter-hardy kale, still thriving in the snow

Lawn Care The Victory Garden is mostly a vegetable and flower garden. We do have a small patch of grass in a corner near the crab apple trees that has seen us through most of our lawn segments, but we have no area large enough to demonstrate starting a lawn from seed, and we receive many questions every year on that subject. So one September we hauled a truckload of television equipment out to a friend's newly reconstructed house and taped the entire procedure, start to finish, on his partly torn up lawn. We did the operation in the early fall because this is the best time to start a new lawn: the rains keep the newly sown grass seed moist, and the frost nips any annual weeds that sprout up.

We began by hiring a tractor to dig up the entire area, loosening soil compacted by months of heavy construction vehicles. Even the tractor wasn't able to take care of the hardness of the soil, though, a problem related more to the lack of organic material in the soil than to anything else. But it did churn the soil enough to make the tilling operation possible.

Tilling: The goal of tilling is to loosen the top 6 or 8 inches of soil. It can be done by hand, but it's much easier with a rotary tilling machine. There are several brands of these machines available, either for sale or rent; the best of them have the tines mounted behind the wheels, so the machine doesn't roll over the very soil it has just tilled.

Grading: My friend's backyard was quite extensive, and only part of it, the area closest to the house, needed reseeding. Beyond that area, and up a slight grade, the lawn was in fine shape. So my job was to make sure that the newly finished lawn would slope gradually up to meet the older grass, without any unexplained peaks or valleys along the way. I did this with a series of grading operations — light

Liming the soil for a new lawn

rakings — to even out the grade of the slope. The first of these operations, the rough grading, didn't leave the soil perfectly smooth, of course, but it did even it out and sweep some of the rocks out of the way.

Soil Test and Lime: I know I run the risk of repeating myself, but nothing matters more in gardening than soil preparation. You can't dig up a lawn periodically to improve the soil; there's only one chance to do the job and do it well. So after the rough grading I did a soil test. The soil looked fine — it was richly colored and well drained — but the test showed a pH of about 5.5, which is far too acid for healthy grass. To correct this situation I used a spreader to add ground dolomite limestone, which contains not only calcium but magnesium as well.

Peat Moss: As I've said, the soil in my friend's yard was hard as nails, even after the tractor had come and gone. So I added 2 to 3 inches of sphagnum peat moss over the soil's entire surface. Peat moss is such a help to the soil that I'm much more generous with it than even the packagers recommend. It holds moisture and fertilizer in light soil, and it improves the texture of heavy soil by providing air spaces and increased drainage capabilities.

Tilling: With the dusting of limestone and the layer of peat on the soil, I used the tilling machine to turn both materials in. Ordinarily I advise walking to the side of a tilling machine to avoid compacting the newly turned soil, but the lawn surface must be firmed before planting the grass seed anyway, so that's not a worry here. Most grass roots lie in the top 4 inches of soil, but as a guard against the inevitable droughts of years ahead, I tilled the peat moss into the soil to a depth of 6 inches.

Grading and Rolling: After the tilling came the final grading, done in two steps. First I raked the surface as carefully as I could and rolled the area to firm the soil. The roller I used was a large drum type designed to hold water, but I did without the water as it would have made the roller sink in too deeply. This first rolling always accentuates the high and low spots that the eye easily misses, so I followed with a careful grading with an iron rake and another light rolling.

Fertilizer: Lawns vary in the specific fertilizer they need. A local garden center is the best source of guidance for a particular area, but as a general principle a lawn fertilizer should have a high percentage of nitrogen, the most important element in grass nutrition. In fact, a lawn needs about 4 pounds of nitrogen for every 1000 square feet annually. On my friend's lawn I used 10-6-4, which is 10 percent nitrogen (see Fertilizing, p. 98). I used a spreader and applied it at the rate of 4 pounds to every 100 square feet to be sure the lawn was receiving the dose of nitrogen it needed.

Grass Seed: Finally, it was time for the grass seed. I wanted to make sure that the new sections of lawn would match the old so I selected seeds of the grasses already in the lawn: Kentucky bluegrass and red fescue. In order to lay the seed down as evenly as possible I made two applications, one perpendicular to the other, each time using half the amount the spreader instructions specified. This takes just a bit longer than one single application but it does result in a more uniform coverage.

Covering the Seed: Grass seeds shouldn't be buried deeply in the soil but it helps if they're covered slightly. I have a device of my own invention for this task: a rubber welcome mat on a leash, which I drag across the soil. The weight of the mat is just enough to turn the seeds lightly into the top $1/8$ inch of soil, and it erases footprints, too.

Rolling: Like most other seeds, grass seeds germinate best if the soil is firm around them; so after I covered the seeds I rolled the whole area again, leaving the soil compacted enough to record only the barest impression of my footprint. For an average-weight adult, that's a pretty good indication that the soil is firm enough.

Watering: All the careful preparation and sowing is for naught unless grass seeds are kept moist through their germination time, so after the last rolling I watered the new seed. I used an oscillating sprinkler because it sets the water down slowly enough to sink into the soil without causing erosion.

One sloped section of this yard presented a special problem. If left unprotected, the rains would have washed the newly sown seed off the slope and the end product would have been a bare gullied hillside with a very grassy base. If the area had been small enough I would have sodded it, as I did a section of the Victory Garden in July. But in view of the size of the slope I relied on one of the oldest grass seeding tricks around. After the soil was prepared, seeded, and rolled I laid a large piece of used tobacco netting — a lightweight gauze available at many garden centers — over the soil, stapling it down with pins fashioned from pieces of wire coat hangers. This blanketed the seeds into place; when they sprouted they grew up through the netting and hid it completely. The pins rusted into the soil, and by the next summer the slope was beautifully grassy without betraying a clue of the webbing underneath.

Lettuce I always have a crop of lettuce seedlings on hand to fill garden vacancies as they occur. During the summer months I plant the heat-resistant varieties, but now in September I can plant the same cool-weather varieties that I do in the spring, such as Black Seeded Simpson, Butter-

a rope-pulled doormat will turn the seeds under just enough.

crunch, and Ruby. Lettuce does well in cool weather so this crop is usually one of the most succulent of the year.

Black Seeded Simpson lettuce

Narcissus Paper white and Soleil d'Or narcissus offer flower lovers their first glimpse of spring, the earliest blooms appearing in November, even before winter is well under way. They grow to be 12 to 15 inches tall; at the tips of their long, slender stems, the paper whites produce clusters of wonderfully fragrant white flowers; the sweet-scented blooms of Soleil d'Or are yellow. In some lucky parts of the country these narcissus are hardy outdoors, but up here in the chilly northeast they're not, so they're grown for a one-shot production of blooms only. The blossoms from each bulb last only about 10 days, so every week from now through December I pot up another few bulbs to keep the Victory Garden greenhouse bright with narcissus blossoms all winter. The bulbs are exhausted after blooming so I put them out on the compost pile and buy new ones each year.

The plants are simple to force, given good firm bulbs. Since the energy for the plant is entirely contained in the bulb, all the gardener need do is give the bulbs enough physi-

cal support to keep them stationary. I generally use pebbles but sand or soil does as well. I set the bulbs on a layer of pebbles in a shallow bowl, and then fill in around the bulbs with more pebbles. Then I add water until the bottom halves of the bulbs are immersed; after about a half a day most of this water will have been absorbed. From this point on I add only enough to keep the base of the bulbs wet.

There are two ways to force the bulbs into bloom. For years I followed the instructions I had learned as a student many years ago: I put the potted bulbs in a cool, dark place until the new growth was about two inches tall, which usually took about 2 weeks; then I set the pots into bright but cool light and waited for the flowers to open. But I've learned an easier way from, strangely enough, a school science project conducted by my youngest daughter, Mary. She experimented with the light needs of these bulbs, putting some into darkness and others into light. The plants grown in full light on a cool, sunny windowsill were so superior to the ones started in darkness that I've never grown them any other way since.

Peonies The peony is the most perennial of perennials. It can easily survive for half a century in the garden, producing its rich green foliage and handsome flowers year after year. There are many eye-catching varieties in shades of pink, red, creamy yellow, and white. The sweetly fragrant flowers can be 6 or 8 inches in diameter or more. The blossom shapes vary from those with a single row of petals with bright yellow centers to huge double blooms that look like floral feather dusters.

Peonies can be left growing in the same spot indefinitely; unlike so many perennials, they don't need periodic dividing. But since the only way to propagate a named variety is by root division, the plants have to be dug up and divided whenever new ones are wanted. The best time to do the job is in the early fall, usually September.

I start out by digging up the whole root system carefully, leaving the foliage as is to continue to build strength for the roots. It's important to be able to see what you're doing with a peony, so after I dig a plant from the ground I shake and wash the soil off the roots so I can identify the small pinkish buds at the crown of the root system; these pointed buds are the beginning of next year's growth, and any division should have 3 or 4 buds to it. I simply use a sharp knife and slice through the root system, with the placement of those buds in mind.

This plant can tolerate a bit of late afternoon shade, but it needs full sun if it's to produce the maximum number of blossoms. And it needs a good-sized hole and an ample supply

Opposite: Tender narcissus bulbs forced into early growth

The root system of a peony plant before dividing

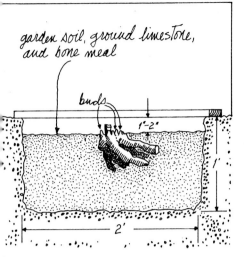

garden soil, ground limestone, and bone meal

buds

1"-2"

1'

2'

of food. I set peony divisions into holes that are about 2 feet across and 1 foot deep. I put about 2 shovelfuls of garden soil into the hole and then add the two ingredients that will keep the plant thriving through its long life: a dusting of ground limestone and bone meal (or, as an alternative to bone meal, superphosphate). I dig these into the soil in the hole, and also mix them with the soil that will fill in around the plant.

The real key to making peonies blossom is in the planting depth. If the tops of the plant's buds are more than 2 inches below the surface of the soil, the plant will seldom bloom, though it will produce foliage without any trouble. To make absolutely sure that the plant is set in at the right depth, I lay a stick across the hole and measure 2 inches from soil line to the bud tips; then I fill soil in firmly around the roots and add a pailful of water to settle the soil and provide moisture so that new root growth can begin.

Peppers The Victory Garden peppers are good in July and again in September, because they form from flowers that open in June and August. Our August crop is sometimes less than perfect because peppers don't set well from blossoms that open in July, our hottest month. Weather conditions aside, though, I sometimes think that a successful crop of peppers is purely a matter of luck. Some years I have good ones and others not so good and I'm not always sure why in either case. The best safeguard against failure is to plant a variety that's appropriate for the area, which means an early variety in the northeast, and to give the plants the rich, well-drained soil they require. The Victory Garden can certainly offer that, but there are other dangers beyond my control — low humidity; hot, drying winds; and excessively high temperatures. These three conditions can dehydrate the flower buds and prevent the peppers from forming blossoms.

So if you've had a good crop of peppers, be thankful. If you haven't, be consoled, do whatever you can to improve your chances, but be ready for problems. And try using a shovelful of compost under each plant. I find this usually produces the best crop.

Phlox Many a gardener has grieved when a brilliantly colored phlox gave way eventually to a muddy purple variety. Although this phenomenon is commonly called reverting, the real story is this: the cultivated varieties of phlox — the clear reds, the snowy whites, and the delicate pinks — are one-in-a-million selections made by plant breeders. The only way they can be perpetuated is by vegetative propagation. Their seeds still carry the genes of their wild ancestors, the muddy purple phlox. If their seedpods are allowed to remain on the plants, the seeds fall to the ground and germi-

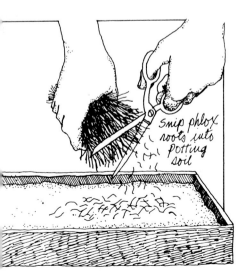

snip phlox roots into potting soil

nate. The wild phlox is far more rugged than the fragile cultivated varieties, so the wild plants overpower the others. Result: magenta-purple phlox. The easy solution is to snip off old
flower heads and seedpods all summer long and throw them
away. In fact, that's good gardening practice for most flowering plants in the garden.

　　Phlox plants need division every four to five years.
Without it the roots compete with one another for moisture
and nutrients from the soil, and crowd out plants nearby. I
divide phlox in the fall or early spring, when the crown buds
are still small enough to make it through the division process
unscathed. The roots may be divided fairly easily by prying
them apart. I try to end up with individual plants that contain
2 to 3 old stalks. Given enriched soil and spaced 12 inches
apart, they will blossom abundantly the following season.

　　There are other ways to propagate phlox plants, too. I
propagate Miss Lingard, our spectacular white Carolina
phlox, by stem cuttings. When 2-inch tips, dipped in rooting
powder and potted in sand, send out roots, I pot them into
ordinary potting soil and set them into the cold frame for the
winter; they begin their growth in the spring and are ready
for setting out into the garden. Because they are still small,

*Above: Snipping phlox flower heads
and seedpods*

Below: Miss Lingard phlox

they usually don't flower their first year, but do beautifully after that.

Garden or summer phlox, such as American Legion, White Admiral, and Prince George, can be propagated by root cuttings. I use a spade to sever a handful of roots from the thick network at the base of the plants' stems, leaving enough of the root system behind for each plant to continue healthy growth. After I shake the soil off the roots I cut them, green bean fashion, into 1-inch sections. I sprinkle these little pieces of roots into a flat of potting soil and cover them with ½ inch of sand. Then I press the sand down to establish firm contact, moisten it, and set the flat into the cold frame for the winter. The first shoots appear in the spring, at which point I move the seedlings to a nursery row until they're big enough to put into the garden.

Poinsettias Poinsettias are Mexican wild flowers grown for their vivid red, pink, white, or multicolored floral bracts that are at the height of their beauty during the Christmas season. Although their brilliant leaflike bracts are the conspicuous feature of poinsettias and are called flowers, they are not true flowers; the real blossoms, tiny and rarely noticed, rest in the centers of the massive colored bracts.

The true poinsettia flower, surrounded by brightly colored bracts

Many a viewer has written to ask me how to make a poinsettia blossom in the home. The theory is easy, but the job is tedious. Poinsettias blossom only when the hours of darkness are longer than those of light. Normally, poinsettias begin the subtle process of flower-bud initiation during the period between September 23 and October 10, following the autumnal equinox, as the days become progressively shorter. This is the key to having flowers at Christmastime, but the strictures are severe. The plants need 9 or 10 hours of light daily and 14 or 15 hours of darkness. This will guarantee flowers, provided night temperatures are about 65 degrees. They must never have artificial light, even for a moment, during those daily periods of darkness. Shading is not sufficient: they need absolute darkness. You can put your plant in a closet, cover it with a light-tight box or black plastic bag, or put it in a room where, no matter what, you won't inadvertently switch on the light. It is a good idea to set up a daily schedule: cover your plant at 5 P.M. and uncover it at 7 or 8 A.M. This is quite a regimen, but it works. One more thing it does, too; it gives a person a high regard for the professional who, as if by magic, offers handsome poinsettias in full bloom at Christmastime.

Primroses At long last the indoor and outdoor primrose seedlings given such careful attention through the summer are of a size to be moved to individual 4-inch pots of potting soil. The tender obconia and fairy primroses, winter-flowering types, will be left in the greenhouse to blossom from mid-February through mid-April; new plants of these species must be grown from fresh seeds each year, so at the end of the blossoming period, I throw these plants away. The hardy polyanthus primrose, loved for its yellow, pink, red, lavender, or purple blossoms that appear late in the spring, will grow along in pots until late October, when the most precocious of the seedlings will begin to show flowers. Generally I leave some of the polyanthus primroses in the greenhouse to blossom in the late fall and midwinter. Others I put into a protected cold frame to induce dormancy, and these are the plants I set into the garden early in the spring to blossom in late April and May. The polyanthus primrose lives for many years; its roots can be divided in early summer after the blossoming season to make additional new plants identical to the parents.

Pumpkins Pumpkins are ready for harvest when they are completely orange. They can be left on the vines beyond that time as long as the weather doesn't get too cold; pumpkins rot and turn black if they're subjected to a freeze, so if cold weather's forecast, I cover the pumpkins with a tarp. To prevent insect damage on the underside of pumpkins, I gently lift each fruit and lay a shingle under it. This provides a quick-drying base for the fruit and deprives the bugs of a hiding place.

    I advise care when harvesting pumpkins: use shears to cut the stem because if the stem pulls away from the fruit, rot will set in quicker than you can say trick-or-treat. For the same reason, avoid scratching the pumpkin's skin. They'll keep well if they're stored in a dry spot in temperatures from 50 to 55 degrees. A garage or attic should do fine.

    (Some young gardeners like to scratch their initials on a pumpkin. The time to do so is when the pumpkin's nearly full grown, but still green. The scratches will heal quickly at that stage and leave permanent markings on the pumpkin skin.)

Radishes If you've decided to do without radishes during the summer in favor of the milder cool-weather yield, September is the month to begin planting again. A crop sown in the beginning of the month is usually ready for harvest by the first of October. Root maggots continue to be a major problem, so I make sure to keep up with diazinon treatments as I do in the spring.

Rosemary I like a winter windowsill garden of herbs, so early in September, I take cuttings of rosemary to

A Cinderella pumpkin beginning to ripen

add to the collection. I take 2-inch cuttings from the tops of a plant's tender, green stems (the older, woodier stems don't lend themselves to rooting). After I remove the lower leaves, I dip the ends of the stems in water to moisten them and then in rooting powder, finally setting the cuttings into a pot of sand. Then I either slip the whole pot into a plastic bag, or turn a plastic drinking glass upside down over the pot and put it in a bright, sunless spot. After about three weeks, when a root system has begun to form but no root is longer than 1 inch, I transplant the rooted cuttings to pots filled with soil-less mix, and when new growth begins, I pinch back the tips of the plants to encourage branching.

Squashes Plant breeders devote their lives to developing varieties with the best and most predictable characteristics, and in my opinion the Waltham Butternut squash is the height of the art. Developed by Professor Robert E. Young at the Suburban Experiment Station of the University of Massachusetts in Waltham, this squash is resistant to diseases and, most importantly, to the squash vine borer, a creature that ruins many other squash varieties. The Waltham Butternut has a smooth beige skin that's easy to peel, and

A harvest of squashes

thick flesh in relation to the seed area, which means more food on the table. The flavor, I should add, is unbeatable. The only mean thing I could say about it is that it's a vine squash and the vines can gobble up a huge chunk of the garden's space, but weighed against this is its tremendous production. I wouldn't be without it in the Victory Garden, and if your squash harvest hasn't been all you've hoped for, you'd be well advised to give the Waltham Butternut a try.

Winter squashes are intended for long periods of storage, but if they're picked in the wrong way, they'll only last a few days. For instance, the vine of the Waltham Butternut, bred for resistance to the attack of the squash vine borer, is woody and tough. The quick and lazy way to harvest this squash is just to pull the fruit from the vine, breaking the stem off where it joins the fruit. But this will leave the squash open to disease and rot. Instead I cut the stem with shears about 1 inch from the fruit, and also take care not to scratch the squash as I harvest. Then I put them into a dry room where the temperature will stay at about 55 degrees, confident that the squash will last through most of the winter.

Tulips There are thousands of varieties of tulips, in different colors, heights, and blossoming seasons. To make the most of these lovely flowers, the bulbs should be planted in a carefully thought-out plan. Early in the fall, I give my attention to the design of the tulip bed, which occupies a narrow strip of the garden along the border of the greenhouse. In the front of the bed I plant the short tulip varieties that bloom early in the spring, and toward the back I put taller varieties that bloom later, giving the garden the longest tulip season possible. I plant several varieties in many different colors, but I take care to cluster 2 dozen or so matching bulbs together so the border will bloom with masses of color, not single random dots. To prevent the bed from resembling an army of marching soldiers, I plant the bulbs in diagonal groupings so the masses of color blend with one another (see the illustration).

Laying out a tulip border

Before the bulbs go into the ground, some soil preparation is needed. I've already added peat moss throughout the Victory Garden, so no more is needed, but if I were working on unprepared soil, I'd dig 2 inches of peat moss into the top 8 inches of soil. Then I'd add ground bone meal, which is rich in phosphorus, an element that will help the plants develop a solid root system for the next spring, spreading it at the rate of 5 to 6 pounds to 100 square feet, digging it into the soil along with the peat moss.

Once the soil is prepared I lay every bulb out on the soil in exactly the location it will be planted; this is the best way to make sure that the design translates from paper to

Hinocrimson Azalea

greenhouse

Grape Hyacinth Blue

Tarda yellow & white

Yew

Yellow Empress

Shakespeare salmon apricot

Joy Bells orange & yellow

Yew

orange Emperor

Foster-iana orange & scarlet

Red Emperor

Red Riding Hood scarlet

Yew

Eichleri crimson & yellow

White Emperor

Chrys-antha

yellow & rose

Yew

0

5'

10'

15'

20'

25'

soil. Then I plant the bulbs, one at a time, with a bulb planter, an ingenious device that twists through the soil to excavate a hole 5 or 6 inches deep. (A good rule of thumb to follow when planting bulbs is to set them three times as deep as the bulbs' greatest dimension. In the case of most tulips, this means a depth of about 5 to 6 inches.) After I set the bulbs into the hole, tip up, I pour the soil from the bulb planter back into the hole, then firm the soil.

The southern end of the tulip bed is the entrance to the Victory Garden, so to dress up this conspicuous spot I plant miniature species that are early bloomers and especially handsome at close range. I also mix other bulbs with the tulips, including grape hyacinths, snowdrops, Siberian squill, and chionodoxa, called glory-of-the-snow.

Q&A

Q: I dearly love celery roots for spicing soups and salads, but all I can find is the celery greens. What do I have to do to grow big roots?

A: You can't get them from celery itself. You have to plant celeriac, a closely related plant. It's also called turnip-rooted celery.

Q: Is there any alternative to drying for storing parsley?

A: Of course you can pot parsley and grow it on a sunny windowsill, but let me also pass along a tip from my wife, Margaret. Pick the fresh parsley, slip it into a plastic bag, roll the air out, and clip the bag shut. Then put it in the freezer and it'll be perfectly delicious all winter long.

Q: It's crossed my mind that my often-used flowerpots are dirty enough to be doing my new young plants a disservice. Should I clean them?

A: Your hunch is right. Dirty flowerpots carry all sorts of disease in them. Before using an old pot, scrub it clean and soak it in a solution of one part household bleach to nine parts water for 10 minutes. Then rinse it and it's all set to use again. Another great suggestion comes from a viewer: run the pots through the dishwasher.

Q: We have a problem with some sort of tomato worm or caterpillar on our ninth-floor terrace. We've used tomato and vegetable dust, but it didn't help.

A: The butterflies have found your terrace and left their offspring behind. There can't be many of them at your altitude, so I'd suggest picking them off by hand. Beyond that the best solution is a nonchemical insecticide known as *Bacillus thuringiensis*.

THE PERENNIAL BORDER

We planted our beautiful perennial border on a cold rainy day in April of our second season. Several days earlier I had personally inspected and chosen the plants at a local nursery and ordered them shipped to the Victory Garden. Due to some mixup, they arrived only hours before we were to tape our show. Luckily, the soil was prepared: we'd added lime and manure and had dug in a couple of inches of compost the day before. And, also luckily, we had the diagram of the border that I had carefully worked out during the winter. So there has never been the least sign of the plants' hurried introduction to the border. Every plant has thrived.

In conceiving a perennial border, the placement of plants is the key to success or failure. I plant clusters of color, at least 3 plants of a type, because isolated single plants will have your garden looking like clowns' pants. Then I plant according to height, in general putting the tall plants in the back, the short plants in front. However, if I maintained that pattern rigidly, I would have a boring border at best. I want the texture of the garden to undulate, not march, so I plant in waves rather than in rows, occasionally bringing medium height plants to the foreground, and the tall plants in right behind them.

The border has remained beautiful year after year with a little faithful attention. We've sprayed it every week during the growing season with an all-purpose spray, a combination of carbaryl, malathion, dicofol, and folpet. We use a soaker hose to water the border, as we want to wet the soil, not the foliage; this helps to prevent disease. And we pick off the faded flowers and seedpods religiously, to encourage the plants to continue flowering. Then every spring we scratch in bone meal to beef up the plants' diet; wood ashes from a fireplace are a good springtime regimen for perennials, too, as they're high in potassium.

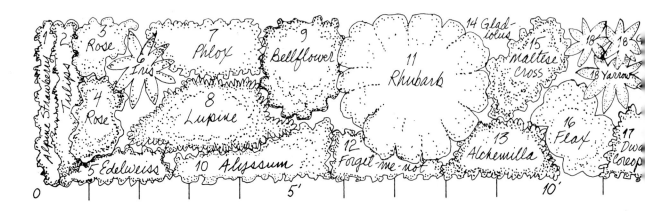

No.	Botanical Name	Common Name	Qty	Variety	Ht. (feet)	Color	Flowering Season
1	*Fragaria mesca*	Alpine Strawberry	6	Alexandria	1–	white/red berries	Jun to Oct
2	*Tulipa* hybrid	Tulip	12	Margaret Herbst	1-1½	scarlet	Apr to May
3	*Rosa*	Hybrid Floribunda Rose	1	Redgold		red/yellow	Jun to Oct
4	*Rosa*	Hybrid Floribunda Rose	1	Europeana		red	Jun to Oct
5	*Leontopodium alpinum*	Edelweiss	3		1–	gray/green	early Jun to mid-Jul
6	Iris, Bearded hybrid	Bearded or "German" Iris	3	unknown		lavender	Jun
7	*Phlox caroliniana (suffruticosa)*	Carolina Phlox	3	Miss Lingard	3–	white	early Jun to Sep
8	*Lupinus* hybrids	Lupine	5	Russell Hybrids	2-3	yel, red, pnk, blu, bicolors	mid-Jun, mid-Jul
9	*Campanula persicifolia*	Peach Leaved Bellflower	3	Telham Beauty	2-3	blue	early Jun, mid-Jul
10	*Alyssum saxatile citrinum*	Basket of Gold	3		2–	pale yel	mid-Apr, late May
11	*Rheum rhaponticum*	Rhubarb	1	Valentine	3		
12	*Myosotis scorpioides semperflorens*	Dwarf Perpetual Forget-me-not	3		1–	pale blue	late May
13	*Alchemilla vulgaris*	Lady's Mantle	3		2–	greenish yel	late Apr
14	*Gladiolus* hybrids	Gladiolus	8		3	mixed	Jul-Aug
15	*Lychnis chalcedonica*	Maltese Cross	3		2-3	or-scarlet	mid-Jun, mid-Jul
16	*Linum perenne*	Perennial Flax	3		2–	pale blue	late May, mid-Jul
17	*Coreopsis auriculata nana*	Dwarf Eared Coreopsis	1		2–	golden yellow	early Jun, mid-Jul
18	*Achillea filipendulina*	Fern-Leaved Yarrow	3	Moonshine	2–	yellow	early Jun, Sep
19	*Gladiolus* hybrids	Gladiolus	8		3	mixed	Jul-Aug
20	*Iris sibirica*	Siberian Iris	1	Tycoon	2–	purple	Jun-Jul
21	*Allium schoenoprasum*	Chives	4		2–	lavender	May-Jun
22	*Digitalis* hybrid	Foxglove		Excelsior			
23	*Santolina chamaecyparissus*	Lavender-Cotton	1		1–	gray foliage	
24	*Chrysanthemum* hybrid	Hardy or Garden Chrysanthemum	4	Baby's Tears	1–	white	Aug-Oct
25	*Lilium* hybrids	Lily	3		3+	yel-pnk, or, maroon	mid-Jun, mid-Sep
26	*Aquilegia* hybrids	Columbine	3		2–	blu/wht, red/wht, bicolors	Jun-Aug

No.	Botanical Name	Common Name	Qty	Variety	Ht. (feet)	Color	Flowering Season
27	*Delphinium elatum*	Candle or Bee Delphinium	5	King Arthur	3+	blu/purple	late Jun-Aug, repeat in Oct
28	*Chrysanthemum coccineum*	Painted Daisy Pyrethrum	5		2−	pink, red, wht	late May to late Jul
29	*Heuchera sanguinea*	Coral Bells	3	Freedom	2−	coral-red	mid-Jun, Sep
30	*Rosa* hybrid	Hybrid Tea Rose	1	Peace		yel-pink	Jun-Oct
31	*Chrysanthemum* hybrid	Hardy or Garden Chrysanthemum	4	Baby's Tears	1−	white	Aug to Oct
32	*Platycodon grandifloris mariesii*	Marie's Balloon Flower	3		2-3	blue	mid-Jun, Aug
33	*Veronica longifolia subsessilis*	Clump Speedwell	3		2−	dark blue	mid-Jun, Aug
34	*Iris siberica*	Siberian Iris					
35	*Phlox paniculata (decussata)*	Phlox		Prince George			
36	*Dicentra eximea*	Plumed Bleeding Heart	3	Luxuriant	2−	deep rose	early May, Aug
37	*Monarda didyma*	Bee-Balm; Oswego Tea	1	Adam	3+	scarlet	mid-Jun, Sep
38	*Rosa* hybrid	Hybrid Floribunda Rose	1	Gene Boerner		pink	Jun-Oct
39	*Artemisia schmidtiana*	Silver Mound Artemisia	3	Silver Mound	2−	gray foliage	
40	*Aster novi-belgii*	New York Aster	1, 3	Eventide	3+	blue; yel cent	Sep-Oct
41	*Chrysanthemum maximum*	Shasta Daisy	3		2−	wht; yel center	mid-Jun-Aug
42	*Geum chiloense*	Geum, Chilean Avens	3	Fire Opal	1-2	or-scarlet	late May-Jul
43	*Dianthus* hybrid	Pink	3	Beatrice	1−	pink	mid-May, mid-Jun
44	*Althaea rosea*	Hollyhock	3	Majorette Dwarf Double	2− (annual)	pink	early Jul-Sep
45	*Phlox paniculata (decussata)*	Garden Phlox	3	White Admiral	3−	white	late Jul/Aug to late Sep
46	*Rosa* hybrid	Hybrid Floribunda Rose	1	Pinocchio		pink	Jun-Oct
47	*Aquilegia hybrida*	Columbine	3	McKana Giant Hybrid	2−	blue/wht, red/wht, bicolors	Jun-Aug
48	Sedum spectabile	Showy Stonecrop	3	Brilliant	1½−	rose-red	Aug-Oct

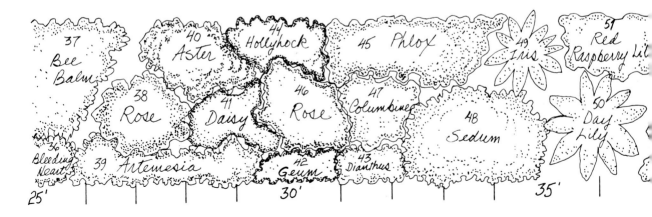

o.	Botanical Name	Common Name	Qty	Variety	Ht. (feet)	Color	Flowering Season
		Japanese Iris					
	Hemerocallis hybrid	Daylily	1		2–	yellow	Jun-Jul
	Rubus hybrid	Red Raspberry	1	Durham	3+		
	Coreopsis lanceolata	Coreopsis	1	Sonnenkind	2-3	golden yel	Jun-Sep
	Gaillardia aristata	Indian Blanket, Blanket Flower	3, 1	Dazzler	3+	red, yel	late June-Oct
	Nepeta mussini	Mauve Catmint	3		1-1½	lavender	early Jun, Aug
	Salvia virgata nemerosa	Violet Sage	3			purple	Jul
	Phlox paniculata	Garden Phlox	3	American Legion	3–	red	late Jul to late Sep
	Gypsophila pankulata	Babies' Breath	1	Bristol Fairy	1½-2	white	Jun-Jul
	Delphinium elatum	Candle or Bee Delphinium	5	Roundtable	3+	blu/purple	late Jun-Aug; repeat in Oct
	Aster novae-angliae	New England Aster	3	Harrington's Pink	3+	pink	Oct-Nov
	Althaea rosea	Hollyhock	3,6	Tall Single	3+	mixed	late Jun to Sep
	Petroselinum crispum	Parsley	3	Darki			
	Chrysanthemum hybrid	Garden Mum	3	Baby's Tears	3+	white	Aug-Oct
	Petroselinum crispum	Parsley	3	Double Moss Curled	1		
	Thymus vulgaris	Common Thyme	3		½		
	Ocimum basilicum	Sweet Basil	1		1½		
	Ocimum basilicum	Sweet Basil Ornamental	1	Dark Opal	1	dark purple foliage	
	Artemisia dracunculus	Tarragon	1		2		
	Anethum graveolens	Dill	3	Long Island Mammoth	3		
	Marjoram hortensis	Sweet Marjoram	3		1½		
	Anthriscus cerefolium	Chervil	6	Double Curled	1		
	Mentha spicata	Spearmint	1		1		
	Rosmarinus officinalis	Rosemary	1		2-4		
	Carum carvii	Caraway	3		1½		

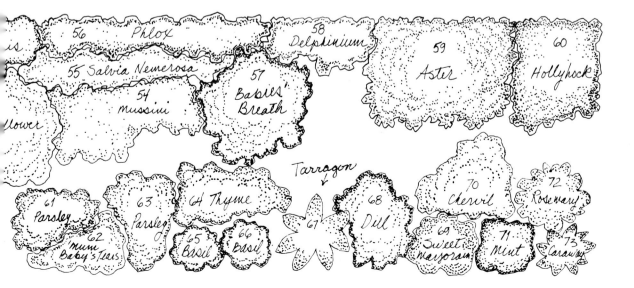

Cinderella pumpkin

OCT

Plant
Evergreens
Garlic
Rhubarb
Shallots

Transplant
Strawberries

Harvest
Cauliflower
Potatoes
Radishes
Rutabagas
Tomatoes

Force
Hyacinths
Tulips

Take Cuttings
Fuchsia

Winter-Over
Begonias
Chrysanthemums

OCT

Many people have long since folded their gardens for the winter by the time October comes along, but the Victory Garden is still flourishing with peas, edible pea pods, tomatoes, brussels sprouts, cauliflower, potatoes, lettuce, regular and winter radishes, kale, pumpkins, celery, cabbage, Chinese cabbage, winter squash, collards, leeks, broccoli, peppers, lima beans, and beets. I'll be harvesting vegetables until the ground freezes hard, and any home gardener can do the same.

The first frost usually hits the Victory Garden at the end of the month, so October is the time for chilly weather preparations. I take in the houseplants that have summered outdoors and put the cold frames to work at their cool-weather jobs: protecting a crop of lettuce and radishes in one frame, so they'll be ready for the Thanksgiving table; and using another frame to winter-over some tender plants. Cold frames are important to us all season long, but they're all but indispensable in the spring and fall. (For more about cold frames, along with hotbeds and cloches, see page 26.)

Concentrating though I am on the coming blast of winter, I've got one eye trained on spring, too, so this month, while the soil is still workable, I plant a crop of garlic and shallots for harvest next August. And to have a breath of springtime later on this fall and winter, I pot up tulips, hyacinths, narcissus, crocuses, and other bulbs so that they will have time to develop the strong roots that help to guarantee large flowers later.

Begonias There are few plants more beautiful in shady gardens than the tuberous rooted begonias, which send out their profuse yellow, salmon, orange, pink, white, or red flowers from early summer until they're finally cut down by the autumn frosts. The flowers can be single, double, frilled, or picoteed (flowers of one color whose petals are bordered with a second color, as if they'd been dipped). They grow either on erect stems about 18 inches tall, or on trailing varieties ideal for hanging baskets or window boxes.

Beautiful as these flowers are all year long, the time will come when they are blackened by frost, so in the fall the tubers must be prepared for their annual period of rest. Immediately after a frost, the tubers should be dug from the ground, along with the stems and some soil, and put in a warm dry spot for a week or two, by which time the stems will have dried out enough to separate easily from the tubers. At this point I shake the dry soil from the tubers, slip them into perforated plastic bags filled with dry vermiculite, perlite, or peat moss, and store them at 40 to 50 degrees until February. Then I pot them up indoors and let them grow until the frost season has passed, when I plant them outdoors again for another season's blooms. The tubers will last for years given this attention, producing larger and handsomer flowers as they gain size and strength.

Purple-headed cauliflower

Cauliflower October is cauliflower month in the Victory Garden, when, along with a continuing harvest of white cauliflower, the Early Purple Head crop sown in June is at long last ready. I harvest the heads when they're about 8 inches across and they've developed that striking purple cast. (The purple coloration disappears with cooking, leaving behind an appetizing pale green vegetable with a mild flavor that can't be bettered.) I'm especially fond of this variety, not only for its taste, but because it doesn't require blanching, that time-consuming process of tying the outer leaves of ordinary white cauliflower into topknots to protect the developing curds from light.

Chrysanthemums Chrysanthemums are a must for the Victory Garden in the fall, and invariably among the dozens of varieties I plant, I have some favorites that I don't want to lose to the winter cold. In a mild winter, hardy chrysanthemums are as sturdy as their name implies, but they die if the winter is harsh, so rather than take the risk I dig up the best of each year's plants in October after they have finished flowering and save them for the next spring.

The wintering-over is a relatively easy task. I dig up the favored plants, along with the roots and a good shovelful of soil, and plant them in the soil in the cold frame. The winter threat for chrysanthemums is repeated freezing and thawing, though they can easily survive a winterlong, solid freeze. So in November after the ground has frozen I cover the plants with salt marsh hay to hold the frost in the ground. In May I take the plants out of the cold frame, divide them, and set them into the garden where they'll become full-sized plants by the end of the summer.

Evergreens One year I decided to dress up the border along the greenhouse with some evergreens. They're really one of my favorite plants, not only because they hold their green foliage all year long, but because they can be planted in the fall, when the garden is making fewer demands on my time.

In buying evergreens, nothing matters more than selecting plants that are suited to their intended growing space. Evergreens come in all shapes and sizes, and it's much easier to train a plant to continue along in its normal growth pattern than to force a tall plant to grow sideward or a spreading plant to grow upright. In the Victory Garden I needed plants that would both fit comfortably in a narrow strip of land along the greenhouse and grow up tall and slim

Hicks yew plants in the tulip and annual border along the greenhouse

Determining the exact planting depth for evergreens

in the limited space between the window boxes. I decided on upright Hicks yew plants, and they've been a great success because they're so well matched to their location.

An evergreen should be dug from the nursery with the soil around its roots intact. Depending both on the type of plant and on the custom of the nursery, the plants will be sold either in nursery cans, or balled and burlapped. The container-grown plants are easy to transplant successfully because none of their roots are severed in the digging. A plant that's been wrapped in burlap can be set into the ground as is, because the roots can push right through the wrapping. I usually peel the burlap a quarter of the way down the root ball to free the top roots and give them an easier job.

As the old nurseryman's adage goes, a one-dollar plant deserves a five-dollar hole — how inflation does wreck those old slogans! — so I set my plants into holes that were no deeper than the root ball, but three times as wide, which kept the plants at the right depth in the soil while giving the roots plenty of space to spread out. I held the plants by their root balls, not by their sensitive stems and foliage, as I set them in, and then I loosened the burlap around the stem and filled the hole in with soil. The soil along this border of the greenhouse hadn't been as thoroughly prepared as had other sections of the garden so I filled the hole with a mixture of 2 parts soil to 1 part peat moss, firming the soil with my foot to leave the new soil as solid as the root ball itself, which closes off any unwanted air pockets and helps keep the plants upright until their roots knit into the new location.

When I finished filling the hole I made a saucerlike depression of soil at the base of the plant to hold water. There is nothing more important to an evergreen, old plant or new, than a good drink before the onslaught of freezing weather. Evergreens take up moisture all winter long and it's essential that the soil be moist before the ground freezes.

Fuchsia Our first spring in the Victory Garden we bought a magnificent purple and pink fuchsia named Dark Eyes and hung it outdoors at the corner of the greenhouse. It thrived all summer, but by the time October arrived, it was a little the worse for wear. There was still life in it, but it had exhausted most of the soil's nutrients during the summer season, so I took some steps to preserve it.

First I took small cuttings, 2 inches long or so, from the tips of the branches, and rooted them to produce grand full plants the following summer. Then I went to work on the main plant: I cut off most of the old stems, leaving 2 or 3 inches of brown branches. As I worked, I found that the pot actually contained not one plant but three, so I knocked the roots out of the pot and used a knife to slice through the root ball and separate the three plants. I potted each of the plants individually in fresh soil, and there was healthy new growth within 3 weeks.

People are often intimidated by the prospect of taking scissors and knives to their plants, but this fuchsia is the perfect model of what some judicious cutting can do. Without this operation, the plant would probably never have blossomed again. As it was, it sired over a dozen new plants, each healthy and full of flowers.

Fuchsia plant in full flower

Garlic Garlic, as most gardeners and cooks know, is a pungent member of the onion family whose root, unlike that of the onion, is easily separated into pointed segments called cloves. These single cloves, planted in the fall, make the big fat bulbs that we dig the following August.

For the October planting I choose a sunny spot with well-drained soil and plant the cloves so that their tips are about 2 inches beneath the surface of the soil. (When I plant the spring crop I barely cover them, but I plant these deeply now because I don't want them heaved out of the soil by winter frost.) I set the cloves in double rows, spacing them about 5 inches apart, and they're up and growing early in the spring.

Hyacinths Dutch hyacinths send up extremely fragrant pomponlike spikes of purple, blue, red, pink, yellow, or white flowers in the spring. Like many other bulbous plants, including crocuses, tulips, and some narcissus, they can be forced into early bloom indoors if they're persuaded that winter has come and gone. By starting bulbs early in October and keeping them in cold temperatures for about 3 months, you'll have flowers inside late in January or early February. (Tulips need some special attention, so see the tulip entry, page 224.)

I start with bulbs that have been marked "for forcing," or "exhibition size" so I am sure they're amenable to this routine. Any size or shape pot containing one or more bulbs can be used, but I often set 4 bulbs together in a container because they make a handsome display when grown this way. I put a layer of ordinary garden soil in the bottom of a 6-inch bulb pan — nothing but a shallow flowerpot half as tall as it is wide — leaving about 3 inches between the soil line and the rim of the pot. Then I set the bulbs in and fill in around them with soil, so the tips are just even with the top of the pot and barely exposed above the soil.

A forced hyacinth ready to bloom

After a drink of water, they're ready for their short winter. They need at least 14 weeks of temperatures that just hover around the 40-degree mark, so I usually set my pots into a cold frame and mulch around them with dry leaves or peat moss. A bulkhead or cool cellar will work, as long as the temperatures are reasonably uniform and the pots are protected from the elements. If you have no place cold enough to store your bulbs, you can bury them right in the garden. Dig a trench deep enough to accommodate the depth of the pots with 3 inches to spare. Line the bottom of the trench with about an inch of straw or gravel to prevent the bottoms of the pots from freezing to the ground, set the pots in, and cover them with about an inch of sand to keep the temperature and moisture uniform. Before the ground freezes hard, cover the trench with leaves and a tarpaulin so that even in the dead of winter you'll be able easily to pull a pot or two out for indoor forcing. Be absolutely sure the soil in the pots stays moist from the time the bulbs are planted until they are covered over for their abbreviated winter sleep.

There's a second kind of hyacinth, known as the French-Roman hyacinth, that produces graceful sprays of blue, pink, or white flowers, and can be forced even more easily than the Dutch varieties. They're not hardy in the north, as are the Dutch hyacinths, so they're treated as tender bulbs and forced into bloom with the same techniques used for paper white narcissus bulbs. I begin with a bowl of pebbles, sand, or soil and set the bulbs — much smaller than those of the Dutch hyacinth — onto this base; then I store them in a moist dark spot with temperatures around 50 degrees until the new growth is about 1½ inches tall, when I put them on a bright cool windowsill and wait for the blossoms to appear, which they sometimes do in time for Christmas.

Potatoes October is the harvest month for potatoes, particularly those late-maturing varieties destined for winter storage. They're ready for digging when the tops of the plants have died away, leaving only dry, withered stalks. By this stage in the plant's life the potato tubers beneath the ground will have reached their maximum size.

In the Victory Garden, we harvest our potatoes on a dry, sunny day, lifting them from the soil as carefully as possible and making every effort to leave the tubers undamaged. Invariably a few will be stabbed by the digging fork, so we use these first because they'd probably rot if they were put into storage. Those that come out of the harvest unscathed I lay out on the surface of the soil just long enough for the skins to become dry. Most of the soil will fall off the skins naturally, so when they're dry I pack them unwashed in baskets or open-mesh bags and put them away for the winter. The best storage temperature is about 40 to 50 degrees; if they're kept any warmer they're apt to sprout. The storage area should also be completely dark because potatoes develop inedible green skins when stored in a light place.

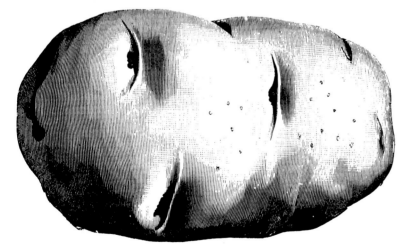

Radishes Approximately two months after planting, the winter radishes sown in the Victory Garden in August are ready for harvesting. These vegetables take very well to storage — in fact they're grown primarily for that reason — so before the ground freezes I dig them up and remove the tops. Then I bury them in barely damp sand or sawdust and store them in a cool spot, around 40 degrees, where they'll last for about 2 months.

Rhubarb Given my fondness for strawberry-rhubarb pie I could quite contentedly grow a dozen rhubarb plants in the Victory Garden, but they're so space-hungry that I set in only one as a demonstration plant. This single plant manages to produce a modest supply of beautiful 3-foot stalks for most of the summer, a vigorous output that is the direct result of

Dividing, digging, and replanting rhubarb

the plant's early upbringing. Its parent was an old but still hardy red-stemmed variety given to me by an uncle. At age four the original plant was ready for division, so I cut its roots and crown into small sections, saving only one of these clumps to put into the Victory Garden.

In preparation for planting, I dug a hole 2 feet deep and just as wide, and put half a bushel of compost in the hole to keep the plant nourished through its long life. Then I positioned the clump in the hole so that the crown of the plant was deep enough to be covered by approximately 2 inches of soil. Once the plant was set in I refilled the hole with equal parts of topsoil, compost, and peat moss, adding a handful of slow-release fertilizer for good measure. Rhubarb plants are heavy feeders, and without this ample menu they tend to become thin-stalked and scrawny, which is why I continue to feed the plants throughout their lives, mulching them with a 2-inch layer of manure every fall.

The first year after planting rhubarb, I let the plants grow unmolested by a harvest, so they can build strength for the following years. The second year I pick a modest harvest, and the third and fourth years the yield is tremendous. In the fifth year I divide the plants again. (By the way, the old line about rhubarb leaves being inedible isn't really an old line at all. They contain acid crystals that will irritate the insides of the mouth. So enjoy the stalks, but don't eat the foliage.)

Rutabagas Rutabagas, sometimes called yellow turnips or Swedes, can tolerate hard frosts, but the roots can't be allowed to freeze or they'll be worthless. So on a sunny day in October, when the July sowing is ready, I pull the roots and cut the tops off close to the crown, along with any small roots the plant is producing.

Rutabagas last for most of the winter if they're stored in cool temperatures — between 32 and 40 degrees. Nowadays most American cellars are heated, so the best bet is to set the roots into a moisture-proof container and bury the container in the ground, keeping it well mulched to prevent freezing. The roots must be protected from dehydration, too: the easy way to see that they don't dry out is to store them in damp sand or sawdust. Another technique is to dip each rutabaga into a pan of warm water that has a skim of melted parafin wax on the surface; the wax coating will seal the roots from the air.

Shallots The shallot is the epicure's onion, a small, delicately flavored bulb that's easy to grow in any sunny garden. At maturity the bulbs are linked together at the base, but when separated and planted, each individual bulb will produce a clump of 6 to 12 bulbs in midsummer. Like garlic, I plant two crops of shallots in the Victory Garden, one in the fall and one in May. Both crops are ready for harvest during the following August.

Shallots need well-drained soil. I plant them about 2 inches deep at this time of the year because if they're planted too close to the soil's surface, there's a chance that they'd be tossed out of the ground by the freezing and thawing of winter. I usually plant double rows, and space the bulbs about 6 inches apart.

Strawberries Many a gardener, surveying the mass of runner-grown strawberry plants in the early fall, has wondered if there were any way to transplant the runners and start new strawberry beds. Indeed there is. Choose a few runner plants that are at the edge of the bed or too close to other plants. Dig them up one at a time, with a good shovelful of soil around the roots, and set them into another garden row or bed. June-bearing strawberry plants set out in the spring need to be given a full season of growth before they're allowed to produce fruit, but because these transplants are moved in the fall with the roots intact in the soil ball, the plants will be vigorous enough in their first summer to be permitted to produce their small harvest.

June-bearing strawberry plants growing in a matted row system

Tomatoes We can expect our first frost in the Victory Garden in October, so just before that fateful day arrives I harvest all the tomatoes, including the green ones. (If the frost seems to be an early freak, I cover the plants with a newspaper tent, and hope for another week or two of warm weather to follow. Tomatoes can tolerate light frost if they're protected.) For some reason, the common wisdom about green tomatoes is that they ripen if left on a sunny windowsill, and that wisdom is absolutely wrong. Green tomatoes shrivel and become pink and bitter-tasting in the sun. They ripen best in darkness, in a spot that gets no warmer than 45 or 50 degrees. I put my tomatoes in an old picnic cooler and set them in the garage. The ripening process is given a boost if a ripe apple is stored with the tomatoes. (One week after I gave this advice on the show, a nine-year-old gardener wrote in to ask me if the apple's job was to help the tomatoes get the hang of turning red. I'm afraid the reason is much less imaginative: ripening tomatoes don't need a lesson in redness so much as they need a dose of ethylene gas, which ripe apples give off.) These ripened tomatoes don't have quite the flavor of the vine-ripened fruit, but they're better than any available in the stores, and they ripen so slowly that they'll last through Thanksgiving. Be sure that all tomatoes to be

Green tomatoes ripening with the assistance of an apple

stored are free of blemishes. Any cuts or cracks in the skin will allow decay to set in and ruin the fruit. It is a good precaution also to wash and dry the tomatoes before storage.

I'm frequently asked at this time of the year if it's possible to save tomato seeds for planting the following year. The answer is yes, but it's not a very good idea if the seeds are from a hybrid plant. Hybrid seeds never reproduce their parents exactly, and often revert to a less desirable ancestor. If the plant isn't a hybrid, go ahead and save the seeds. Cut the fruit apart and strew the seeds out on a piece of paper. After about 2 weeks, when the seeds are perfectly dry, put them in an envelope and start the seedlings indoors the following spring. And good luck. (I always buy my tomato seeds because I know I can depend upon true-to-name varieties with guaranteed performance. Seeds, after all, are the least expensive part of gardening.)

Tulips Most bulbs are symmetrical and it makes no difference how they are planted as long as the tops point up. Tulip bulbs are not regular in shape, so although the procedure for forcing tulips is nearly the same as for forcing hyacinths and other bulb plants, the actual arrangement of the bulbs is a little different. Tulip bulbs have a curved side and a flat side. I always set the flat side against the inside of the pot so that the large leaf that grows from the flat side will arch over the side of the pot. The result is a very graceful plant in a pot nearly masked by foliage.

Some tulip varieties take to forcing more willingly than others. Single early or double early varieties are usually the best bets. If you are in doubt, look for bulbs marked "for forcing," and always buy the largest possible bulbs, usually called "top size."

A pot of forced tulips

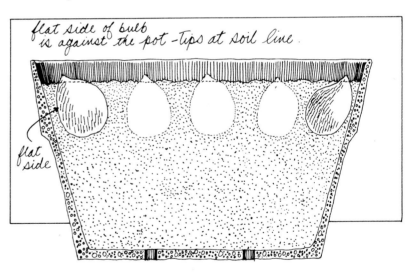

flat side of bulb is against the pot - Tips at soil line.

flat side

Remember that the soil in forcing pots acts only as a physical support for the bulbs and does not have to be expensive potting soil. I use soil straight from the garden.

Q&A

Q: My grapevines are well pruned. Even though I live in coastal Maine I have a good yield of grapes but they're way too sour to use. What can I do?

A: Nothing, I'm afraid. The only way to grow sweet grapes is to have warm, long summers, and in coastal Maine your summers are cool. Unless you get a warm summer your grapes will always be sour.

Q: I have a spiderless spider plant. What's up?

A: Don't worry, the spiders are on their way. They form most quickly when the days are short; in fact they do their best with only 8 hours of daylight, so you'll have spidery spider plants beginning in the fall.

Q: I have an old, tired potted geranium that has seen better days. In its prime, it was a beauty. Can I save it somehow?

A: The best way to perpetuate a geranium is by taking cuttings. But at this time of year, if you are intent on saving the whole plant, the old-time way may work. Knock the plant out of the pot and remove all the soil from the roots. Then pick off all the leaves so that nothing remains but bare roots and stems, and hang the plant upside down in a cool, humid room with good ventilation. A cellar is usually perfect. Next March bring it back up and repot it. It will grow, but slowly; that's why I like to start new plants from cuttings.

Q: How and when should I harvest sunflower seeds?

A: Wait until the seeds are fully grown and firm, then cut the head with about a foot of stem attached. Hang it in a dry, airy spot to finish ripening. Don't stack the heads in a box or they will all rot. (The biggest problem with harvesting sunflower seeds is that the birds often get to them first. Some gardeners cover prize seed heads with cheesecloth to keep the birds away and yet allow the seeds to mature fully on the plants.)

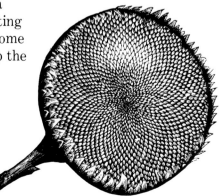

NATURAL-IZING BULBS

Some of us, with orderly minds, like all of our flowers in neat little rows; others, I among them, prefer to see a more natural order of things. Bulbs, especially daffodils, seem to me to be at their best when apparently growing at

Crocuses in bloom

random in a meadow or under trees. Thanks to the busy lives we lead (or our natural procrastination) we often think of bulbs only in the spring when they blossom, so I must remind you that they have to be planted in the fall if they are to bloom in the spring. Be consoled, however, that the job need be done but once in a lifetime; the bulbs live on for years, becoming more beautiful every springtime.

It's a simple thing to create a natural garden of bulbs in any lawn by a process called, rightly enough, naturalizing. When the bulbs are planted in the lawn in October, they develop a sturdy root system before the arrival of freezing weather and then grow up through the grass in the spring. There is one hitch to naturalizing, however, and that

is that the bulbs' foliage must mature before the grass is cut, and that means no mowing until early summer. They must be left alone to wither in peace after they've blossomed, as this is the critical period during which they build strength for the following year. In the Victory Garden's naturalized area we don't mow the grass until mid-June, by which time the bulb foliage has browned and dried.

Some types of bulbs can be naturalized easily, but others aren't well suited to this method of culture. Neither tulips nor hyacinths are good candidates for naturalizing, because unless they are dug up and separated every year, they produce fewer and fewer

blooms. We've planted narcissus of several kinds, grape hyacinths, snowdrops, chionodoxas, crocuses, and squills, a combination that provides a variety of color and blossoming sequences through the spring.

In the first October of the Victory Garden I put about 150 bulbs in an area of about 200 square feet, assuring a blizzard of blossoms the following springtime. Because the goal in naturalizing is to follow nature's haphazard ordering, I use the most random possible method to place the bulbs: I toss them on the ground and plant them where they fall. Believe me, peculiar as that sounds, it's the best way to achieve a natural effect. If some human hand starts arranging things, a geometric pattern is bound to show up.

Bulbs should be planted at a depth three times their height, measured from the base to the shoulder of the bulb. I plant the bulbs one at a time by digging the hole to the right depth with a spade, keeping the surface sod undisturbed as I remove it from the turf. Then I add about 1 tablespoon of bone meal and scratch it into the soil at the bottom of the hole, distributing this phosphorus-rich nonburning fertilizer to help the bulbs develop sturdy root systems. After I set the bulb in,

tip up, I replace the hunk of sod and firm it down with my foot. There isn't so much as a clue that there's been work done on the lawn until the following spring, when the bulbs bloom as naturally as on a field in their native Spain or Portugal.

Left: Snow drops
Right: Grape hyacinths

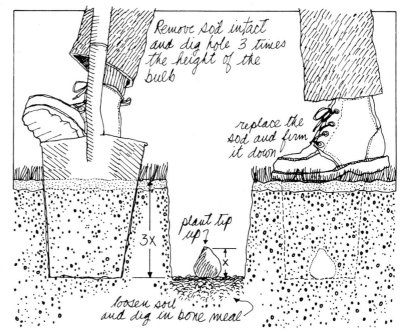

Remove sod intact and dig hole 3 times the height of the bulb

replace the sod and firm it down

plant tip up

3X

X

loosen soil and dig in bone meal

Winter squashes

NOV

Plant
Amaryllis
Calla Lilies
Marigolds

Start Seedlings
Streptocarpus

Harvest
Broccoli
Brussels Sprouts
Cabbage
Cauliflower
Celery
Collards
Jerusalem Artichokes
Kale
Leeks
Lettuce
Parsnips
Peas
Radishes

Take Cuttings
African Violets
Lantana

Winter-over
Asparagus
Dahlias
Gladioluses
Pansies
Roses

Special Events
Peas
Rhubarb

NOV

I would have to argue that November is the most important month in the gardener's calendar because it's the month the soil should be prepared for the next spring's plantings. The hows, whys, and wherefores of this most critical of gardening jobs are given in this month's feature (pages 246–249).

We expect our first frost on the last day of October, and while it sometimes comes earlier, it hardly ever comes later. So the November harvest includes only those vegetables that can stand up to a frost: broccoli, brussels sprouts, cabbages, leeks, celery, parsnips, Jerusalem artichokes, lettuce, cauliflower, radishes, collards, kale, and peas. Hardly a harvest to be ashamed of this late in the season.

November is also the month to get the garden in shape for the winter, and to collect any of its products that are usable. For instance, I always pick up the pea-sized nasturtium seeds that will have fallen from the plants, dry them on a sunny windowsill for a couple of weeks, and save them for planting the next spring. Then I clean all the vegetable refuse from the garden, shred and compost it. There's more than neatness behind this job. It's a sanitary move that clears the garden of cozy wintering shelters for unwanted pests.

Last, I turn my attention to the lawn. I rake up all the leaves, saving them for the leaf mold pile (see the feature on soil preparation, pages 248–249). Then I mow the grass to about 1½ inches tall to prevent matting through the winter, and I remove the clippings to control snow mold. Once these tasks are done, the garden is free to rest for the winter.

African Violets I hear many complaints about how difficult it is to grow African violets, but personally I don't know of an easier plant to cultivate indoors. They're the most popular flowering houseplants in the country; so they can't be as temperamental as some people think them to be. If their few basic needs are met, their single or double pink, blue, purple, white or two-toned blossoms will appear month after month without ceasing.

The African violet isn't a violet; it's a close relative of the gloxinia. But it is African. It was discovered growing wild in eastern African in 1893 by Baron Walter von St. Paul, which is why its proper botanical name is *Saintpaulia*. The Baron came upon these plants growing at the base of trees in an area that was warm — 70 degrees or so — day and night.

And that combination of partial shade and shirt-sleeve weather is still the key to successful African violet culture.

What makes a good African violet? For one thing, rich green foliage that grows horizontally to form a flat rosette; this is an indication that the plants are receiving the right amount of light. I grow most of mine on a north-facing windowsill so they get bright reflected light, and they blossom 12 months of the year. Second, the foliage should be clean and unspotted. (Most of the disfiguring blotches on African violet leaves are the result of watering the plants with cold water. Always moisten African violets with warm water. You can even wash the leaves, provided the water is warm.) The next thing I look for in a healthy plant is a single crown; the plants blossom most freely if all the foliage grows from one crown. Finally, a plant with young flower clusters showing from the crown is a plant with promise.

African violets will do beautifully until they're about 4 years old, when the stem will begin to show the thick stalkiness of advancing age. There's no way to rejuvenate an old plant — cutting back won't work — but it's quite simple to propagate a new one from a leaf of the old. The propagating

African violets in flower

firm the sand around the stem

builder's sand

leaf should be neither the oldest nor the youngest leaf on the plant, but a healthy leaf of medium growth. The leaves will separate easily from the parent if you simply reach in and press the leaf stem from the crown with your finger. (If you cut the leaf stem and leave part of it behind, it will decay.)

The propagating leaf should be set into a pot of builders' sand at an angle of about 45 degrees. I usually poke an angular hole in the sand with a pencil or label, slip in the stem, firm the sand around it, and set the pot into a bright, warm spot. After about 3 months there will be several new leaves growing at the base of the leaf stem and it will be time to transplant. It's not unusual at that point to find that a single leaf stem has produced two or three different plants; they may need to be cut from one another, but planted individually in potting soil or soilless mix they'll begin to grow right away, and in fact can double in size in the month after transplanting.

Most African violets are in blossom within 5 months of propagation if they are given bright filtered light, warm temperatures, and the right water and fertilizing care. I keep my African violets barely moist by bottom-watering, putting warm water into a saucer beneath the plants every day or so. After an hour and a half, I empty the saucer so the roots don't sit in the water. When I fertilize, which is once every 4 weeks, I water the plants from the top with a half-strength solution of fertilizer. They don't need a great deal of food, but they do need frequent modest feedings. In this case, the top-watering insures that the fertilizer is evenly distributed through the soil. Sometimes gardeners overfeed these plants, which causes the surface of the soil to turn white, but they can be rescued by top-watering for several days in a row, which will flush away some of that extra fertilizer.

Amaryllis Amaryllises are undoubtedly among the most dramatic houseplants around. From the top of each tall, thick flower stalk they produce 4 enormous lilylike flowers — 8 or 10 inches in diameter — in red, white, orange, pink, or striped combinations. They also bear strap-shaped leaves and occasionally a second flower stalk. Considering the size of the grown plants, it's hardly surprising that the bulbs from which they grow are huge, nearly the size of a grapefruit. Nor is it surprising that the bulbs are expensive, although they last for so many years that the initial outlay goes a long way.

An amaryllis in full bloom

As a rule, the plants are in bloom by Christmas if they're potted up in November. I begin with a pot that's about 2 inches larger in diameter than the bulb itself, which allows a 1-inch margin all around between the bulb and the pot. I line the bottom of a standard pot — one that's as deep as it is wide — with a ½-inch layer of pebbles or coarse gravel and then ½ inch of potting soil. Because the planted bulb should be about two-thirds of the way out of soil, I hold the bulb suspended over the pot, letting the roots hang down, and fill in around the bulb with potting soil, firming the soil against the roots as I do so. Once the bulb is planted, I soak the soil thoroughly and let it drain. Overwatering is a poten-

Amaryllis bud about to bloom

tial problem for these plants, so they get no more water after planting until there's a sign of growth. There's no way to predict how long that will be, as amaryllises have minds and blossoming schedules of their own.

The plants will be at their best if they have at least 4 hours of direct sunlight every day until they flower, and warm temperatures, at least 60 degrees at night and 70 or warmer during the day. Once they flower, I take the plants out of the direct sunlight to preserve the bloom, which lasts for about 3 weeks.

When they've finished blooming I set the plants back into the full sun and allow the foliage to grow as luxuriantly as possible throughout the spring and summer. During this period the soil should be moist and the plants fertilized monthly. When the foliage begins to yellow late in the summer I reduce the amount of water and omit the fertilizer entirely. Then about a month before I want the plant to bloom again I cut the old, withered foliage back to within ¾ inch of the bulb, and to make way for new soil I wash and brush away as much of the old soil around the bulb as possible without disturbing the roots. Replacing the soil is a better idea than repotting because larger pots encourage leaf growth at the expense of flowers.

This routine can go on indefinitely as long as the bulbs are given a 1-inch-larger pot every 3 to 4 years, and any young bulbs that develop alongside the main one are separated and planted individually.

Asparagus Asparagus foliage is an ideal place for borers to spend the winter, so for reasons of sanitation it should be cut down to soil level in the late fall, after it has turned brown and withered. This is true both for new and for established beds. The foliage is very rich, having grown in a thick layer of compost, so I put it onto the compost pile to make sure the nutrients eventually find their way back to the garden. I also give the asparagus bed an autumnal top dressing of 2 inches of cow manure to help the soil build up strength for the next year.

Calla Lilies In South Africa, calla lilies grow wild in roadside ditches, with their roots in the mud and their flowers shining in the sun. This native environment provides the plants with the constant moisture they demand. There are several kinds of calla lilies, ranging in height from a modest 1½ feet to a commanding 4 feet. Their snowy white, yellow, or pink blossoms last for months; in fact the white calla will bear its richly fragrant 6- to 8-inch flowers continuously all year long, provided it's given enough fertilizer, moisture, sunshine, and warmth.

A bouquet of fragrant calla lillies, the result of a steady diet of moisture, fertilizer, bright light, and warmth

The thick calla lily roots can be bought at almost any time of the year, but like most indoor gardeners, I start them into growth in the fall so I can enjoy the first of the flowers on the young plants during the bleak days of winter. On one show I planted a white calla in a 6-inch standard pot, a container well proportioned for the plant's fast-growing roots. I put a ½-inch layer of drainage pebbles in the bottom of the pot, half filled the pot with potting soil, set the roots in so they were 2 or 3 inches below the rim of the pot, and filled in around the roots with soil. The plant is a very speedy grower and was about 7 inches tall 2 weeks after potting. The first flowers appeared about 2 months after planting.

As calla lilies grow, I shift them into ever-larger pots to accommodate their increasing growth, and feed them once a month with houseplant fertilizer. I also make sure that the saucer beneath the plants always has a bit of water in it to satisfy the plant's need for moisture; this is an unusual step, as most plants would die if they were forever sitting in water, but calla lilies would suffer if they weren't.

A clump of dahlia tubers ready for storage

Dahlias These Mexican natives simply cannot live through our New England winters outdoors. Their roots need to be dug up and stored at temperatures just above freezing. So in November, after the foliage has been killed by frost, I cut the stems off at the soil line and carefully dig up the clumps of potato-sized tubers that lie just beneath the soil. (The tubers are connected to the crown of each plant by very fragile, slender "necks" that are easily broken.) Dahlias' large hollow stems are usually full of water, so I drain them by leaving the clumps outside for a half a day with the stems turned downward. They dehydrate and wither quickly, so as soon as they're dry I put them into storage.

To keep the tubers plump, I line a wooden box with a sheet of black plastic to help hold moisture and set the tubers inside, covering them with moist peat moss, vermiculite, perlite, or sawdust to help keep the tubers from drying out. Then I staple another piece of black plastic over the box and take it into my cellar, where I tilt the whole thing up against the cellar wall, an area that in most houses stays reasonably cool and damp all winter. (Another suggestion comes from a viewer who buries tubers in a hole about 18 inches deep which he digs right outside the foundation wall of his house, a spot that stays cool and damp, preventing dehydration, and where the temperature hovers just above the freezing mark. It's an idea I'm going to try because, like most other gardeners, I have a heated basement that makes dahlia storage tricky.)

The tubers should be left in winter storage until March, when they're resurrected to begin their spring growth for another season.

Gladioluses Every week or 10 days through the spring and early summer I plant a few gladiolus corms to maintain the Victory Garden's supply of these tall, stately flowers. Gladioluses are tender plants, and they die if their corms, or roots, freeze, so I dig them up in the fall, winter them over, and save them for the next spring. After digging the plants, I cut the foliage back to ½ inch from the tip of the corm, and lay the corms one layer thick in a warm, well-ventilated spot out of the sun.

During the season's growth, each single planted corm produces a number of offspring, ranging in size from tiny pea-shaped cormels to corms larger than the original size of the parent, now shriveled and exhausted from its season's work. So after a couple of weeks, when the corms are com-

Gladiolus corms dug from the Perennial Border and ready for winter storage

pletely dry, I first break off the parent corm and discard it; then I split up the new corms and cormels and slip them into a paper bag along with a few moth flakes and a light dusting of captan. The moth flakes kill thrips that might be clinging to the corms, and the captan helps prevent disease. After a month, I transfer the corms from the paper bag into an old nylon stocking that I hang in my cellar, where the temperature ranges from 40 to 50 degrees, and they keep well until spring.

Jerusalem Artichokes It's seven months since the Jerusalem artichokes were last heard from. We plant the tubers in April and leave these rock-strong plants to grow in the rich soil near our composter; by November, when the foliage has completely dried, it's time to begin the harvest. I say begin, because we harvest only as many tubers as we want at one time, leaving the bulk of the crop in the ground for a continuing fresh supply all winter long. To harvest, I just lift an entire plant up out of the ground and separate the potato-sized tubers from the stalks. In order to keep the ground soft enough to harvest through the snow we mound leaves over the roots of the plants left behind after the initial harvest.

This is an obscure but valuable vegetable. It's absolutely no trouble in the garden, and it can be grown from wild tubers so it's not expensive either. It produces carbohydrates in the form of inulin, not starch, which makes it a particularly good food for diabetics.

Lantana Early one November someone brought to the greenhouse the most straggly lantana imaginable. It had three or four stems, mostly devoid of foliage. The few leaves that clung to its stems had brown edges. The plant was in a hanging basket and apparently had been suspended in such a way that the owner could not see the soil to check its moisture. I have a feeling that it received water only after it became so dry that it wilted.

Healthy lantanas are beautiful, abundant plants, so I hoped to nurse this one back from the grave. It was a bushy type called *Lantana camara*, a variety that bears 1-inch clusters of fragrant flowers in yellow, orange, white, pink, or red. Originally from Jamaica, it grows wild throughout the tropics. The trailing lantana, *L. sellowiana*, sometimes called *L. montevidensis*, has smaller rosy purple flowers and comes from Uruguay. Both require bright sunshine, moist soil, and monthly feedings with a houseplant fertilizer to promote new growth and flowers. The stems need an occasional cutting

A lantana flower cluster, beloved of red spider mites and white flies

back or the plants get lanky and the stems lose their lower leaves.

The unhappy plant brought to me was badly in need of rejuvenation. First, I repotted it in fresh soil; then I snipped the stems back to 2-inch stubs. Within a few weeks the plant was covered with new growth, so I decided to propagate it by taking cuttings of the fresh new stems. I simply removed a few 4-inch tips from the stems, dipped their ends in rooting powder, and set them in damp sand. The cuttings formed roots within a month so I transplanted them to ordinary potting soil. The old plant became even bushier from having its new stems pinched back, and although it delayed its flowering a few weeks it eventually became a beautiful specimen again.

Plants blossom only when they are in active growth, and the lantana is no exception to the rule. Ordinarily, young plants purchased in the spring are set outdoors where they blossom all summer. By fall, they are woody and have exhausted the soil's nutrients, so they stop growing and blossoming. If they are repotted at that time in fresh soil and cut back severely, they will make handsome new growth and produce flowers indoors during the winter. As houseplants, they grow best with night temperatures about 60 degrees and daytime readings in the 70s. They need the sunniest windowsill in the house.

Lantanas are apt to be attacked both by spider mites and by white flies. The spider mites can usually be held at bay by keeping the plants relatively cool and spraying them forcefully every week with water to dislodge the mites; if that doesn't work, dicofol usually will. White flies can be controlled by regular use of pyrethrum and rotenone.

Lettuce Surprising as it may seem, we usually harvest succulent lettuce in the Victory Garden throughout the month of November and sometimes into early December. We're able to keep the crop growing for a full month or more beyond the first killing frost because we use our cold frames and cloches, and because we can usually count on a brief but sunny Indian summer to help spur the lettuce growth along. It's sometimes a bother to open and close the covers on the frames and to pull a tarpaulin over the cloches on nights when the temperature dips into the 20s, but the reward of those tender leaves more than makes up for the trouble involved.

Lettuce can be kept in the open garden through the fall without the protection of cloches or cold frames if the temperature drops steadily from night to night, allowing the plants to harden their growth. But if freezing weather arrives overnight even these ordinarily frost-tolerant plants will be killed outright unless they're covered with leaves, which will afford them all the temporary protection they need.

Marigolds Because they're such rugged, showy plants, there are probably more marigolds seen on the air in the Victory Garden than any of our other flowers. And though they're seldom thought of in this way, they make excellent houseplants as well. They grow quickly and are tolerant of the less-than-perfect conditions of house and apartment growing. Their yellow, orange, maroon (and now white) flowers are great for splashes of color, whether indoors or out.

For growing indoors, I recommend the dwarf French marigolds or the French-African hybrids. The ordinary African varieties grow too tall and are so late in coming into blossom that I prefer to use them in the outdoor garden only. By the way, the names French and African are a bit misleading. Both marigolds are native to Mexico, regardless of the names that they now carry. All marigolds are free-flowering, but the French-African hybrids are especially so; they are sterile and do not set seeds, but the plants keep trying to do so by sending out more and more flowers. To get seeds of these hybrids, plant breeders must make individual flower crosses between selected forms each year.

Except for the French-African hybrids, the germination rate of marigold seeds is reliably high, so I sow only about 6 or 7 seeds in a 3-inch pot filled with soilless mix. (For French-African hybrids I sow twice as many seeds to get the same number of plants.) After a couple of weeks, when the seedlings are about 2 inches tall, I transfer each one to an individual 3-inch pot. Given the minimum 4 hours of sunlight that they need every day, they soon grow large enough to produce their lovely flowers and pungent fragrance.

One warning about these plants. They're very susceptible to red spider mites, which hide on the underside of the leaves and suck the plants' nourishment, first turning the leaves yellowish and finally disfiguring the whole plant. The problem is easily taken care of with a weekly washing with a forcible spray — the kitchen sink spray is fine — making sure the water hits the underside of the foilage.

Parsnips This is one of the few crops that can stand up to winter, actually improving in flavor with the arrival of cold weather. The early spring harvest is by far the best, but I can never resist a fall pulling to have a first taste. I use a spading fork to lift a sneak preview out of the soil, and leave the rest for later diggings through the winter. It's conceivable that we could pull the parsnips from the ground during a stretch of mild winter weather, but rather than run the risk of their freezing solid in the soil, I mulch the ground with a 12-inch layer of leaves to keep the soil soft enough to dig even in midwinter.

Pansies One of the reasons we've been so successful with our pansies in the Victory Garden, managing to produce a crop in full flower as early as the first week in April, is that we protect them through the winter with a 3-inch layer of pine needle mulch. I wait until November, and put the mulch on after the ground has frozen, in order to spare the plants the hazards of alternate freezes and thaws that heave them out of the ground and leave their roots exposed to dehydrate and die. The plants are very hardy and will even send out a few flowers during a mild winter. As soon as the spring sun appears, though, they'll begin to grow and produce an impressive number of early spring blossoms. (If we had the space, we'd turn over a few of our trusty cold frames to the wintering pansies. The cold frames would bring the plants into blossom even sooner by warming the soil earlier in the spring.)

Peas Ordinarily I plant peas in a trench so I can hill them up as they grow and keep the roots of the plants deep in the cool earth. But by doing a little work in the fall, I can actually plant the peas as soon as the ground thaws in the spring, even if the soil is still too soggy to work.

In November, while the soil is still mellow and warm and easily worked, I choose a south-facing row that borders one of the garden paths, where the soil is light and well drained. Then after I do the normal fall soil preparation (see this month's feature, page 246), I rake the soil smooth. That's all there is to it. In the spring I just stand on the garden path, sprinkle the seeds on the surface of the soil, and poke them in with my finger. They come up quickly and are completely toughened against frost, even in their infancy.

Rhubarb One year I dug up the roots of a 4-year-old rhubarb from my home garden and brought the plant into the Victory Garden to force the plant to produce stalks in mid-winter. There was nothing much to this. First of all, the roots needed to freeze solid. This would have happened, of course, if the plants had been left in the ground, but they would've been almost impossible to dig up when they were needed in January. So I dug them in November, set them in a box lined with plastic, and left the box uncovered in the garden, resting on a couple of bricks so the whole thing wouldn't freeze to the ground. In mid-January I put them into a warm, dark place for the actual forcing.

Roses In November, when I make the winter care of roses part of one of the television shows, I am acutely aware that in some parts of the country this process isn't necessary. Our oldest daughter, Carol, and her family live in southern California, where I once helped her plant a rose garden one January while New England was blanketed with snow. My sister Jean and her family live in Houston in a climate so mild that she picks roses all year long. Friends in Florida are similarly blessed.

But most of us live in areas where tender varieties of roses need protection in order to survive winter's cold. Some shrub roses become dormant during the cold weather and are perfectly hardy without any protection at all. But most of the hybrid tea roses have in their ancestry certain species from the warmer climate of southern China, and they try to keep growing in spite of the cold. All gardeners can do for them is to temper the wintry blasts by protecting the plants from the direct cold and from dehydration by icy winds.

The simplest protection is a mound of soil around the base of the plant to safeguard the bud union. This mounding soil should be brought from another part of the garden, and

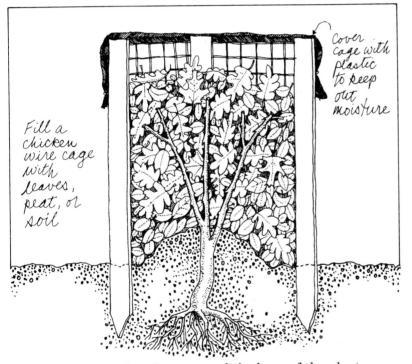

Cover cage with plastic to keep out moisture

Fill a chicken wire cage with leaves, peat, or soil

not simply scraped up from around the base of the plant, as this would expose the rose roots to extra cold. In areas where temperatures are very severe it pays to erect, in addition to the soil mound, a circle of chicken wire as tall as the plant and fill it with leaves, peat moss, or even soil. By all means, though, remember to remove this deep mulch early in the spring, before the new growth starts.

Streptocarpus In spite of its name, this is a plant, not a disease. It's also known as the Cape primrose, but it isn't a primrose either. It's a handsome flowering houseplant from South Africa related to the African violet and the gloxinia, and it thrives under the same moist, warm, well-fed conditions as its relatives. Streptocarpus blossoms are slipper-shaped and range in color from pure white through many shades of pink to deep red and from pale lavender to deep purple.

If you already have a favorite streptocarpus, the only way to propagate plants identical to the parent is by leaf cuttings or division. But it's perfectly possible to start the plants from seed, as I do in November. The seeds are barely visible, and their size requires some special attention. If they were planted in a regular pot, most of them would wash down into the soil and smother, so I give the germinating seeds the shelter of their own little greenhouse.

I begin by laying a quart mason jar on its side in a bed of sand, which helps keep the jar stable. Then I scoop a layer of pasturized sifted compost (see the August feature, pages 180–181) into the jar. about ½ inch deep and I'm all set to carry out the most delicate step in this operation. I sprinkle the seeds onto a wooden label and with a steady hand put the label into the jar, shaking it to distribute the seeds over the compost. I don't cover the seeds at all.

Sprinkle seeds over ½" of pasturized compost in a 1 quart mason jar

Place the jar on a bed of builder's sand for stability

For the next 2 months, while the seedlings are young, they need both water and light, so I mist inside the jar with a hand sprayer — enough to dampen the soil but not soak it. After I cap the jar I set it into a bright warm spot out of the direct sun until it's time for the delicate transplanting operation in January.

Q&A

Q: What do you think of seaweed as a fertilizer or mulch?

A: I think you're lucky if you've got it. Seaweed absorbs every known mineral when it grows in the ocean, and it adds those minerals to the soil, providing some critical trace elements. You can either dig it into the soil in the fall and let it decay, use it as mulch around your plants, or add it to your composter.

Q: Can you suggest a plant that will thrive in an office with no windows?

A: Yes, the aspidistra, also called the cast-iron plant, which gives you some idea of the tolerance this plant has to bad growing conditions. It does magnificently with careful attention, but if deprived it can withstand drought, flood, heat, cold, neglect, dust, and poor light. No room can be *that* bad.

Q: How do you husk black walnuts?

A: Not with your standard nutcracker, I can tell you. They need a more barbaric touch. Crack the husks by laying them out in the driveway and driving over them with your car. The tires won't hurt the nuts and the husks won't hurt the tires. I hope you won't mind the stain the husks leave on your driveway — and on your hands when you pick them up.

Q: It's November and some of my spring bulbs are already up and growing. What do I do?

A: Stop worrying. It's normal for Madonna lilies and grape hyacinths to come up at this time of the year and spread their leaves on the surface of the soil. Other bulb plants may peek through the soil, but the bulbs themselves are still safe in the ground, waiting for the spring.

SOIL PREPA- RATION

Soil is not dirt. It's the top few inches of the earth's surface, the layer in which most of the world's vegetation grows. There are three basic types of soil. Sandy soil, which best identifies the Victory Garden soil, is a good planting medium because it drains quickly and can be worked early in the spring; the problem with it is that moisture and nutrients leach out very quickly. Clay soil is at the other end of the spectrum. Clay is the material from which crockery and bricks are made, and it's brutal to plants' roots. Clay soil is easily spotted because it forms a hard clod when it's dry, and when wet it feels greasy. The middle ground, so to speak, between sand and clay is loam, an approximately equal mixture of the two. Loam is the kind of soil gardeners pray for: it drains efficiently but not so quickly that drying out is a constant fear; and it contains abundant supplies of organic material.

Soil quality is the most controllable of garden variables: all sorts of deficiencies can be corrected in one way or another, whether these deficiencies are caused by years of neglect or by a season of garden production. Any type of soil, even loam, can and should be improved and rejuvenated yearly by replenishing the supply of organic matter, correcting the soil's level of acidity or alkalinity by adding lime or sulfur, and tilling to loosen and aerate the soil.

We prepare the Victory Garden soil in two phases. In November, when the garden has been emptied of all but the few winter-hardy crops, we take care of the rougher preparations, adding the materials that will work slowly through the soil all winter long. First we test the soil and add a dusting of ground limestone: generally at the end of our growing season the production effort leaves the soil with a pH of 5.5 to 6.0, so I add lime at the rate of 3½ to 5 pounds per 100 square feet to raise the pH to about 6.8, a good level for vegetables. Then I add organic material: 2 or 3 inches of fresh cow or horse manure, along with any leaf mold or other organic materials that we have on hand, and till all these materials into the soil with a rotary tilling machine, making as many passes with the machine as are needed to turn the soil 8 to 10 inches deep. (In our first year, because we were preparing the soil in the spring, we used several bales of peat moss as our organic material. In subsequent years we've been able to save ourselves the expense of peat moss by using our own garden refuse and well-rotted manure, which, although it isn't free, is much cheaper

For a new garden, invert sod into trench and cover with at least 12" of earth ⊢ 10" ⊣ 12"

than peat.) As our last step in the fall we plant a crop of winter rye grass as green manure. Then we leave the garden for the winter.

In the spring, as soon as the soil dries out enough to work, we turn the rye grass into the soil with the tilling machine. Then we do another soil test and add a bit more lime if it's needed, and till the lime in. (If a tilling machine isn't available, my advice is to hand-dig the garden in small, manageable sections, turning over only the area you plan to plant immediately.) Whether by hand or by machine, though, the soil should be tilled 8 to 10 inches deep. The last step is to add fertilizers just at planting time. They leach through the soil very quickly, and if they're put on in advance of planting

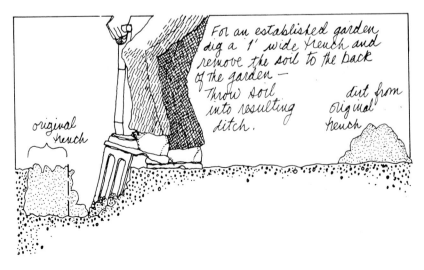

For an established garden dig a 1' wide trench and remove the soil to the back of the garden — Throw soil into resulting ditch.

original trench

dirt from original trench

they'll wash away before the plants have a chance to take advantage of them. (See more about fertilizing on page 99.)

There is nothing that matters more in gardening than soil preparation, so even though we give the Victory Garden such loving attention in the fall and spring, we continue to monitor the soil all through the growing season, adding lime as it's called for and giving certain plants an added boost of organic material at planting time. If there's a key to successful gardening, it's thorough soil preparation.

Organic Matter Soil is more than pulverized rocks. It is a living laboratory of many forms of life, including earthworms, fungi, and bacteria. Each of these organisms plays a vital part in the overall life and productivity of the soil, but the usefulness of these live creatures depends on the amount of dead vegetation in the soil. By adding organic materials — leaves, decayed vegetable matter — gardeners improve the structure and texture of their soil as well as its ability to retain nutrients and moisture. Growing crops use the decayed residue of organic materials as they grow, so these materials have to be replenished in the soil year after year.

Organic materials do wonders for any soil. Worked into sandy soils they act like sponges, holding water and nutrients so the plants can get at them. They open dense clay soils to air and water. Although organic materials were for years the only fertilizer farmers had at their disposal, they are not particularly rich in nutrients. For improving the soil's texture, though, none of these materials can be beaten.

Peat moss, expensive but worth every penny

Compost: This is the caviar of organic materials. It can't be bought; it can only be made by letting piles of garden refuse decay over time. It improves the soil's water-holding capacity and returns its rich store of nutrients to the soil. (For more about compost, and instructions for building a composter, see pages 180–181.) It's so precious that I parcel it out to selected crops, including asparagus, leeks, and some of the long-range perennials. It's far superior to manure in nutritive value. And in spite of its origins in decay, it doesn't smell or draw flies if it's properly made.

Peat Moss: Peat moss is the partially decayed remnants of plants from ancient bogs. It isn't cheap, and it doesn't contain the trace elements found in some other organic materials, but it is certainly the easiest to use and one of the best organic materials available. It's fast too; it alters the soil structure as soon as it's dug in. Many gardening books advise using peat, but I advise using it in large doses. When we began the Victory Garden, our local supplier sent over 6 bales of peat, an amount he considered sufficient for the job. But I ordered another 19 bales because, with neither compost nor well-rotted manure on hand, peat was by far the best organic material I could add to the soil. That 3-inch layer of peat moss did wonders for the Victory Garden's generally lifeless soil. In fact it's hard not to launch into superlatives about peat moss. It improves any soil it's added to. It helps sandy soil retain moisture, it helps clay soil breathe, and it even improves loam. It makes the soil easy to work, eases weeding, and generally makes the entire plot more productive. (Peat moss is naturally acidic, so a soil test should always be done after the peat has been added.)

The most popular form of peat moss is sphagnum peat moss, a fibrous, pale brown material that can hold many times its weight of water. It's available either milled or ground, long-fibered, or shredded; in the Victory Garden, we use the shredded peat, because its coarse structure helps to separate the hard soil particles.

Manures: For years, manures were the only source of nutrients and the only material available to improve a soil's texture. These days, the nutritional duties are performed by the new concentrated fertilizers (see page 99), but there is still nothing like a layer of manure to improve the structure of soil. Cow manure is the best, but horse manure is much easier to come by.

Leaves: Leaves are excellent mulches, but they're most valuable when they're composted and then added to potting soil or spread on the garden to help rejuvenate tired soil. Leaf mold is a decayed organic material composed entirely of leaves. It's made by first chopping the leaves with a shredder or mower, which speeds the decay process, and then storing them in a chicken-wire bin in layers to which some soil, lime, and 10-10-10 fertilizer are added. After 2 or 3 years it decays into brown crumbly material every bit as useful as peat moss.

Green Manures: These are grassy or leguminous cover crops that are planted at any time and dug into the soil to add organic matter. In the Victory Garden we use winter rye

Above: Turning leaves into the soil

Below: Spreading manure

grass. We plant it in the fall and leave it through the winter (it will grow whenever there's a mild day), and then turn it into the soil in the spring. We dig it in when the grass is at the peak of its succulent vegetative growth, before the stems are tough and woody, turning it into the soil either by hand or by machine. Unlike animal manures, green manures are not caustic even when first dug in; so sowing can take place immediately after tilling.

Tilling We have our own rotary tilling machine in the Victory Garden, and it's one of the best on the market. The tines are mounted behind the wheels so the machine doesn't roll over the very soil it has just tilled. (In the majority of tilling machines the tines are mounted in front of the wheels.) These machines have simplified the tilling process enormously, saving thousands of gardeners their posture and their Saturday afternoons. They're great

for blending materials into soil that's already been worked.

The goal of tilling is to loosen the top 8 to 10 inches of soil, and this can rarely be accomplished with one pass of the tilling machine. In light soils the first pass may dig through the top 5 inches of soil, but it's apt to penetrate only an inch or two of heavy soil. For the machine's sake, it's wise to go over the garden several times, reaching a few inches deeper with each pass.

Useful as tilling machines are, though, they can't stand up to virgin or rocky soil; only the centuries-old technique of hand digging can. It's one of the hardest and most exhausting of gardening jobs, but it's simpler if it's done the right way, as the illustrations show.

Lime and Sulfur The level of a soil's acidity is important in gardening because it affects the availability of nutrients to the crops. In very acid or very alkaline soil the nutrients are locked in where the plants can't get at them. Slightly acidic soil is best, but

very few gardeners are lucky enough to have it naturally. As a rule of thumb, land east of the Mississippi is acid and land west of the Mississippi is alkaline. But the way to positively determine a soil's alkalinity or acidity is with a soil test kit. These kits are easy to use and inexpensive — there are costly versions but they're beyond the needs of most home gardeners. With a kit it's easy to get a reading of the soil's pH, the 0–14 scale used to measure acidity and alkalinity. The neutral point is 7.0 pH; zero is extremely acid and 14 is extremely alkaline. Most vegetables do best in soil that is just a bit below neutral (6.5–6.8).

To lower the pH of alkaline soil, add ground agricultural sulfur; ground limestone will correct acidity problems. The amount of either of these materials to use depends upon the original pH level and the composition of the soil.

Above: Tilling, the easy way

Below: A fall application of lime is best

Poinsettias

Plant
Easter Lilies
Oxalises

Start Seedlings
Browallias
Strawberries

Take Cuttings
Evergreens

Special Events
Christmas Trees
Poinsettias
Rubber Trees

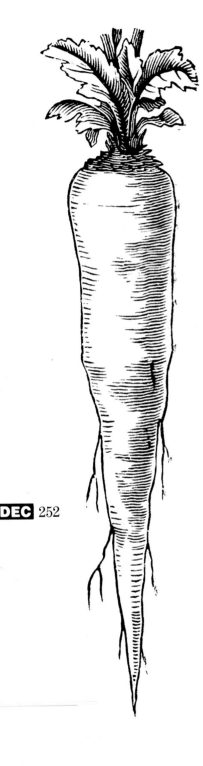

DEC

December brings hard winter to the Victory Garden, emphasizing the need some of our plants have for winter protection. Evergreens, for instance, are unable to take up moisture during the winter if the ground is frozen, and there are few things so dangerous to these plants as dehydration. So we blanket the ground around all our evergreens, especially our rhododendrons, with a 4- to 6-inch layer of leaves, watering the soil ahead of time. Herbaceous plants such as perennials and biennials face a different winter hazard: the months of alternate freezing and thawing of the soil surface can "heave" the plants out of their locations, exposing their roots. The best prevention is to keep the ground frozen all through the winter, so as soon as the soil has frozen hard we mulch all the herbaceous plants with a 2- to 3-inch layer of pine needles, salt marsh hay, or straw. The shade provided by these mulches keeps the ground frozen. To protect young fruit trees from damage by mice or rabbits we put permanent cylinders of ½-inch galvanized hardware cloth around their trunks, extending from the ground up to the lowest branches.

Then, except for the continuing harvest of parsnips, Jerusalem artichokes, and some of the other winter-hardy plants, we leave the garden to rest for the winter, and move indoors. The gardening chores are fewer at this time of the year, so we often take the opportunity for tidying up the potting shed, cleaning, sharpening and oiling our hand tools, and sending the garden machinery out for an annual tune-up.

Of course, not all the month's jobs are simple housecleaning chores. We continue forcing amaryllises, tulips, and paper white narcissuses this month, and we watch the mail for the first of the next year's seed catalogues. We root more cuttings from our indoor geranium plants so we'll have a large supply of healthy plants by the time the spring comes. December is the time to sow indoors seeds of alpine strawberries; they will begin to blossom and bear fruit in May and will continue until freezing weather in the fall. And we devote some of the year's pleasantest hours caring for such so-called Christmas plants as poinsettias, azaleas, cyclamens, and kalanchoes.

Browallias If you have a browallia plant, it's a simple matter to take stem cuttings and propagate new plants. In fact, this in the only thing to do with a plant that's become woody and bedraggled with age, as browallias do not respond well to cutting back. If you don't have a plant of your own you can start browallias from seeds, as long as you don't mind waiting for the results. The plants are very slow growers, so I usually sow the seeds around Christmastime and have plants large enough to go into the garden in May. I'm especially partial to rich blue browallia varieties because the color is so effective in the summer garden. There is a handsome large-flowering white variety also, but the small-flowered white type seems somewhat weedy to me.

The seeds are minute, much too tiny to cover after sowing, so I fill a 3-inch pot with soilless mix, sift a ⅛-inch layer of milled sphagnum moss over the surface, and then sprinkle the seeds into the moss and let them settle down in as they please. I water the seeds by setting the entire pot in a dish of water until the moss is moist. At that time, I set the pot aside to drain, later putting it on a tray filled with gravel and water to humidify the plants' atmosphere. After about a month the seedlings are large enough for a delicate transplant

Browallia seedlings will begin to flower even at this young age

to six-packs where they grow on until May, at which point I put them into a shady spot in the garden, or pot three together in a hanging pot. Because of their trailing habit of growth, browallias are especially effective along the edges of window boxes in shady spots.

Christmas Trees Time was when Christmas trees were chopped down from woods and dragged into the house on Christmas Eve to be decorated with candles, then lit for no more than an instant while the family stood by with buckets of water in case one of the candles should spark the tree. Now Christmas trees are grown as crops, carefully spaced, fertilized, and pruned for 15 or 16 years in preparation for a week or two of glory. There are many fine trees available; the balsam fir, Douglas fir, Scotch pine, and several varieties of spruce are among the most popular.

A living Christmas tree, a reminder of a holiday past

Christmas trees last longest indoors if they're fresh, and the way to test for this is to grab hold of some of the needles and pull: if they stay on the branch, the tree's been freshly cut. As soon as the tree is taken indoors, it will start to lose moisture to the dry inside air, and there are few things that will burn so suddenly or completely as a dry Christmas tree. So it's a good idea to keep the tree sitting in a couple of inches of water for the entire time it's in the house. Cut off about an inch from the base of the trunk, exposing fresh cells, so it will be able to absorb the water efficiently. The tree will not only be safer for this, it'll stay attractive longer.

Although most Christmas trees are cut and then sold, many garden centers are now offering live Christmas trees that have been dug from the nursery to be enjoyed indoors then planted outdoors after the holidays. We have a handsome 40-foot Norway spruce in our yard that was a family Christmas tree when our kids were small; my father and I dragged it out after New Year's and planted it together. It makes a nice memory.

If you plan to buy one of these live trees, decide ahead of time where the tree will be planted, and dig the hole early in December before the ground freezes. (If you live in an area where the ground is still workable in December, you needn't dig the hole in advance.) Fill the hole with leaves and cover it with plastic until planting time. Then select a tree that will, at maturity, fit the spot you're giving it. By the way, live Christmas trees are heavy and it'll take some muscle to cart them around.

Don't plan on having a live tree indoors for more than 10 days. If you can, buy the tree on Christmas Eve and take

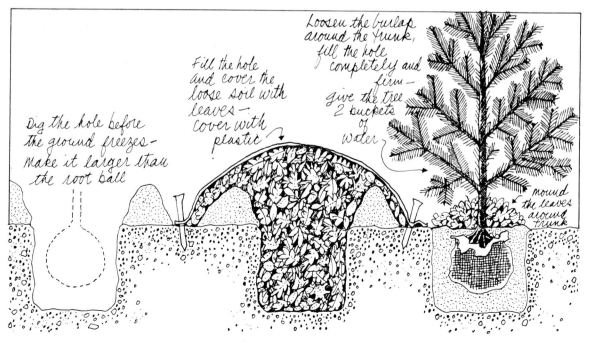

Dig the hole before the ground freezes — make it larger than the root ball

Fill the hole and cover the loose soil with leaves — cover with plastic

Loosen the burlap around the trunk, fill the hole completely and firm — give the tree 2 buckets of water

mound the leaves around trunk

A small Norfolk Island pine

it out on New Year's Day so that it has to put up with dry, warm air for only a short time. Because you want this tree to survive, it is extremely important that the soil around its roots stays moist at all times. Lay down a piece of plastic to protect the floor, and as an added precaution, before you bring the tree indoors, wrap the root ball in plastic so you'll be able to water the soil without damaging the floor. Some Christmas trees come in containers that enable the trees to stand erect. Others, with burlap-covered soil around their roots, may need a brace.

After the holidays, carry your tree out to its prepared spot and take the plastic off the root ball. Then scoop the leaves out of the hole, set the tree in, and loosen the burlap slightly around the trunk. Add soil to fill in the hole completely, firm it well with your feet, and give the tree several buckets of water. The tree will die if it dries out during the winter, so to keep the soil from freezing deeply and to allow the moisture to be taken up by the roots, mound the leaves over the soil around the trunk.

For indoor gardeners, the Norfolk Island pine makes a fine small potted Christmas tree. On its native Norfolk Island, a tiny speck of land about 1,000 miles east of Australia, this tree grows to be 200 feet tall, but indoors it makes a slow-growing, long-lived plant that's handsome all year long. The Norfolk Island pine can take anything from full sunshine to rather dim light. Keep the soil barely moist and feed it every 6 months with any houseplant fertilizer. Except in southern California and Florida it's not hardy outdoors.

Easter Lilies Gardeners are often advised against trying Easter lilies on their own, but the only risky part of this undertaking is in getting the plants to bloom on schedule for Easter Sunday. If you don't care when their snowy white, sweetly fragrant blossoms appear and you can provide them with the chilly temperatures they need, you will find that they're not any more complicated than many another houseplant.

Easter lilies grow from fat bulbs, composed of thick scales that are really modified food storage leaves. When the bulbs arrive in the fall, they are relatively dormant, but will begin growth soon after being planted. They grow slowly through the winter months on a sunny windowsill, producing one or more stems lined with rich green slender leaves. Eventually the flower buds appear at the tops of the stems, opening into lovely perfumed blossoms.

In planting an Easter lily, start by putting a 1-inch layer of gravel in the bottom of a 6-inch standard pot, and set the bulb directly on the gravel; this is rather an unusual procedure, but it helps keep the bulb from decaying. I use a mix-

A greenhouse full of Easter lilies in bloom

ture of equal parts potting soil and compost fortified with about a teaspoonful of slow-release fertilizer to fill in around and over the bulb to within ½ inch of the rim of the pot.

Planted in this way, the bulbs do not need additional fertilizer, but they do need full sunshine and constant though moderate moisture in a cool room (40 to 55 degrees at night and 68 or lower during the day). The first leaves show above the soil about a month after planting. When the flowers fade, set the plants into the garden. They will live and blossom outdoors for many years.

Evergreens It takes years to grow an evergreen plant large enough to make an impact in the garden; the little 15-inch plants sold by nurseries are already 7 or 8 years old. But many evergreens can be propagated from cuttings, if time is no issue, and it cuts down dramatically on the expense. The best time to take the cuttings of most evergreens is late in the fall when the current growth is completely mature. Not all kinds of evergreens can be propagated from cuttings. For instance, pine, spruce, fir, and hemlock are extremely difficult to grow in this manner. However, expensive yews as well as arborvitae, false cypress, some junipers, and

ne-year-old Hicks Yew, making fine root system

evergreen ground covers such as pachysandra, pachistima, and myrtle are relatively easy to propagate.

Among the evergreens I propagated for demonstration purposes was a Japanese yew. First I took 3-inch to 4-inch stems from the tips of the plant, where the growth was young and tender enough to root. After I peeled away the needles from the bottom 1½ inches of each stem, I dipped them briefly into water to moisten the ends and then into rooting powder. I set the cuttings together in a flat of coarse builders' sand, covering the entire flat with our own miniature greenhouse. After a couple of months, when there was a sign of a callus or thickening forming on the base of the stems, I transferred the cuttings to individual 3-inch pots filled with potting mix and gave each a drink of transplant solution.

All winter long I kept the soil moist and the plants cool in a brightly lighted spot in the greenhouse until the roots formed. It can take as long as a year for the root system to be large enough to set the plants out into the garden.

Another method of handling hardwood evergreen cuttings is to set the flats directly into a well-protected cold frame for the winter, covering them with excelsior, salt marsh hay, pine needles, or other light, airy material. The flats should be left undisturbed in the spring, except for the removal of the mulch, until new growth signals the development of roots. The cuttings can then be transferred to a nursery bed for further growth. One lesson evergreen propagation teaches the home gardener is that the professional nurseryman is not overpaid for all his labor, patience, and skill.

Oxalises Oxalises are short, tidy plants with profuse pink, yellow, white, or lavender flowers clustered above foliage that resembles giant clover. They make economical as

well as attractive houseplants because the bulbs, which multiply rapidly, can be saved and used year after year. Even the tiniest bulbs will send out flowers the following season. The plants are also, like some people I know, moody: they open their flowers only when the days are sunny, closing them against darkness and cloudy weather.

Oxalises seldom grow more than about 6 inches tall, so it's not surprising that the bulbs themselves are small, usually no more than ½ inch in diameter. In order to have full, bushy plants, I pot 6 bulbs in a 6-inch shallow pot, filled to within ¾ inch of the rim with ordinary potting soil. I keep the soil barely moist and set the pots on a sunny, cool windowsill.

The plants are quick to grow, often up and looking like a tiny field of clover within 10 days or so. They usually begin to blossom within a month, continuing for 4 weeks or more.

When the flowers cease to appear and the foliage begins to turn yellow, I gradually reduce watering until the leaves wither away completely. After resting dry for two or three months, the bulbs can be replanted and started into another growth cycle.

Poinsettias In 1825 our Ambassador to Mexico, Joel Poinsett, brought these wildflowers — reputed to be Montezuma's favorite — back to this country, and we've been growing them ever since, mostly as houseplants, though in the warm southern climates they're hardy outdoors. For the first 138 years of their popularity here, any gardener who could manage to keep them in full foliage past New Year's Day was considered a real pro. Then in 1963 someone discovered a mutation that didn't drop its leaves and ever since we've had poinsettias that last for months, bringing on a whole new era in the plants' popularity. (One summer, I confess, I finally threw away a poinsettia that was still in flower, simply because I needed room for new plants.)

In the Victory Garden we usually propagate our own poinsettia plants from cuttings, but they demand the fussiest care, and many people prefer to let the professionals worry

Poinsettia plants in bloom for the holidays

about the plants' early days and simply buy a mature plant already in blossom. In either case the care of poinsettias once they are in bloom is very easy indeed. They put up with a range of light and temperature conditions, and need be watered only when the soil's been allowed to dry slightly. We fertilize our plants every couple of weeks during the spring and summer when they are growing — not at all during the rest of the year — and cut them back and repot them when they lose their blossoms, usually in midsummer.

Rubber Trees The most common rubber tree grown as a houseplant, *Ficus elastica* and its varieties, was originally found in Burma. These trees are very popular as houseplants, and have been for generations because they're long-lived, easy to care for, and there's a lot of plant for the money. In fact, they can grow so tall that eventually most of the foliage is clustered at the top of the plant while the bottom of the stem is bare and woody. We had a plant in this condition in the greenhouse, so we decided to give it a new lease on life by air-layering it, a technique that encourages new roots to grow high on the plant's stem; eventually the plant can be cut just below those new roots and repotted.

A young rubber tree with new leaves forming from the red leader

The theory behind air-layering is based on a plant's circulatory system. Sap runs upward along the center of the stem, and downward close to the outside edge of the bark, distributing nutrients to the extremities of the plant as blood does to our fingers and toes. In air-layering, the stem is cut so the returning sap is dammed up; nutrients accumulate and produce roots. It's as simple as that, and it requires little more than a steady hand and patience.

First of all, about 3 inches below the main top cluster of the rubber tree's foliage, I made an upward slanting cut with my knife about ¼ of the way through the woody part of the stem, propping the cut open with a toothpick while I dabbed the exposed tissue with rooting powder. During the next few weeks the area around the cut needed to be kept moist to give the roots a chance to form, so I wrapped the stem with a baseball-size wad of damp long-fibered sphagnum moss, using string to secure the moss to the stem. To keep the moss from drying out I wound a sheet of medium-weight plastic food wrap around it, securing the wrap with more string. Then I set the plant into the greenhouse, checking the moss periodically and adding water whenever necessary to keep it moist.

When the moss was entirely filled with roots — which took months — I removed the plastic, cut the stem below the moss, and planted the newly rooted top, moss and all, in a new pot. For the first few weeks the young plant needed to be misted regularly to prevent wilting, but soon its root system

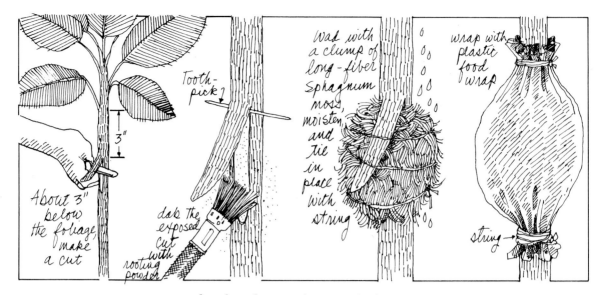

About 3" below the foliage, make a cut

3"

Tooth-pick?

dab the exposed cut with rooting powder

Wad with a clump of long-fiber sphagnum moss, moisten, and tie in place with string

wrap with plastic food wrap

string

developed strongly enough that the new plant was self-supporting.

This is a procedure that will work for most of the stiff-branched, large-leaved plants that can't be treated as cuttings because they would lose too much of their moisture through their large foliage surfaces. Among the suitable candidates for this operation are pleomele, dieffenbachia, dracaena, calliandra, hibiscus, schefflera, croton and monstera, or Swiss Cheese plant. Perhaps the most famous plant ever to be propagated by air-layering was Captain Bligh's breadfruit tree, which he brought from the South Pacific to provide inexpensive, nourishing food for slaves in the Caribbean. Breadfruit is entirely seedless, so new plants had to be propagated vegetatively, and air-layering was and is the easiest and most productive of these techniques, since every branch can be made to root.

Strawberries More people write in to ask us where they can buy everbearing alpine strawberry seeds than any other single question. Considering the number of questions we get week after week, that's quite a statement of interest. They are, indeed, obscure plants, but I can't for the life of me imagine why, as they have it all over the June-bearing varieties in many respects. For one thing, they produce a modest yield all summer long, from June through October. For another, they live for years with a minimum of attention. Third, they don't send out runners; they grow as neat plants 8 to 12 inches tall that will never take over whole sections of the garden. Last, their fruit is handsome, deep red, and sweet-tasting. Our variety is known as Alexandria; we buy seeds from the DeGiorgi Company (see the feature, page 267.)

In order to have fruiting-size plants in May, the seeds must be sown indoors in December. I sprinkle the contents of

Opposite: *Everbearing alpine strawberries*

one seed package onto the surface of a 6-inch pot filled to within ¼ inch of the top with potting soil, cover the seeds with ⅛ inch of milled spaghnum moss, and bottom-water. I transfer the seedlings to six-packs when their first true leaves appear. Then they go to individual 3-inch pots when they're about 2 inches tall. Early in April I set them into the cold frame to harden-off, and plant them outside later in the month. Beginning late in May the plants have an abundance of white flowers, followed by the first fruit in early June. In the Victory Garden I grow my alpine strawberries above a low railroad-tie retaining wall. You may want yours to edge a garden walk, to grow in a strawberry barrel, or to add interest to a rock garden.

Q: What can we do with our office plants when we close for two weeks during the December holidays?

A: First of all, give them a good drink of water, so the root balls are wet all the way through. Then group them together and make a tent over them out of a light plastic bag (use a dry-cleaning bag if you've got one). Put them in bright light but out of the direct sun; when you get back after the holidays give them another drink and they'll never know you've been away.

Q: I tried to grow the top of a pineapple, but it rotted. Can you tell me how I should've done it?

A: I think the problem probably was that you didn't give the top a chance to dry out before you planted it. Next time, take a sharp knife and cut the foliage off with about ½ inch of the pineapple, and leave it lying on a sunny windowsill for a week or so. Then plant it with the bottom 2 inches in potting soil, firm it well, and set it on a sunny windowsill. It'll form roots, and the plant will eventually be 1½ to 2 feet tall. If you cover the plant with a plastic bag when it reaches full height, and put a couple of ripe apples inside the bag with the pineapple for 2 to 3 weeks, you're apt to encourage blossoming. With luck, you'll have a little pineapple for yourself.

Q: I have a few 50-foot spruce trees. I've piled soil about 1 foot deep and 3 feet around the radius of the trees in order to make a rock garden. Now I understand that wasn't a good idea. Will the trees die?

A: They might. Trees send out their roots at the optimum depth for their species. By piling soil over the roots, you've buried them, and they may suffocate. I'd suggest that you remove most of the soil. By the way, to have a successful rock garden, you need a sunny, not a shady, location.

Q: I'm taking some plants home for Christmas. Any advice about transporting them in the cold weather?

A: Many plants will die even if only briefly exposed to freezing weather. So before you take them outside, wrap them completely, pot and all, in 3 or 4 layers of newspaper, and staple the newspaper shut over the top of the foliage so no air will blow in. This is how professional florists protect their plants for delivery in cold weather.

Q: I've just bought a female English holly that I'd like to plant outdoors. When and how should I do this?

A: First of all, well over half the country is too cold to grow English holly outdoors, so if you're north of zone 6, you won't have any luck (see page 306). If you're in a warm enough area, you'll have to buy a male plant, too, if you want berries. Grow them about 15 to 20 feet apart in a slightly shady spot.

THE VICTORY GARDEN VARIETIES

We order seeds off and on all through the year in the Victory Garden, but the major effort comes in December and January when we plot our garden for the following year. This timing may seem premature, but it isn't. The delivery time for seed orders often runs 3 weeks or more; by ordering them as soon as the catalogues arrive, we have the seeds in hand by the time we begin sowing indoors in January and February.

Many gardeners throw away extra seeds at the end of the season, but there's no need to. Most seeds can be saved and planted a second year or even a third. In fact, the seeds sold from seed houses are not necessarily new: they've been carefully stored and tested for viability. (The date stamped on the seed envelope is the date of the test, not the seeds' birthday.) The best way for home gardeners to store seeds is to keep them in their original packages, so the critical planting information isn't lost, and store the packages in an airtight container, a mason jar, or some such, in the back of the refrigerator or in a cool room. If they're stored at room temperature inside the house, they're apt to lose viability. Most seeds are relatively inexpensive, but this isn't so with some of the hybrids. Hybrid tomato seeds, for instance, may cost several cents each, and a package may contain many more seeds than are needed for a single year. If they're stored properly, they can supply top-quality plants for 2 or 3 years.

When it comes time to plan the following year's garden, the seeds are easily tested for viability. Just take a pinch of seeds from the packet and lay them out on a damp paper towel in a warm place. Remember that the normal germination period of seeds varies according to the kind of plant. If after the proper length of time has expired you can see developing roots, the untested seeds in the package are still usable. Don't expect every seed to germinate; this rarely happens. But if 50 to 60 percent of the seeds sprout, you can plant from that package

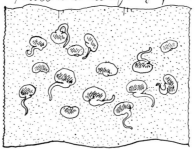

Sprinkle a few test seeds on a wet paper towel and see if they sprout

with confidence of harvesting a good crop. If only a few seeds sprout, then buy fresh ones.

After we've tested our seeds and know what we'll need for the upcoming season, we begin shopping. We order most of our seeds directly from mail-order houses because it affords us the opportunity to compare the various catalogues for the best selection and price. These catalogues, usually offered at no cost by the seed houses, list every seed available, along with descriptions of the plant, the time, space and weather requirements, the number of seeds to a package, the price, and sometimes a photograph. Seed catalogues are indispensable sources of information for veteran and beginner alike; there's no other systematic way to keep up with the latest varieties and techniques. We have well over 100 catalogues in the Victory Garden, some solicited and others not, and we consult them frequently both for ordering new seeds and for reference through the year.

Still, it's well to keep in mind that these catalogues are designed as selling tools. Some of the copy is a little glorious, and the predictions for a crop's performance optimistic, based as they are on ideal growing conditions. As a matter of rule, for instance, the maturation rates for certain crops such as tomatoes, peppers, and eggplants are measured from the time of transplant, not sowing. So some 2 months must be added to the maturation time listed in the catalogue for the entire sowing-through-harvest time. And even with the seedling time added in, the predictions are subject to weather and soil conditions.

Most seed houses advertise in gardening magazines through the fall and winter. The houses listed below are a few of the ones we've used and found reliable.

Burnett Brothers
92 Chambers Street
New York, New York 10007

W. Atlee Burpee Company
(three regional locations)

Warminster, Pennsylvania
18794
Clinton, Iowa 52732
Riverside, California 92509

DeGiorgi Company, Inc.
Council Bluffs, Iowa 51501

Joseph Harris Company
Rochester, New York 14624

Olds Seed Company
P.O. Box 1069
2901 Packers Avenue
Madison, Wisconsin 53701

Park Seed Company
Greenwood, South Carolina
29647

Stokes Seeds
(two regional locations)

P.O. Box 548
737 Main Street
Buffalo, New York 14240

P.O. Box 10
37 James Street
St. Catharines, Ontario 6R6
Canada

In general, most of the seed houses offer the same varieties, although each has a few house specialties that were developed in their experimental laboratories and of which they are particularly proud. The classic varieties — Black-Seeded Simpson lettuce, or Ruby Queen beets — are available from any of the houses, though the price may vary. I order a few new varieties every year both to keep up with new developments and to make the garden interesting. Whenever I can, I buy varieties noted as All-America Winners, a designation of All-America Selections, a nonprofit organization founded by seedsmen in 1932 to promote the development of new varieties; winners indeed they are.

It would be impossible for us to list every vegetable and fruit variety we've ever grown in the Victory Garden, but here follows a partial list. I change the garden a little every year, and I hope you do the same. Most of these varieties are suitable throughout the country, but I'd advise that you use this list as no more than a guideline. Buy your seeds to suit your own soil, weather conditions, and personal preference. Many area seedsmen have varieties particularly bred for local growing conditions.

Bean (Bush)
Green
Tendercrop
Executive
Bush Blue Lake
Lima
Fordhook 242
Yellow (Wax)
Gold Crop (All-America Winner)
Sungold
Pencil Pod
Black Wax
Novelty
Royalty
Italian
Bush Romano
Shell
French Horticultural

Bean (Pole)
Lima
King of the Garden
Green
Blue Lake

Beet
Early Red
Ruby Queen
Main Season
Detroit Dark Red
Pacemaker II
Novelty
Burpee's Golden
Formanova

Broccoli
Early
Cleopatra
Main Season
Premium Crop

Brussels Sprouts
Jade Cross Hybrid

Cabbage
Early Green
Stonehead Hybrid
(All-America Winner)
Main Green
King Cole Hybrid
Late Green
Harris Resistant
Danish
Autumn Marvel
Savoy King

Red
Red Acre
Ruby Ball
Red Ball
Red Head

Chinese Cabbage
Springtime
Summertime

Carrot
For Rock-free Soils
Waltham Hicolor
For Average Soils
Pioneer
Scarlet Nantes
For Rocky Soils
Baby Finger-Nantes
Short n' Sweet

Cauliflower
Snow Crown Hybrid
Early Purple Head

Celery
Summer Pascal

Collards
Georgia

Corn
Extra Early
Extra Early Super Sweet
Earlivee
Early Sweet Hybrid
Buttervee
Polarvee
Early
Spring Gold
Sprite
Midseason
Butter & Sugar
Tastyvee
Main Season
Seneca Chief
Wonderful
Late
Silver Queen Hybrid
Illinichief
Sweet Sue

Cucumber
Saticoy
Marketmore 70
Burpless Hybrid
Sweet Slice
Victory Hybrid
Pickling
Bravo Hybrid

Eggplant
Burpee Hybrid
Early Hybrid
Early Beauty Hybrid

Endive
Salad King
Green Curled
Full Heart Bavarian

Kale
Scotch Curled

Kohlrabi
Early White Vienna
Early Purple Vienna

Leek
Early
Titan
Main Season
Broad London
Giant Musselburgh

Lettuce
Butterhead
Buttercrunch
Loose Leaf
Salad Bowl
Ruby
Black-Seeded Simpson
Oakleaf
Heat Resistant
Slobolt
Matchless or Deer
 Tongue
Cos (Romaine)
Paris White

Melon
Cantaloupes
Ambrosia
Harper Hybrid
Burpee Hybrid

**New Zealand
Spinach**
No Varietal Listings

Okra
Emerald
Clemson Spineless

Onion
Sets
Stuttgarter
White Storage
White Portugal
Yellow Storage
Early Yellow Globe
Spanish
Yellow Sweet Spanish

Red
Red Weathersfield
Bunching
Beltsville Bunching

Parsnip
Harris' Model

Pea
Dwarf 15"
Little Marvel
Medium 30"
Lincoln
Tall 4–5'
Alderman
Heat-Resistant 30"
Wando
Green Arrow

**Pea (Edible
Podded)**
30"
Oregon Sugar Pod

Pepper
Bell
Earliest Red Sweet
Bell Boy Hybrid

Potato
White Early
Superior
Early Gem
White Midseason
Kennebec
White Late
Russet Sebago
Red Midseason
Red Pontiac

Pumpkin
Nonvining
Cinderella
Spirit

Radish
French Breakfast
Cherry Belle
Burpee White
White Icicle
Winter
Black Spanish
White Chinese

Raspberries
Durham

Rutabaga
Purple Top
Altasweet

Spinach
Early
America
Melody

Late
Winter Bloomsdale
Fall Planting
Cold Resistant Savoy

Strawberries
Everbearing Alpine
Alexandria
June-bearing
Fairfax
Sparkle
Sure-Crop

Squash (Summer)
Zucchini
Aristocrat (All-America
Winner)
President Hybrid
Yellow
Golden Girl
Goldbar Hybrid
Scallop
Patty Pan

Squash (Winter)
Vining
Waltham Butternut
Bush
Gold Nugget
Table King

Sweet Potato
Centennial

Swiss Chard
Green
Large White Rib
Red
Rhubarb

Tomato
Early
Early Girl
Midseason
Spring Giant
Main Season
Better Boy
Jet Star
Ultra Boy
Yellow
Sunray
Cherry
Small Fry
Pink
Beefmaster

Turnip
Tokyo Cross
Purple Globe

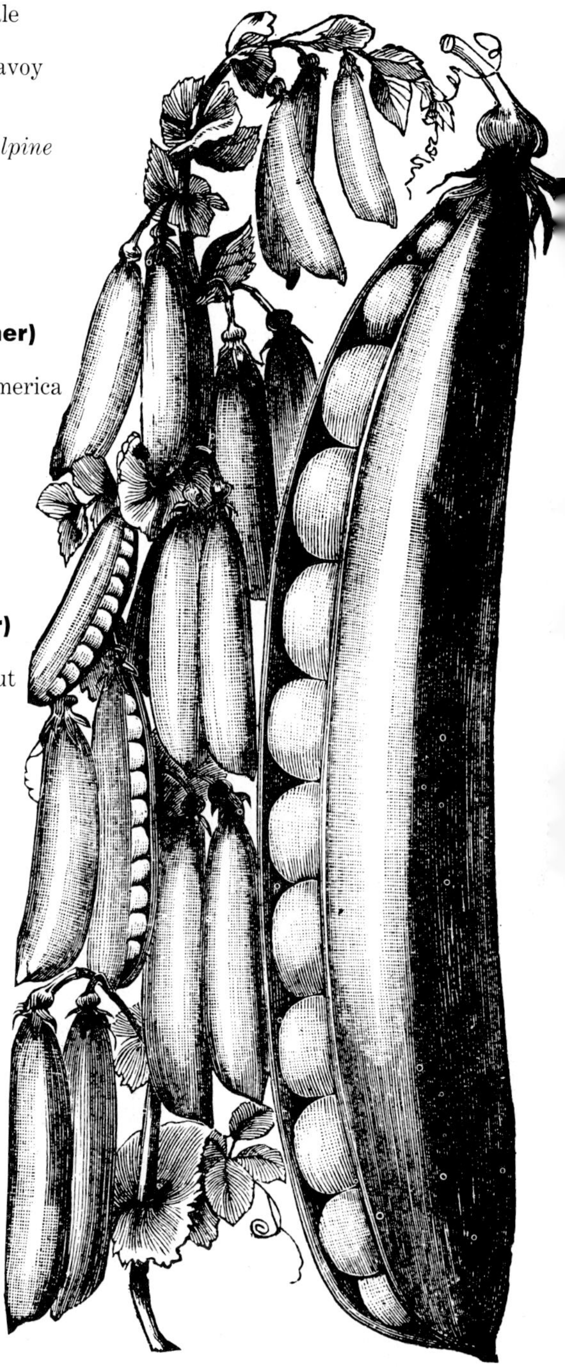

Paper white narcissus

Plant
Shamrock

Start Seedlings
Ageratum
Begonias
Petunias

Force
Rhubarb

Transplant
Streptocarpus
Strawberries

Special Events
Bean Sprouts
Hyacinths
Orchids

JAN

It's the dead of winter in the Victory Garden, but our sights are on spring. Toward the middle of the month we bring in the first of the forcing bulbs in order to have flowers early in February. After we take them from the cold frame, we set the bulbs into a semishaded, cool spot — 50 degrees or so — for a week. When the sprouts are 2 to 3 inches tall we move them to a bright sunny area where they'll mature. (Hyacinths need some special attention: see the entry on pages 275–276.)

January is the last of the slow winter months, so we take the opportunity to sow indoors some flowering plants for next year's garden, including ageratum, baby's breath, begonias, salpiglossis, statice, sweet peas, and snapdragons, as well as gloxinias for summer-flowering indoor potted plants.

This is also the time of the year to lavish some attention on the houseplants, before the outdoor garden begins to clamor for all the gardener's time. Once a month I give all our plants a soap and water bath to remove the winter's dust. (I never use anything designed to make the foliage shiny because I don't like houseplants that look as if they're made of vinyl; besides, some of those home polishing concoctions can actually kill plants by clogging the stomata, or breathing pores, of the leaves.) While I'm at work in the greenhouse, I take cuttings from fuchsias, heliotropes, lantanas, and geraniums so I'll have plants large enough to make a difference in the garden in the spring. I also inspect the dahlia tubers for rot, cutting away any diseased areas and dusting them with sulfur. Then I transplant last summer's sowing of cinerarias to their final homes in 4 or 6-inch pots; those planted in the smaller pots will develop into smaller plants, but because their roots are more confined, they'll blossom a little earlier.

Out in the garden, I sometimes use the branches of discarded Christmas trees as a mulch over roses, bulb beds, evergreen perennials, and in the cold frames. My soil preparation is long since done by January, but if it weren't, I would lay manure and ground limestone over the soil — or over the snow if need be — and let them leach down through the soil.

Finally, it's a good month to undertake indoor construction projects — for instance, making a composter, a set of cloches, or a cold frame — that are too time-consuming for the busier gardening months.

Ageratum The ageratum is one of the most free-flowering and cheery of annuals. The clustered flowers are small and fuzzy, and the colors, though limited mostly to shades of blue, are delightful. (There are white ageratums, too, which are reasonably effective in the garden, and pink ones as well, though these are often disappointing.) We've used ageratum in the Victory Garden in containers with taller plants, as edging plants along the walks, and to brighten the window boxes along the outer wall of the greenhouse. They have a long season of bloom and thrive in full sunshine. The ones that have particularly distinguished themselves are Blue Blazer, a clear light blue, and Royal Blazer, closer to purple in color. Both are compact varieties, usually growing no more than 6 inches tall at maturity.

Ageratum grow from tiny seeds and are slow to develop. We start our plants in late January to make sure that they are sturdy enough to make a good showing in the garden when we set them outdoors in the spring. Because ageratum are susceptible to damping-off fungi, we sprinkle the seeds sparingly over a ⅛-inch layer of milled sphagnum moss in a pot filled with potting soil. To prevent washing the minute

Blue Blazer ageratum plants along Main Street in the Victory Garden

seeds away, we bottom-water the pots. When the true leaves develop we transfer each seedling into private quarters in a six-pack. We move them a second time, into individual 4-inch pots, early in March and set them into a cold frame to harden-off before they go into the open garden in late April.

Bean Sprouts Sprouted seeds have everything to recommend them. They need very little care, grow within a matter of 3 or 4 days, require no light whatsoever to germinate, and are among the most nutritious foods available. For instance, ½ cup of sprouted alfalfa seeds contains as much Vitamin C as 6 glasses of orange juice, and the Vitamin B$_2$ will increase 1000 percent just in the process of germination, which also converts the seeds' starches to a form that's readily digestible. Many different kinds of beans can be sprouted, as well as alfalfa, chick peas, oats, sunflower seeds, and many others.

A jar of bean sprouts ready to eat

They could hardly be simpler to grow. Since they increase in bulk sixfold in the process of sprouting, I usually put about a ¼-inch layer of beans in the bottom of a quart mason jar, covering the seeds with about 1 inch of tepid water. After standing overnight, during which time they will soak up much of the water and increase in size by 100 or even 200 percent, I drain away the remaining soaking water and rinse the seeds with fresh water. During the next two days, I rinse the seeds three times a day with tepid water. By that time they will have sprouted and be ready to eat.

The germination process requires air circulation, so I cover the top of the jar with gauze or netting to let the air in while keeping the seeds clean. Also, since the seeds must be damp, but without standing water around them, I invert the jars to assure good drainage. Darkness isn't absolutely necessary for sprouting, but it does speed the process up and keeps the sprouts tender. Moreover, most of us find it easier to come up with a needed dark spot than with the sunshine most gardening projects require. Sprouts do well at average household temperatures, between 68 and 72, and given these conditions most seeds sprout within 3 to 4 days.

Begonias The wax begonia's botanical name is *Begonia semperflorens,* and it certainly lives up to its name; it is always in flower, whether indoors or out, in the shade or in full sun. Plants destined for the outdoors need to be started 4 to 6 months before the last expected frost, so many gardeners opt to buy the seedlings from garden centers in the spring, rather than wait half a year for these slowpokes to grow. But personally I mind their leisurely pace less than the price of garden center seedlings, so I start our plants from seed.

In the Victory Garden, where our frost-safe date is about April 20, we sow the seeds indoors early in January. The seeds are dustlike, so I just sprinkle them as evenly as possible onto potting soil that has been lightly covered with milled sphagnum moss. Tiny as the seeds are, they nevertheless have a high rate of germination and are often crowded as they emerge from the soil. The resulting poor air circulation is an invitation to damping-off fungus that could destroy the lot; so about three weeks after germination, while the plants are still very tiny, I move them to roomier quarters. They aren't large enough at this point to need a great deal of space, so I double them up and put two seedlings into each compartment of a six-pack, using the tip of a knife blade to prick them from their original locations.

While their size makes them rather difficult to handle at this age, it ultimately works to the gardener's advantage, as the root systems are too immature to feel much, if any, transplant shock. They grow rapidly in the six-packs; when they're about 2 inches tall I move them to individual 4-inch pots and let them grow on until May, when they're ready for the garden or window box.

Hyacinths In the Victory Garden greenhouse, January is the first month of spring, thanks to the spring-flowering bulbs that can be forced into bloom. Most of the

Fragrant French Roman hyacinths forced into bloom

bulb plants that have been rooting in cold frames since October can be brought indoors in January and will bloom with no further assistance from the gardener. Hyacinths, though, need a bit of special attention.

When the hyacinths are brought indoors in January, there are usually flower buds about 1 inch high peeking up from the bulbs. If the plants were put into bright light as is, the flowers would begin to open immediately, even though many of the buds would still be hidden within the bulbs. An easy way to prevent this abortive type of bloom is to keep the bulbs relatively warm, about 50 to 55 degrees, and to keep them in the dark a bit longer. I do this by inverting an empty flowerpot over each potful of plants, leaving it there until the stems grow tall enough to touch the inverted pot. Then I remove this dunce cap and set the plants into a bright spot to flower, keeping them as cool and moist during this period as nature would in the spring.

When they've finished flowering, I let the foliage continue growing because although the plants can't be forced indoors again, they can be planted outdoors as soon as the ground can be worked. There they will bloom for many years, and though the flowers will be small, they will have the full-scented fragrance for which hyacinths are famous.

Orchids This is the time of the year that orchid societies across the country hold their annual shows, so one January I decided to take advantage of the timing to indulge one of my own gardening pleasures: I devoted a major portion of one show to the wonders and needs of these spectacular plants.

There are over 25,000 different kinds of wild orchids scattered from the arctic to the tropics. The ones most suitable for greenhouse or indoor gardening are those that originate in the forests of Central and South America, Malaysia, and Southeast Asia. There are two general types of orchids that can be grown successfully indoors: terrestrial orchids, which, like most other plants, require soil for balance and nutrients; and epiphytes, or air plants. The latter are the more common of the two: in nature they actually live on the branches of trees, drawing their sustenance from the air, the

A collection of orchids, as easy to grow as African violets

rains, and from decaying plant matter caught on the trees' coarse bark. There's a dazzling range of possibilities within these two groups. Among the terrestrial ones are the so-called lady slipper, moth, and cymbidium orchids, while among the epiphytes there is great variety, the most common being the cattleya orchid. With some attention paid to their need for constant humidity, orchids do very well indoors and they can last practically forever. I have one that I bought for $3.00 twenty-five years ago and it still blossoms every year. I've divided it and given away portions to friends, and it's still a reliable and attractive resident of my greenhouse.

Among amateur gardeners, orchids have a forbidding reputation, but without reason. Their care isn't particularly complicated. They need moisture with good drainage and high humidity. I usually set the pots on trays with a layer of pebbles and water in the bottom. The evaporating moisture is enough to keep the air around them sufficiently humid. They need very little plant food: after all, most of the varieties of orchids suitable for indoor culture are air plants that simply cling to the bark of trees, using the bark for support. And true to their nature, epiphytes should not be planted in soil; chipped fir bark is the potting medium preferred by many or-

A single Cattleya orchid

chid fanciers, although others use the fibrous roots of *osmunda* fern or the stems of tree ferns.

Orchids can't usually be bought from garden centers, but they can be purchased through the mails. A good source of orchid dealers can be found in gardening magazines such as *Horticulture*, *Plants Alive*, and *Flower Grower*, but the best information is given in the American Orchid Society Bulletin, Botanical Museum of Harvard University, Cambridge, Massachusetts 02138. In each monthly issue dozens of reliable growers advertise plants that vary immensely in price depending upon their size and rarity. It's also a good idea, and an unforgettable treat, to visit an orchid show where there will be orchid devotees eager to pass on the fine points of their culture.

If you want to grow orchids, you will probably be happiest with your results if you begin by buying a few mature plants at the stage called "in sheath." This means that the flower buds are nearly ready to open. There are so many different kinds of orchids that you can easily get a selection of kinds whose flowers will open at a predictable time each year. Try your hand with some inexpensive varieties. The blossoms of these older varieties will still be outstandingly beautiful and will inspire you to add to your collection. As you become more skilled in orchid culture I suggest that you invest in some young seedlings. They may require several years' care before their first flowers open, but when they do you will be rewarded by some of the most glorious blooms known.

Petunias Petunias are among the most popular bedding plants in America. Originally from Argentina, where muddy white and magenta species still grow, they have been so improved by plant breeders that their colors now range from snowy white through hundreds of shades of pink and red to rich purple and yellow. They're available in an extraordinary variety of flower sizes and shapes, including some with frilled or double blossoms. Most petunias grow to be about a foot tall, and are useful in borders, hanging baskets, container gardens, and as spectacular additions to window boxes. The young plants grow very slowly and have to be started in January in order to be large enough for the garden in May. They're still worth the time needed, though, because the seedlings sold in the spring can eat up a surprisingly large portion of one's gardening budget.

Petunia seeds are so tiny that they can't tolerate covering after they're sown. Instead, I just sprinkle them as evenly and sparingly as possible over the surface of a thin layer of milled sphagnum moss on top of regular potting soil. To prevent washing the seeds away I water the soil by submerging the base of the pot until the soil surface is moist.

Once the pot has drained I slip it into a plastic bag until the seeds germinate; then I remove the plastic bag. When the plants' first true leaves appear, I transplant the still tiny seedlings into individual compartments in six-packs. Early in March they go into the cold frame for a period of controlled chill to toughen their cells so they can go into the open garden in May.

Rhubarb Rhubarb is one of the joys of the spring garden, and of the winter cellar as well if a gardener is foresighted enough to dig and store a few roots outdoors in the fall for forcing inside in midwinter. In November I dig a few mature rhubarb roots and put them in boxes set on bricks. With the arrival of cold weather, the roots freeze solid, inducing the plants' dormancy. (If you don't have freezing weather in your area, rhubarb will be difficult to grow or force.) Now as I need them, I carry boxes into my dark cellar and let them thaw. I keep the soil moist and watch the rhubarb sprouts appear. The leaves are tiny and insignificant, but the stems are long, pink, juicy and ready to be made into delicious sauce or pie. So January can be a time of snow or a time of harvest: it all depends on you and that eternal bugaboo of gardening, planning ahead. The rhubarb roots will be quite exhausted after production ceases, but they will still be alive and can be planted in the garden again. After growing for 2 or 3 years they will have regained enough strength to tolerate forcing again.

Shamrock In Ireland, there are two or three different kinds of shamrock. The most popular is one that we know, for 11 months of the year anyway, as white clover. It's a quick and simple thing to sow a few seeds in January, producing a potted crop of shamrock about 2 inches tall by St. Patrick's Day. I just sprinkle a pinch of seeds into ordinary potting soil in a 3-inch pot, and cover them with a ⅛-inch layer of milled sphagnum moss. They need water, sunshine, and warm temperatures to grow, but they don't need much else.

Strawberries By January, the alpine strawberries sown in December have developed their first true leaves, and although they're still no more than ½ inch tall, they're ready to be pricked out and transplanted into individual sections in six-packs. It's important when transplanting most plants that they be set into their new soil at the same depth they grew in the old, but it's especially important with strawberries: if they're too deep, the crowns of the plants are smothered; if they are too shallow, the roots dry out and die.

The seedlings increase in size very rapidly indoors in January and February. The next step for these plants is the

Opposite: Cyclamens will bloom all winter

281 JAN

cold frame in March. Then it's into the open garden in April. By June the first berries are ready to pick.

Streptocarpus   After 2 months in their little greenhouse, the streptocarpus seedlings have developed their first true leaves and deserve new surroundings, but they're still so small that the transplanting operation is nearly as delicate as the sowing. Even the gentlest finger-hold would squeeze the life out of them, so they have to be lifted from their protected surroundings on the tip of a knife. I don't try to remove individual seedlings from the jar; instead, I just

Streptocarpus, a unique flowering house plant

slip a cake spatula under the soil and remove a section of seedlings, then lift them one by one on my knife tip.

I usually put them 1 inch apart in a flat of ordinary potting soil. Several dozen will fit together in a 12 × 18–inch flat, small as they are. After about 2 months, they'll be a whopping ½ inch tall, and ready for individual 2-inch pots or six-packs. They won't flower until about 10 months after the seed is sown, but the blossoms are so lovely that the wait is well worthwhile.

Q&A

Q: What causes a white mold on the soil surface of my houseplants?

A: If it's a wet mold, it could be caused by over-watering, the primary houseplant killer. Or it may be an encrustation of fertilizer salts, in which case you should scrape away as much of it as you can, and then water the plant every hour for three or four hours to wash some of that fertilizer away. Or you can just repot it in fresh soil.

Q: The lower leaves of our bird's nest fern are forever turning brown, shriveling up, and dying, even though there are always 1 or 2 new leaves growing from the center of the plant. What's wrong?

A: Your plant needs more humidity. Set it on a tray of pebbles and water so the evaporating moisture will keep the area humid. It's also a good idea to group a few of these plants together, rather than isolating one lone plant.

Q: We've started apples, oranges, avocados, and Chinese dogwoods, but we've never been able to find the seeds for a banana tree. Can you help?

A: I'm afraid not. You can't buy the seeds of edible bananas because those little brown specks in the fruit are only vestigial seeds — bananas are sterile and have to be grown from suckers that arise at the base of old plants. There are ornamental bananas, though, that will grow very rapidly from rather large seeds. Try the George Park Seed Company in Greenwood, South Carolina, for seeds.

Q: Can I root a twig of a holly tree in water?

A: No, you'd have to set it in damp sand. And you'll need the patience of Job, as these plants are very slow to send out roots. They can be started from seed, too, but the first seedlings don't appear until 14 months after planting.

Q: My sunny windowsill space is limited. Can I grow vegetable and flower seedlings under artificial light?

A: You can grow very husky seedlings under artificial light. Make sure to keep the lights on about 16 hours a day, and you'll have better seedlings than if you put the plants on a windowsill that received insufficient natural light.

SOWING SEEDS INDOORS

In our first year in the Victory Garden, we were so late getting started that we had no time to grow our own seedlings. We had to join the procession to the local gardening center, where we bought our young plants. This is not the way I like to start a garden: the seedlings are expensive, and if one shops at the wrong time they're apt to be old, woody, and leggy. What is more, it was our bad luck to pick up some cauliflower seedlings that were infected with clubroot, one more reason to grow your own plants when possible. Ever since that first year we've started the seedlings in our greenhouse or hotbed, and we've had the benefit of perfect little plants at almost no cost. January may seem early in the year to start thinking about seedlings for next summer's garden, but it isn't. We put some of our early crops out in March, so the seeds must be sown in January to give them sufficient time to reach proper size.

Seed-sowing doesn't call for a great deal of equipment, but a few items are crucial. Light and heat are essential, whether provided by a greenhouse, hotbed, sunny windowsill, or artificial lights. The other necessities are containers, planting medium, seeds, milled sphagnum moss, and labels.

Containers Plants will grow in almost any kind of container, whether an old soup can or a styrofoam coffee cup, but it's easier to grow uniform, husky plants with the more traditional materials used by commercial growers. Nowadays this means mostly plastic pots, trays, and flats, as well as small pots made of compressed peat moss. We avoid clay pots because they're porous and dry out quickly, and there's no greater danger to newly sown seeds than drought. The advantage to the plastic containers is that they are lightweight and can be easily cleaned and used over and over again. The peat pots, on the other hand, are relatively expensive because they can only be used once, but they're gentle on the plants because the entire thing is planted, pot and all, with a minimum of shock to the seedling.

Planting Medium It's possible to make up one's own potting mix, and it may be cheaper than buying it, but I usually use the commercial products, either potting soil or soilless mix, primarily because it's more convenient but also because I can depend upon it to be uniform and free of insects, been improved with such materials as peat moss, perlite, vermiculite, coarse sand and fertilizer, then pasteurized to kill insects, diseases, and weed seeds. Soilless mix is a combination of equal parts peat moss and vermiculite, plus ground limestone and nutrients, and contains no true soil at all. Generally the potting soil is more expensive than soilless mixes. Soilless mixes, incidentally, were developed at various agricultural colleges in response to the needs of commercial growers who found too much variation in the soil mixes available to them.

Seeds I plant only the best true-to-name seeds I can buy because I know that it's the most economical thing to do. It takes as much time, effort, and fertilizer to grow an inferior variety as it does to grow a superior one. When it comes to seeds, it doesn't pay to gamble. When I sow, I take into account the percentage of germination given on the seed package and sow extra seeds if necessary. For instance, if the package indicates a 60 percent germination rate, I sow roughly 40 percent more seeds than I need plants. (For more about the seeds we use in the Victory Garden, see the December feature.) Above all else in seed sowing, allow enough space between the seeds so that the seedlings will not crowd each other before they are large enough to transplant. To ignore this warning is to risk losing all of the seedlings to damping-off fungi or to have thin, spindly seedlings that never outgrow their initial weakness.

Milled Sphagnum Moss During World War I, sphagnum moss was used as a wound dressing because it aerated an injury while keeping it sterile. It performs essentially the same function with plants. For seed sowing we use milled sphagnum moss, which means that the ordinary long-fibered material has been ground to a nearly powderlike consistency that allows it to be spread evenly on the soil surface. For large seeds, such as tomato, pepper, etc., we use a light sprinkling — ⅛ inch or so — over newly sown seeds, and it has all but eliminated damping-off disease from our list of plagues in the Victory Garden. For tiny seeds, we first

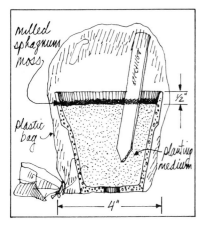

cover the soil with a layer of moss, then sow the seeds on top of the moss without covering them. The moist moss assures good germination. There is one peculiarity about milled sphagnum moss that is not commonly known. It concerns water absorption: when cold water is applied, it runs off as though from a duck's back; but when hot water is used, it is absorbed instantly.

Labels These needn't be fancy, but some sort of labels are a must. Without a record of the variety, color, and planting date, there's very little way for a novice gardener to distinguish one unfamiliar pot of seedlings from another. I prefer 3- to 4-inch white-painted wooden pot labels because if they should become lost in the garden, they

will disintegrate. Plastic labels last forever, are expensive, and are prone to breaking.

The procedure for sowing seeds indoors varies with the particular seed and the container, but there are some general rules. First of all, begin with a clean pot large enough to accommodate the number of plants expected — in the Victory Garden, we usually use a 4-inch pot — and fill it with firmed-down planting medium to within ½ inch of the rim. Then sow the seeds, add milled sphagnum moss as the size of the seeds determines, and bottom-water by setting the pot into a pan of water until the moss feels damp to the touch, a sign that the water has been drawn all through the soil. I recommend bottom-watering the seeds at first because it protects them from a disturbing overhead shower. To avoid the necessity of watering newly sown seeds before they germinate, I usually slip the pots into clear plastic bags, which helps to maintain a highly humid atmosphere around the seeds. I put them in bright light, but not sun, and remove the plastic as soon as sprouts appear. The object is to keep the seeds from drying out, maintaining dampness without saturation. Most seeds sprout quite uniformly when they are kept at 65 to 75 degrees. Once their growth is visible above the soil, they should be removed to a spot where they'll receive direct sunlight all day long.

New gardeners soon discover that all seedlings are not alike. Even from the beginning, some seedlings, such as grass, onions, and corn, emerge as a single blade; others, such as cabbage, tomatoes, and pansies, have twin leaves as they appear above the soil. Onion relatives, such as leeks and chives, should be transplanted when they're about 1½ or 2 inches tall, but

Prick out the seedlings by their seed leaves not the stem.

for most other vegetables, the transplanting time is judged not by the seedlings' height but by the development of the third leaf, called the first true leaf, that arises between the twin leaves, known as seed leaves.

When I transplant seedlings, whether to another container for growing on, or into the garden, I prick them out of the medium, usually with the point of a wooden label, and hold them by the seed leaf, not by the stem, as even the gentlest pressure on tiny stems could injure the tender cells. I use a pencil or label to make holes for them in their new locations, and generally set them in at the same level they had been growing in the other container. If, however, the seedlings are slender and weak, I set them so that their seed leaves are just above the soil line, where they should be if the plants were of normal growth. Some seedlings are still very small — under ½ inch — when they form their true leaves, but they need to be transplanted anyway, as the poor air circulation around crowded seedlings invites damping-off disease. Besides, seedlings transplanted at such a tender age rarely feel the shock of relocation.

Primroses

Plant
Begonias (Tuberous-rooted)

Start Seedlings
Annuals
Beets
Celery
Leeks
Lettuce
Onions

Take Cuttings
Camellias

Special Events
Cactus
Japanese Pittosporum
Terrariums

FEB

In the Victory Garden February is the bridge month between winter and spring. We continue through the month to force bulb plants, including tulips, crocuses, hyacinths, freesias, and both paper whites and hardy types of narcissus. At the end of their flowering period, we throw the paper white narcissus bulbs away, because they can't be forced again and aren't hardy enough to survive outdoors in our garden. But the other bulbs we keep growing for as long as we can, as this is the period during which the bulbs are building strength for their next blossoming stage. We give them bright sunshine and feed them now and then with a liquid fertilizer. When the tops turn yellow we stop watering them and store them in a shed to dry, still in their pots. The freesia bulbs can be forced again, but the others can't, so we store the hyacinths, crocuses, hardy narcissus, and tulips in a cool dry place until we plant them in the garden in the fall. There they will blossom again the following spring and for years to come.

February is also the month to begin forcing branches of flowering trees and shrubs, including forsythia, spirea, Japanese quince, apple, plum, peach, and pussy willow. There are two reasons that some gardeners don't have success with forcing branches: they try to force flowers too quickly in a warm room; or they fail to counteract the arid indoor air, so the latent flower or buds dehydrate instead of opening. But there's a way to avoid both these problems. First of all, wrap the bunches of stems in several layers of damp newspaper; then set them into water in a cool, brightly lit but not sunny room. The buds will stay springtime-moist and will open to their fullest beauty.

Outside in the Victory Garden, it's time to put the hotbed to use, sowing some of the crops that will be transplanted into the garden later in the spring. And it's time to survey the effects of the winter: frost can heave plants up out of the soil — recently planted perennials are especially vulnerable to this problem — so if a stretch of mild weather comes along, it's a good idea to press the plants back into place in the soil. That midwinter thaw is a good time to prune grapevines, too. If they are allowed to go without pruning until the buds begin to swell, the cut stems will "bleed" great quantities of sap.

Annuals I must confess that I've never grown an all-vegetable garden. Flowers are what really make my world go around, and besides, I think other people like them too, especially when I pick a summer bouquet for them.

Most summer flowers, like summer vegetables, are annuals. (Some, like petunias and peppers, are really perennial in nature, but we grow them as annuals because our growing seasons are limited by cold weather.) To circumvent the shortness of our seasons we give both annual flowers and many annual vegetables a head start by sowing their seeds indoors several weeks or even months before we set them outside.

Just as some of our vegetable seedlings require more lead time than others, so do our annuals. For example, we sowed the seeds of browallias in December and begonias in January. Now, in February, the pace quickens. Because the plant list is so long and because it is more useful for you to know when to plant the seeds in your garden than when I plant them in mine, I have divided the annuals into three groups according to the length of time normally required from seed sowing to plants large enough to set into the garden. There is some overlapping of plants from one list to another because plants grow faster later in the spring than they do

Alyssum plants in the Victory Garden annual border

closer to winter; in a sense some of them nearly make up for lost time, practically catching up with similar varieties planted a week or two earlier. The ever-longer hours of sunshine that occur as springtime advances account for the more rapid growth of late-planted seedlings.

Group I includes plants that require a minimum of seven to nine weeks from seeding indoors to planting in the garden: fibrous-rooted begonia, seed-grown geranium, impatiens, browallia, lobelia, ice plant, sensitive plant, petunia (fringed, ruffled, and double-flowering types), scarlet sage, verbena, and Madagascar periwinkle.

Group II includes plants that require a minimum of six to eight weeks from seeding indoors to planting in the garden: ageratum, sweet alyssum, globe amaranth, arctotis, China aster, bells of Ireland, blue lace flower, castor bean, cardinal climber, cathedral bells, cosmos (yellow and orange types), dusty miller, lupine, cape-marigold, nemesia, flowering tobacco, petunia (bedding types), China pink, portulaca, annual phlox, painted tongue, snapdragon, stock, and strawflower.

Group III includes plants that usually require four to five weeks from seed sowing until they are ready to set into the garden: sweet alyssum, globe amaranth, arctotis, balloon vine, calendula, celosia, annual chrysanthemum, clarkia, spider flower, cornflower, cosmos, Chinese forget-me-not, Swan river daisy, winged everlasting, annual gaillardia, godetia, marigold, nemophila, petunia (bedding types), pincushion flower, poor man's orchid, and zinnia.

Beets Beets are one of the few root vegetables that can be successfully transplanted, so we take advantage of this fact late in February by starting the seedlings either in the hotbed or the greenhouse. I handle the hotbed sowing just as I do the open garden planting, putting the seeds in at 1-inch intervals in 2 rows about 5 inches apart. Beet seeds are composite seeds, meaning that each seed is capable of producing 3 or 4 plants, so if the planting interval isn't kept under control, thinning will be a bother. I leave the hotbed crop right there in the protected warmth until early April, when I transplant the seedlings into the garden.

If I start a crop in the greenhouse instead of a hotbed, I just sprinkle the seeds thinly onto a flat of ordinary potting soil and cover them with milled sphagnum moss. I thin them to stand about 1 inch apart when the true leaves develop, and transplant them into the garden in April.

Begonias In the last few years the Rieger begonia, a spectacular new member of this popular family, has taken the greenhouse business by storm, but beautiful as the Rieger is, it will never overshadow the tuberous-rooted begonia, one

A *Rieger begonia, popular new addition to the begonia family*

of the plants from which it was developed. Tuberous-rooted begonias are mimics in the plant world, with flowers that look like carnations, camellias, narcissus, and roses; the petals may be smooth, ruffled, frilled, picoteed, bi-colored, or crested. The blossoms come in every imaginable color except blue and green, and may be as much as 10 inches in diameter. Some types have trailing stems that make them ideal for hanging containers; others have upright stems that vary from eight to fifteen inches in height. Tuberous-rooted begonias bloom from June through October if they're planted in rich, organic soil in a shady, cool spot in the garden, and kept moist all summer.

The tubers from which these plants grow are rough-textured brown knobs about the size of plums. The round side of the tuber is the bottom, and the concave side is the top. I usually plant the dormant tubers in shallow flats of damp peat moss late in February, setting the tubers so that the tops barely show above the moss. The growth rate varies from tuber to tuber, so as each sends out strong growth, I transplant it into a 6-inch pot of rich soil composed of 2 parts compost and 1 part each of peat moss and soil. When the weather becomes warm enough, around the first of June, I move the plants outdoors where they'll bloom until the fall. When frosts kill the top growth, I dig the tubers and store them for the winter. (For storage information, see the October entry.) Properly cared for, the tubers will live and produce handsome flowers for many years.

Cactus Cactuses are sometimes called the camels of the plant world because they can withstand the toughest droughts simply by relying on their own reserves. In fact, one of the theories about cactus thorns is that, in addition to discouraging thirsty animals interested in taking advantage of this natural reservoir, they protect the plants from the harshest rays of the sun. In their native environment some cactuses grow in full sun and others grow in the shadow of taller desert plants, so contrary to popular belief, not all cactuses can sit happily in the scorching sun. Cactuses can nevertheless tolerate some rather severe conditions; of all houseplants they are probably the most immune to owners' mistakes. Indoors they like a bright windowsill with sun most of the day. During the summer we put ours outdoors but we introduce them to the hot sun gradually so they don't come down with cactus sunburn. (If the plants are kept inside through the summer they can stand bright reflected light without direct sun at midday.)

Cactuses produce gorgeous flowers if they're handled correctly. First, they need cool temperatures during the winter; 45 to 50 degrees is ideal. Second, they shouldn't be watered from November through February except to prevent the tissues from shriveling. The coolness and lack of moisture trigger the formation of flowers later in the season. The rest of the year the soil should be kept barely moist. I know of one woman who takes her watering cues from a Tucson, Arizona, newspaper to which she subscribes. When the paper reports rain, she waters her cactuses. Her system must work because her cactuses are healthy and free-flowering.

About every 3 or 4 years, cactus plants should be repotted, a job that terrifies most beginning cactus growers who fear for their fingers. If some precautions are taken, though, there's nothing much to this job. Obviously the main thing to avoid is touching the cactus, because the thorns easily become embedded in the skin, causing no end of discomfort. When I handle cactuses, I wear thick gloves. Also, to repot cactuses without being pierced by thorns, I make a cactus-gripper by folding a few sheets of newspaper into a strap, and use the strap to hold the plant as I knock it out of its pot and set it into larger quarters.

I always pot cactuses in clay pots because the moisture content of these plants make them very top-heavy, and the weight of the pots helps keep them stable. Besides, the loss of moisture through their porous walls that I usually complain of

with clay pots actually works to the plants' advantage here, as cactuses demand excellent drainage.

When it comes to potting soil, there are as many different mixtures as there are cactus growers. My basic recipe calls for 3 cups each of potting soil and coarse sand, mixed with about ¼ cup of aquarium charcoal. To this mixture I add a tablespoon of ground limestone to sweeten the soil and help the plants form sturdy, showy thorns, and another tablespoon of bone meal, a mild slow-release fertilizer that will feed the plants through their long life. I start off by putting a little of this mixture in the bottom of a pot and then use the newspaper strap to grip the plant, knock it out of the old pot, and set it into the new one. Rather than putting my hand in close proximity to those dangerous thorns I use a long blunt-ended stick to tamp the soil around the roots. Once repotted, the plant will thrive for another 3 or 4 years before it needs shifting to a larger pot.

There is a relatively new bit of creative cactus gardening that produces dramatic results with a minimum of effort. Cactus growers have known for years that whenever cactus seeds are sown, some of the seedlings emerge from the soil in bright colors; these seedlings live only a short time because they have no chlorophyll in their systems and are unable to manufacture food on their own. A few years ago an enterprising Japanese gardener began experimenting with these heretofore doomed young seedlings, and found that they could be grafted to healthy green cactuses if the graft was done while the seedlings were still young. As a result of his work, garden centers now carry a whole range of unique cactus plants topped off with brightly colored domes.

The technique is also easily done at home. Any cactus plant may be grafted onto any other cactus plant, but for the sake of aesthetics and balance, I chose for our Victory Garden specimen a round small section from an Easter Lily cactus as the top of the graft, or scion, and a slender, single-stemmed cactus as the understock. The graft requires nothing more than putting the freshly cut tissue of the scion against the similar tissue of the understock and holding it firmly in place until the cells knit together. I began by slicing off the tip of the understock. I also pared the sides of the understock slightly, so it wouldn't continue to grow and push off the newly grafted section. Then I used a pair of tongs to set the bristly scion atop the understock. I anchored it with two lengths of lightweight chain crisscrossed over the scion, providing just enough weight to hold the sections in place as they grew. In 2 weeks I removed the chain and tested the graft by gently tugging on it. It had knit perfectly and has been growing and blossoming each spring since the graft was made.

Camellias These natives of China and Japan need the same cool, shady, moist, acid-soil conditions that keep azaleas thriving. Depending on the variety, each shrub produces its white, pink, red, or multicolored flowers for a 4- to 6-week period through the late fall, winter, and early spring. They last for years in the same pot.

Camellia plants are occasionally available through garden centers or mail-order catalogues, but if you have the patience, you have an almost perfect chance of rooting a cutting from a friend's plant. Our Victory Garden cutting took months to root, but it didn't ask much of me in the process. I began with a 4-inch tip of a stem, stripping it of all but 2 leaves at the tip. Then I dipped the lower end in water, moistening it to hold the rooting powder, and set it into damp sand. Some 4 months later when I noticed new leaf growth at the tip of the cutting, I knew the plant had rooted and was ready for repotting, so I transferred it to a soil rich in peat moss.

Camellias are garden shrubs in mild parts of the country and even in cool areas they benefit greatly from being put outdoors in a lightly shaded spot for the summer. It is a good idea to dust the soil with a slow-acting acid-type fertilizer such as cotton seed meal about the time the last flowers fade

Slow-growing camellia cuttings after one year

and the new vegetative growth begins. During the summer outdoors, a period in which the soil must be kept moist at all times, the current season's growth matures and fat flower buds develop at the ends of the twigs. Often clusters of buds develop and some fanciers, looking for the largest possible flowers, remove all but one bud on each stem tip. If the excess buds are not removed, the flowers will be a bit smaller, but there will be more of them, usually over a longer period of time.

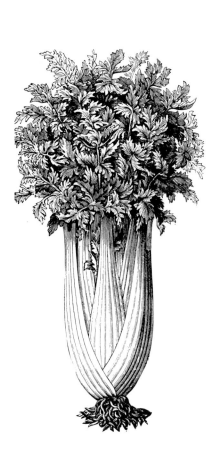

Celery It's with good reason that most gardeners don't bother with celery. This vegetable thrives on soil so wet and full of organic matter that it could double as swampland. It needs a long head start in warm temperatures, a long growing season, and some time-consuming care as it develops. Still, the crop we've grown in the Victory Garden has done well. (For more on our techniques of celery growing, see the March, June, and September entries.)

We have to sow celery seeds in February in the Victory Garden in order to give the plants time to develop. I buy fresh celery seeds each year — old seeds aren't dependable and those packaged for use in kitchens usually aren't viable. Planting is easy: I sift the seeds sparingly over regular potting soil, then I cover them with about ⅛ inch of milled sphagnum moss, firm them down, and water them. They need to be kept moist and at about 65 degrees during their slow germination period, which often requires as much as 3 weeks. About a month after they germinate, they're ready for transplanting.

Japanese Pittosporum I occasionally am asked to play Dr. Crockett to friends' troubled houseplants. And I have, in my days, seen some of the sorriest patients imaginable, but the Japanese pittosporum dropped off one day holds the record as the sickest ever. It was gigantic — a good 3½ feet tall — but even for its great size it was overpotted. It had been chopped in the name of pruning. The leaves were pathetic, and a gang of red spider mites was at work on their undersides.

The first remedial step was to prune all the straggly stems back to about 10 inches from the soil line. The plant was grossly lopsided anyway, so this wasn't much of a sacrifice. Then I knocked the plant out of the pot, pulled away about half the ball of earth, and repotted it in a smaller pot. I took care of the insects with a forcible spray of water. It was a simple prescription, but it was all that was needed. When I gave it back to its owner, I included a list of the conditions that would keep the plant healthy: 4 or more hours of direct sunlight every day (or at least bright indirect light); night

temperatures between 40 and 55 and day temperatures between 65 and 80; a chance to dry out a bit between waterings;
and feedings twice a year, once in the early spring and once in
the early summer.

Leeks These members of the onion family are among
our most successful crops in the Victory Garden, a success
they owe both to their very early start and to the rich bed of
compost in which they grow in the garden. We always start
some seedlings in the greenhouse in March, and if we have
the space, we start a backup crop in the hotbed in February.
Both these crops mature at about the same rate and are ready
for the open ground in April.

First I make shallow rows in the hotbed soil and
sprinkle the seeds in thinly. When they're about 1 inch tall I
thin them to 1-inch intervals. Around the first of April I turn

the heat off in the hotbed, which in effect converts it to a cold frame; in this cold-frame atmosphere the plants harden-off so they're sturdy enough to transplant outdoors by the middle of the month.

Lettuce The lettuce that I sow in my hotbed in February is on the table in May, a welcome early bonus from the garden. I just sprinkle the seeds in a shallow row in the hotbed, and thin them as they grow large enough to touch each other. When they're about 2 inches tall I move them to individual 3-inch pots and set them into the cold frame for a couple of weeks of hardening-off. I transplant them into the open garden in April.

Onions We find in the Victory Garden that one of the most satisfactory ways to grow onions is from sets — small onion bulbs that we plant in the open garden in March. The disadvantage to sets is that relatively few varieties — only those that tolerate storage — are available in this form; other varieties less tolerant to storage must be started from seed.

We sow seeds indoors in February to give them 2 months of growing time before they go into the ground in April. This not only gives them a head start, it means they mature before the arrival of hot weather, helping to keep their flavor mild. We sow the seeds sparingly in small rows in a flat of soilless mix, cover them with milled sphagnum moss, and water the flat. They germinate quickly and when the seedlings, which resemble small blades of grass, begin to crowd one another we thin or transplant them to 1-inch intervals and let them grow on until they're ready for moving into the open garden in early April.

Terrariums Terrariums are small gardens grown entirely within clear glass or plastic containers. Almost any container will do, but those with hand-sized openings are easier to work with; small-necked bottles require the deft use of specialized tools.

Assembling a terrarium takes some time and a steady hand but there's nothing complicated about the job. I usually make what's known as a tropical terrarium, composed of plants native to warm, jungle atmospheres. (There are also woodland terrariums, made up of plants that grow on the forest floor, but many of these plants are on the endangered list and shouldn't be removed from their natural location.) When I select the plants from the florist I try to pick those with a variety of foliage shape and color, usually making sure that no plant is taller than 4 inches. I also pick slow-growing plants of types that thrive under similar growing conditions.

The first step is to decide ahead of time how the plants are to be arranged in the terrarium, which is purely a matter of personal choice. They're easy to move around while they're still in pots on the counter top, but rearranging them once they're in the container is considerably more difficult.

In planting a terrarium, I begin by putting a layer of planting medium on the bottom of the container. I use 3 parts of ordinary potting soil to 1 part crushed charcoal; the charcoal is the same material used as a filter in aquariums, and it purifies soil just as it does aquarium water. There should be about 1 inch of the soil mix in the container. To make sure it lands neatly without splattering up on the sides of the jar where it would be all but impossible to clean off, I drop the soil into the container through a funnel. If the pot is particularly tall I use a paper tube as an extension on the funnel.

Before I set the plants in I peel away about half of the soil around the roots, leaving the root balls tidy and shallow and easy to manage. To set the plants into the container I use a variety of tools, most of them borrowed from the kitchen or easily constructed. For example, a wooden label tied to a long dowel can serve as a sort of trowel, scooping a hole for the plant in the soil. For holding the plants and setting them into a shallow container, a pair of kitchen tongs is perfect; for deeper pots, long specialized tongs are available from garden

A flourishing new terrarium

centers. All plants, whether in a terrarium or not, need to be firmed into their new soil; my tool for this is nothing more elaborate than a wine cork impaled on a long pointed stick.

Once the plants are in place I cover the soil surface with a layer of ground fir bark, which gives the little forest an attractive natural-looking floor.

Terrariums don't require much in the way of maintenance. The primary danger is overwatering, which means certain death. The best idea is to keep the plants so dry they nearly wilt, which keeps their growth under control in addition to keeping them healthy. They need bright light, but not direct sunlight: the sun's heat, concentrated by the glass, would parboil the plants in a matter of a few minutes. Lastly, they shouldn't be given so much as a drop of fertilizer. The object of terrarium culture is to keep the plants small and healthy for years in cramped surroundings; if they're fertilized they'll outgrow their container very quickly.

There's a controversy of sorts as to whether it's best to cover terrariums or not. With tightly fitting covers, they don't need watering at all, as the moisture will circulate through the containers in a miniature eco-system. However, the condensation along the sides of such containers may make it all but impossible to see the plants. My preference is to leave the covers off and attend to their infrequent watering needs, though covering a terrarium is a good way to help it survive an owner's month-long vacation.

Q&A

Q: I bought myself a beautiful gardenia plant a while ago. It hasn't produced any new buds since it's been in my house. What's wrong?

A: When gardenias have budding problems, temperature is usually the villain. They like their nights at around 60 degrees and their days at 70 to 75 degrees. If they're subjected to warmer nights, they don't produce new flower buds. They also need bright sunshine, constantly moist soil, fertilizer once a month, and occasional applications of either iron sulfate or iron chelate if the plants' foliage becomes pale in color. All in all, these plants are a challenge to any gardener.

Q: I have a lovely ivy geranium plant. Can I grow another plant from a cutting?

A: Sure. Just take a tip cutting about 3 or 4 inches long, dip the lower end in rooting powder, and set it into damp sand. When new top growth appears, you'll know the roots have formed, so you can transplant the cutting to potting soil.

Q: Can you give me some guidance in misting my houseplants?

A: During the winter, when plants are indoors in a heated house, the dry air can be very hard on them. It's a good idea to spray daily with an atomizer, using lukewarm water. Keep the sprayer about 18 inches from the plants, as the goal is to create a humid atmosphere, not to wet the foliage. (Don't spray fuzzy-leaved plants such as African violets.) Another tip: if you grow a number of plants close together on a tray of moist pebbles, misting will not be necessary.

Q: Mealy bugs have attacked the crowns of all my African violets. Can I save them? What can I do to prevent this from happening again?

A: The only thing to do with those infested plants is to throw them away and begin again with new plants; mealy bugs are very difficult to get rid of. In the future, quarantine new plants when they come into your house and inspect them carefully before you add them to your collection.

Q: I have a recipe that calls for marrow squash. What is it?

A: It's the name the English have given to the vegetable we call zucchini or summer squash.

Q: Why can't I keep my English ivy plants safe from red spider mites?

A: Probably because your house or apartment is too warm. These plants can take any amount of cold indoors: they do best when the night temperatures fall below 60 degrees and the days are no warmer than 70 degrees. In the heat they attract the red spider mites. To control the mites without chemicals, wash the plants weekly with a forceful spray of cold water directed at the undersides of the leaves.

TOOLS OF THE VICTORIOUS GARDENER

Gardening tools are one of the biggest and longest lasting investments that gardeners make, so my advice is to buy the best you can afford. There are no bargains in this area except that good tools are practically indestructible. And once you've got them, take the best care of them that you can: store them under cover, and keep them sharpened, cleaned, and coiled as they need it.

The Victory Garden potting shed shelters quite a collection of gardening tools, some that are absolutely critical, others that are time-saving but nonessential, some that can be easily constructed in a home workshop. Here are the ones we use.

Indispensables *Cold Frame:* For complete use and construction, see pages 26–27.

Bulb planter

Bulb Planter: A simple, toothed cylinder that cuts tulip-planting time to a fraction of what it takes with a spade or trowel.

Cultivating Tools: There's no doing without hoes and weeders in the garden. For more on the ones we use, see the May feature, page 99.

Spading Fork: I recommend that gardeners buy the best 4-tined spading fork they can afford, as this is a tool that will be called on for some of the heaviest tasks in the garden.

Long-Handled Shovel: In this case, a medium-sized tool is best; the smaller ones make jobs last forever, and the larger ones are too taxing for the weekend gardener.

Rakes: We have two, a medium-sized iron rake and a leaf rake.

Shears: Again, we have two pairs, one hand shears and one hedge shears. Poor shears are abominable; good ones are a joy.

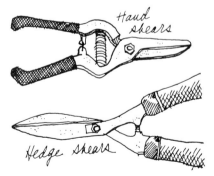

Hand shears

Hedge shears

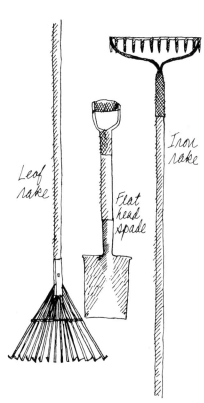

Leaf rake

Flat head spade

Iron rake

Spade: An invaluable tool for slicing down through tough, grassy surfaces. We sharpen ours with a file after every use.

Hand Trowel: The critical factor in trowels is one-piece construction, which eliminates the danger of bending or breaking the tool.

Hand Trowel

Sprayer: The hose-end attachment is the cheapest and easiest to use, but the compressed air sprayers are more portable and don't depend on a nearby water supply. We use both in the Victory Garden for spraying fertilizers and insecticides.

Wheelbarrow or Garden Cart: A good wheelbarrow is well-balanced so that it is smooth and stable as it moves, and has a pneumatic tire for easy pushing. A large-wheel garden cart is even better than a wheelbarrow because it doesn't tip over easily and can carry heavy loads with little effort.

Watering Can: We use a 2-gallon galvanized steel can with a fine spray or rose.

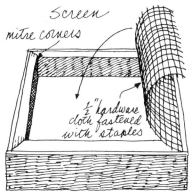

Screen

mitre corners

½" hardware cloth fastened with staples

Homemade Indispensables

Planting Board: A 4-foot length of wood that's beveled along one of the long sides so it can be used to make a furrow, and notched along the other side to serve as a guide to planting intervals. Ours has large notches at the 1-foot intervals and shallow notches at the 6-inch intervals. We rarely go a day without using a planting board.

Screens: We've made a variety of simple sifting screens in the Victory Garden. Our largest has ½-inch-gauge hardware cloth stretched over a 3-foot-square frame of 2 by 4s; we prop it up on stakes and

use it for sifting large quantities of either compost or soil. We also have 2 smaller screens for use in the greenhouse, one of ¼-inch gauge and another of ⅛-inch gauge, both set on 8-inch-square frames.

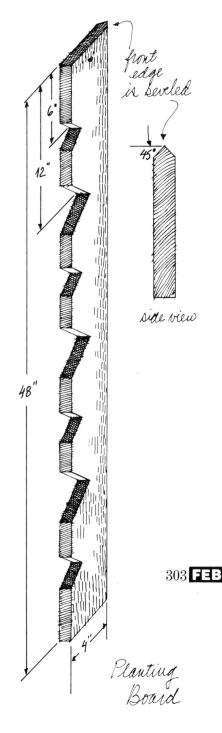

front edge is beveled

45°

6"

12"

side view

48"

4"

Planting Board

multi-dibble

Dibbles: These tools have been around for years; single dibbles are nothing more complicated than metal-pointed hole-pokers for small plants or bulbs. We've made two multi-dibbles in the Victory Garden, and they're very time-saving little tools. Ours are simply short lengths of dowels pegged in a board at established intervals. With them we can make 8 to 16 holes simultaneously. It speeds the planting of seedlings and insures accurate spacing.

Row Marker: There are row markers available commercially, of course, but we've made one of our own in the Victory Garden, and it's a dandy. We use wooden stakes that are notched to secure the line, and we've added a baler to

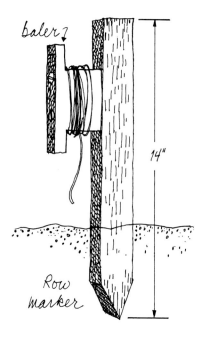

baler

14"

Row marker

the stakes so the extra line is conveniently stored when not needed. Our line is 50-foot nylon.

Handy But Not Crucial
Crowbar: We use ours for fence-post holes and for parsnip-planting holes in stiff clay or rocky soils.

Lopping Shears: For pruning anything up to 1 inch in diameter.

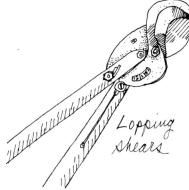

Lopping shears

Pruning Saw: For some pruning jobs a standard carpenter's saw will do, but a pruning saw is specially designed both for ease of motion and to fit into awkward spots. It can simplify an otherwise tiring task because its teeth are set so that the saw doesn't stick in wet or "green" wood.

Army Trenching Tool: These are usually available only through army surplus stores, so they can be hard to acquire. They're useful in setting out plants for which a trowel is too small and a spade is too big.

Trenching Tool

Sledge Hammer: Not usually considered a gardener's tool, but useful the few times of the year when some heavy pounding is needed.

Spreader: Grass seed and fertilizer can both be spread by hand, of course, but for large jobs it's a laborious process. The spreader cuts down on time and does the job more evenly.

Necessary But Rentable
Shredder: A lawn mower will do much of the work of the shredder, but it can't do it all, and the shredder has the added qualities of tidiness and speed.

Rototiller: No gardener who values his or her back would tackle large-scale soil

Roto tiller

preparation without one. Make sure to get one with rear-mounted tines, so the wheels of the tiller don't compact the very soil that's just been turned.

Lawn Roller: A must for those putting in a new lawn. It's a good tool to rent for the few occasions it's needed. Otherwise it clutters up the garage.

VEGETABLE GARDENING GUIDE FOR DIFFERENT CLIMATES

How to use this Guide:
First determine the zone in which you live from the Zone Map. Then select the vegetable you want to grow and look on the Vegetable Chart on page 308 under your zone to determine the planting date or dates. For example, if you live in Zone 3 (the same zone as the Victory Garden) and want to grow potatoes, look on the chart under Zone 3 and find that the planting period extends from March 15 to June 15. If you live in Zone 6, you will find that potatoes can be planted at two different seasons, January 1 to February 15 and August 1 to September 15. With this chart and the Zone Map you will be able to determine when to plant any vegetable, no matter where you live in the United States or Canada. When an asterisk (*) appears in place of dates, the crop is not suited for growing in that zone: lima beans, for example, need a long, warm growing season and are difficult if not impossible to grow in Zones 1 and 2. If two asterisks (**) appear after the name of a vegetable, the plants are usually set into the garden as 4- to 6-inch seedlings at the specified date: these plants have to be started from seeds several weeks earlier in a hotbed or greenhouse. The frost dates under each zone refer to the last frost expected in spring and the first frost expected in fall for that area.

Planting schedule for annual flowers: Since this is a book devoted primarily to vegetables, the planting dates of annual flowers are not included in the Vegetable Chart. Instead, you will find annuals in the February chapter, grouped according to the length of time normally allowed between sowing the seeds indoors or in a hotbed or greenhouse and setting the plants out in the open garden. Some annuals are more resistant to cold weather than others and can tolerate light frosts if they have been properly hardened; however, all plants can be set out after frost danger has passed. Those annu-

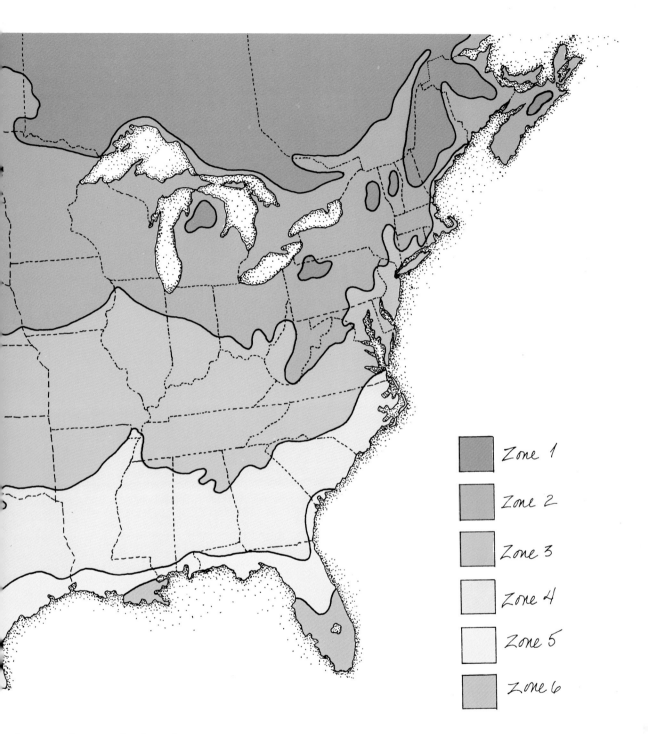

Zone 1

Zone 2

Zone 3

Zone 4

Zone 5

Zone 6

als grown from seeds planted
directly in the garden can usually be sown about the time of
the last anticipated frost or any
time thereafter. The spring
frost date for your area can be
determined from the Zone Map
and Vegetable Chart.

Vegetables *=vegetable not suited for zone **=set out plants, not seeds	Zone 1 *Frost Dates* *Spring: Jun 10* *Fall: Aug 20*	Zone 2 *Frost Dates* *Spring: May 20* *Fall: Sep 20*	Zone 3 *Frost Dates* *Spring: Apr 20* *Fall: Oct 10* *(Victory Garden)*	Zone 4 *Frost Dates* *Spring: Mar 20* *Fall: Oct 30*	Zone 5 *Frost Dates* *Spring: Feb 20* *Fall: Nov 20*	Zone 6 *Frost Dates* *Spring: Jan 30* *Fall: Dec 20*
Asparagus**	May 15-Jun 1	Apr 20-May 15	Mar 15-Apr 15	Feb 1-Mar 10 Nov 15-Dec 31	*	*
Beans, lima	*	*	May 1-Jun 20	Apr 1-Aug 1	Mar 1-Sep 1	Feb 1-Oct 1
Beans, snap	*	May 15-Jul 1	Apr 25-Jul 20	Mar 15-Aug 15	Mar 1-May 1 Jul 1-Sep 10	Feb 1-Apr 1 Sep 1-Nov 1
Beets	May 15-Jun 15	Apr 25-Jul 1	Mar 20-Jul 25	Feb 15-May 15 Aug 1-Sep 1	Jan 20-Apr 1 Sep 1-Dec 1	Jan 1-Mar 15 Sep 1-Dec 31
Broccoli**	May 1-Jun 10	May 1-Jun 15	Mar 25-Apr 20 Jun 15-Jul 15	Feb 15-Mar 15 Jul 1-Aug 15	Jan 15-Feb 15 Aug 1-Sep 15	Jan 1-Jan 30 Sep 1-Dec 31
Brussels sprouts**	May 1-Jun 10	May 1-Jun 15	Mar 25-Apr 20 Jun 15-Jul 15	Feb 15-Mar 15 Jul 1-Aug 15	Jan 15-Feb 15 Aug 1-Sep 15	Jan 1-Jan 30 Sep 1-Dec 31
Cabbage**	May 20-Jun 1	May 1-Jun 15	Mar 10-Apr 1 Jun 1-Jul 15	Feb 1-Mar 1 Aug 1-Sep 1	Jan 1-Feb 25 Sep 1-Dec 1	Jan 1-Jan 15 Sep 1-Dec 31
Carrots	May 15-Jun 15	May 1-Jul 1	Apr 1-Jul 20	Feb 15-Mar 20 Jul 1-Aug 15	Jan 15-Mar 1 Sep 1-Nov 1	Jan 1-Mar 1 Sep 15-Dec 1
Cauliflower**	May 1-Jun 15	May 1-Jul 1	Mar 15-Apr 20 Jun 1-Jul 25	Feb 10-Mar 10 Jul 15-Aug 15	Jan 10-Feb 10 Aug 1-Sep 15	Jan 1-Feb 1 Sep 15-Nov 1

Vegetables *=vegetable not suited for zone **=set out plants, not seeds	Zone 1 *Frost Dates* *Spring: Jun 10* *Fall: Aug 20*	Zone 2 *Frost Dates* *Spring: May 20* *Fall: Sep 20*	Zone 3 *Frost Dates* *Spring: Apr 20* *Fall: Oct 10* *(Victory Garden)*	Zone 4 *Frost Dates* *Spring: Mar 20* *Fall: Oct 30*	Zone 5 *Frost Dates* *Spring: Feb 20* *Fall: Nov 20*	Zone 6 *Frost Dates* *Spring: Jan 30* *Fall: Dec 20*
Celery and Celeriac**	Jun 1-Jun 15	May 10-Jul 1	May 10-Jul 15	Apr 1-Aug 15	Jan 20-Feb 10 Jul 15-Sep 1	Jan 1-Feb 1 Oct 1-Dec 1
Chervil	May 10-Jun 10	Apr 15-Jun 15	Mar 10-Apr 10	Feb 10-Mar 10	Jan 1-Feb 1 Nov 1-Dec 31	Jan 1-Feb 1 Nov 1-Dec 31
Chinese cabbage	May 15-Jun 15	May 1-Jul 1	Jun 15-Aug 1	Aug 1-Sep 15	Sep 15-Oct 15	Sep 1-Dec 1
Chives	May 10-Jun 10	Apr 15-Jun 15	Mar 10-Apr 10	Feb 10-Mar 10	Jan 1-Feb 1 Nov 1-Dec 31	Jan 1-Feb 1 Nov 1-Dec 31
Chicory, witloof	May 15-Jun 15	May 15-Jun 15	Jun 1-Jul 1	Jun 1-Aug 10	Jul 20-Sep 1	Aug 15-Oct 15
Collards**	May 20-Jun 15	May 1-Jun 15	Mar 10-Aug 1	Feb 15-May 1 Aug 1-Sep 15	Jan 1-Mar 15 Aug 25-Nov 1	Jan 1-Feb 15 Sep 1-Dec 31
Cornsalad	May 15-Jun 15	Apr 15-Aug 1	Feb 15-Apr 15 Aug 15-Sep 15	Jan 1-Mar 15 Sep 15-Nov 1	Jan 1-Mar 15 Oct 1-Dec 31	Jan 1-Feb 15 Oct 1-Dec 31
Corn, sweet	*	May 15-Jul 1	Apr 25-Jul 10	Mar 15-Aug 1	Feb 20-Apr 15 Jun 1-Sep 1	Feb 1-Mar 15
Cucumbers	*	Jun 1-Jun 15	May 1-Jul 1	Apr 1-Aug 1	Feb 15-Apr 15 Jun 1-Aug 15	Feb 1-Mar 15 Aug 15-Oct 1
Eggplant**	*	Jun 1-Jun 15	May 10-Jun 15	Apr 1-Jul 1	Feb 20-Aug 1	Feb 1-Mar 1 Aug 1-Sep 30
Endive	May 15-Jul 1	May 1-Jul 15	Mar 25-Apr 15 Jul 1-Aug 15	Mar 1-Apr 1 Jul 15-Aug 15	Jan 15-Mar 1 Sep 1-Oct 1	Jan 1-Mar 1 Sep 1-Dec 31
Fennel, Florence	May 15-Jun 15	May 1-Jul 1	Mar 25-Jul 15	Mar 1-Apr 1 Jul 1-Aug 1	Jan 15-Mar 1 Aug 15-Sep 15	Jan 1-Mar 1 Sep 1-Dec 1
Garlic	May 15-Jun 1	Apr 15-May 15	Mar 10-Apr 1	Feb 1-Mar 1	Aug 15-Oct 1	Sep 15-Nov 15
Horseradish**	May 15-Jun 1	Apr 20-May 20	Mar 20-Apr 20	Feb 1-Mar 1	Aug 15-Oct 1	Sep 15-Nov 15
Kale	May 15-Jun 15	Apr 20-Jul 1	Mar 20-Apr 10 Jul 1-Aug 1	Feb 20-Mar 10 Jul 15-Sep 1	Jan 20-Feb 10 Aug 15-Oct 15	Jan 1-Feb 1 Sep 1-Dec 31
Kohlrabi	May 15-Jun 15	Apr 20-Jul 15	Mar 20-May 1 Jul 1-Aug 1	Feb 20-Mar 10 Aug 1-Sep 1	Jan 20-Feb 10 Sep 1-Oct 15	Jan 1-Feb 1 Sep 1-Dec 31
Leeks	May 1-Jun 1	May 1-Jul 15	Mar 15-Apr 15	Feb 1-Mar 1	Jan 1-Feb 15 Sep 1-Nov 1	Jan 1-Feb 1 Sep 15-Nov 1
Lettuce, leaf	May 15-Jul 15	May 1-Aug 1	Mar 20-May 15 Jul 15-Sep 1	Feb 1-Apr 1 Aug 15-Oct 1	Jan 1-Mar 15 Sep 1-Nov 1	Jan 1-Feb 1 Sep 15-Dec 31
Melon	*	May 1-Jun 15	May 1-Jun 15	Apr 1-Jul 15	Feb 15-Apr 15	Feb 15-Mar 15
Mustard	May 15-Jul 15	May 1-Aug 1	Mar 20-Aug 15	Feb 20-Apr 1 Aug 15-Oct 15	Feb 15-Apr 15 Sep 1-Dec 1	Jan 1-Mar 1 Sep 15-Dec 31
New Zealand spinach	*	May 20-Jun 15	May 1-Jul 15	Apr 1-Aug 1	Mar 1-Aug 15	Feb 1-Apr 15 Jun 1-Oct 1
Okra	*	Jun 1-Jun 20	May 1-Jul 15	Apr 1-Aug 10	Mar 1-Sep 10	Feb 1-Oct 1
Onion**	May 1-Jun 10	Apr 20-May 15	Mar 15-Apr 10	Feb 10-Mar 10	Jan 1-Jan 15 Oct 1-Dec 31	Jan 1-Jan 15 Oct 1-Dec 31

Vegetables *=vegetable not suited for zone **=set out plants, not seeds	Zone 1 *Frost Dates* *Spring: Jun 10* *Fall: Aug 20*	Zone 2 *Frost Dates* *Spring: May 20* *Fall: Sep 20*	Zone 3 *Frost Dates* *Spring: Apr 20* *Fall: Oct 10* *(Victory Garden)*	Zone 4 *Frost Dates* *Spring: Mar 20* *Fall: Oct 30*	Zone 5 *Frost Dates* *Spring: Feb 20* *Fall: Nov 20*	Zone 6 *Frost Dates* *Spring: Jan 30* *Fall: Dec 20*
Onion (seeds)	May 1-Jun 10	Apr 20-May 15	Mar 15-Apr 1	Feb 10-Mar 10	Jan 1-Jan 15 Sep 1-Nov 1	Jan 1-Jan 15 Sep 15-Nov 1
Onion (sets)	May 1-Jun 10	Apr 20-May 15	Mar 10-Apr 1	Feb 1-Mar 20	Jan 1-Jan 15 Nov 1-Dec 31	Jan 1-Jan 15 Nov 1-Dec 31
Parsley	May 15-Jun 15	May 1-Jul 1	Mar 20-Aug 1	Feb 15-Mar 15 Aug 1-Sep 15	Jan 1-Jan 30 Sep 1-Dec 31	Jan 1-Jan 30 Sep 1-Dec 31
Parsnip	May 15-Jun 10	May 1-Jun 15	Mar 20-Jun 1	Feb 15-Mar 15	Jan 1-Feb 1 Aug 1-Sep 1	Sep 1-Dec 1
Peas, black-eye	*	*	May 10-Jul 1	Apr 1-Aug 1	Mar 1-Sep 1	Feb 15-May 1 Jul 1-Sep 20
Peas, garden	May 10-Jun 15	Apr 15-Jul 15	Mar 10-Apr 10 Aug 1-Aug 15	Feb 1-Mar 15 Aug 1-Sep 15	Jan 1-Mar 1 Oct 1-Dec 1	Jan 1-Feb 15 Oct 1-Dec 31
Peas, podded	May 10-Jun 15	Apr 15-Jul 15	Mar 10-Apr 10 Aug 1-Aug 15	Feb 1-Mar 15 Aug 1-Sep 15	Jan 1-Mar 1 Oct 1-Dec 1	Jan 1-Feb 15 Oct 1-Dec 31
Peppers**	*	May 25-Jun 20	May 10-Jun 1	Apr 10-Jul 20	Mar 1-Aug 15	Feb 1-Apr 1 Aug 15-Oct 1
Potatoes	May 15-Jun 1	Apr 15-Jun 15	Mar 15-Jun 15	Feb 10-Mar 15 Jul 20-Aug 10	Jan 15-Mar 1 Aug 10-Sep 15	Jan 1-Feb 15 Aug 1-Sep 15
Pumpkins	*	May 20-Jun 10	Jun 1-Jul 1	Jun 10-Jul 10	Jul 1-Aug 1	Aug 1-Sep 1
Radishes	May 1-Jul 15	Apr 15-Aug 15	Mar 10-May 10 Jul 15-Sep 15	Jan 20-May 1 Aug 15-Oct 15	Jan 1-Apr 1 Sep 1-Dec 1	Jan 1-Apr 1 Oct 1-Dec 31
Rhubarb**	May 15-Jun 1 Sep 1-Oct 1	Apr 15-May 10 Sep 15-Nov 1	Mar 10-Apr 10 Oct 15-Nov 15	Nov 1-Dec 1	*	*
Rutabaga	May 15-Jun 15	May 1-Jun 20	Jun 15-Jul 15	Jan 15-Mar 1 Jul 15-Aug 1	Aug 1-Sep 1	Oct 15-Nov 15
Salsify	May 15-Jun 1	May 1-Jun 20	Mar 20-Jul 1	Feb 15-Mar 1 Jun 1-Jul 10	Jan 15-Feb 20 Jul 15-Aug 15	Jan 1-Feb 1 Sep 1-Oct 31
Shallots	May 10-Jun 1	Apr 20-May 10	Mar 1-Apr 15	Feb 1-Mar 10	Jan 1-Feb 20 Aug 15-Oct 1	Jan 1-Feb 1 Sep 15-Nov 1
Soybeans	*	*	May 10-Jun 25	Apr 10-Jul 15	Mar 10-Jul 30	Mar 1-Jul 30
Spinach	May 1-Jul 1	Apr 10-Aug 1	Mar 1-Apr 15 Aug 1-Sep 1	Jan 15-Mar 15 Sep 1-Oct 1	Jan 1-Mar 1 Oct 1-Dec 31	Jan 1-Feb 15 Oct 1-Dec 31
Squash, summer	Jun 10-Jun 20	May 15-Jul 1	May 1-Jul 15	Apr 1-Aug 1	Mar 1-Aug 1	Feb 1-Oct 1
Squash, winter	*	May 20-Jun 10	Jun 1-Jul 1	Jun 10-Jul 10	Jul 1-Aug 1	Aug 1-Sep 1
Sweet potatoes	*	*	May 20-Jun 10	Apr 10-Jun 15	Mar 20-Jul 1	Feb 15-Jul 1
Swiss chard	May 15-Jun 15	May 10-Jul 1	Apr 1-Jul 20	Feb 20-Sep 10	Jan 20-Apr 15 Jun 1-Oct 1	Jan 1-Apr 1 Jun 1-Dec 31

Vegetables *=vegetable not suited for zone **=set out plants, not seeds	Zone 1 *Frost Dates* *Spring: Jun 10* *Fall: Aug 20*	Zone 2 *Frost Dates* *Spring: May 20* *Fall: Sep 20*	Zone 3 *Frost Dates* *Spring: Apr 20* *Fall: Oct 10* *(Victory Garden)*	Zone 4 *Frost Dates* *Spring: Mar 20* *Fall: Oct 30*	Zone 5 *Frost Dates* *Spring: Feb 20* *Fall: Nov 20*	Zone 6 *Frost Dates* *Spring: Jan 30* *Fall: Dec 20*
Tomatoes**	Jun 15-Jun 30	May 25-Jun 20	May 5-Jun 20	Apr 1-Jul 1	Mar 1-Aug 1	Feb 1-Apr 1
Turnips	May 15-Jun 30	Apr 15-Jul 15	Mar 10-Jun 15	Feb 10-Mar 10 Aug 1-Sep 15	Jan 10-Mar 1 Sep 1-Nov 15	Jan 1-Mar 1 Oct 1-Dec 31
Watermelon	*	Jun 15-Jul 1	May 1-Jun 15	Apr 1-Jul 15	Feb 15-Jul 30	Feb 15-Mar 15

GLOSSARY

Acid Soil Soil with a pH reading below 7.0. Ground limestone sweetens acid soil. (See the November feature, page 249.)

Alkaline Soil Soil with a pH reading above 7.0. Ground agricultural sulfur corrects alkaline soil. (See the November feature, page 249.)

Aphids One of the most prevalent of garden insects. They usually congregate on the undersides of plants' foliage and suck the nourishment from the stems and leaves. (See the July feature, page 152.)

Annual A plant that lives for only 1 year or one season.

Biennial A plant that lives for 2 years, producing leaves the first year and flowers and seeds the second.

Blanching The process of depriving a plant of light in order to leave it pale and tender. A technique used with celery, endive, and forced rhubarb, among other plants.

Bolting The premature flowering of a plant, which makes it inedible. Spinach, lettuce, celery, and endive are plants that are prone to bolting.

Cloche A portable glass or plastic cover for a row, making it possible to sow some crops weeks ahead of time in the spring or late in the fall. (See the March feature, page 26.)

Cold Frame A low structure with a translucent top, used for protecting plants from the weather and for hardening-off young seedlings. (See the March feature, pages 26–27.)

Commercial Fertilizers Chemical compounds, available in a number of forms, including liquid and granular, that provide plants with needed nutrients.

Compost The richest of organic materials, the remains of decomposed vegetable matter. (See the August feature, pages 180–181.)

Crown The part of a plant where the root and stem meet.

Drill A shallow furrow in which seeds are sown. The planting board (see the February feature, page 303) is a helpful, time-saving tool for making drills.

Foliar Spray A solution of water and fertilizer sprayed directly on the foliage of plants, where it can be quickly absorbed.

Force To speed growth with the artificial changing of the seasons. Many bulb plants can be forced, as can rhubarb (see October for more).

Fungicide A chemical that kills fungi or prevents their growth.

Germination The sprouting of seeds.

Green Manure A crop of growing plants, such as rye grass, that is plowed under while still green and allowed to decay and enrich the soil. (See the November feature, pages 248–249.)

Grow on Transplanting a plant to a larger container for continued development.

Harden-off The process of gradually toughening a plant's cell structure by exposing it to controlled cold weather, as in a cold frame.

Humus The end product of decaying organic material.

Hilling-up The process of periodically pulling soil around the stems of plants to keep the roots deep and cool, as with potatoes, or to protect growing plants from the sun, as with leeks.

Hybrid A plant produced by crossing different species.

Intercrop One crop grown between the rows of another. It is also used to describe the practice of alternating the plants of two crops within a row, like slow-growing cabbage and fast-growing lettuce.

Leader   The primary or top stem of a plant.

Loam   Soil composed of roughly equal portions of clay and sand. The best of garden soils. (See the November feature, page 246.)

Mulch   A covering spread around plants to control weeds and hold moisture in the soil.

Neutral Soil   Soil that has a pH around 7.0, which is neither acid nor alkaline. Most vegetables do their best in soil with a pH of 6.0 to 6.8, just on the acid side of neutral.

Organic Fertilizers   Natural materials, such as manure, compost, bone meal, and blood meal, that nourish plants slowly as the material decays.

pH Factor   A reading of acidity or alkalinity, based on the 0–14 pH scale. A pH of 7.0 indicates neutral soil; below 7.0 indicates acid soil, and above 7.0 indicates alkaline soil.

Pelleted Seeds   Tiny seeds that are coated to give added bulk and make them easier to handle.

Perennial   A plant that lives for more than 2 years.

Pricking out   Gently lifting a seedling out of its seed container to be transplanted elsewhere.

Rootstock   A growing plant onto which a scion, a piece of another plant, is grafted.

Runners   Above-ground stems that send out roots when they come into contact with moist soil. The most familiar of the runner plants is the June-bearing strawberry.

Scion   A young shoot of a plant that is joined to a rootstock during the grafting process.

Seed Leaves   The first two leaves — sometimes only one leaf — that grow after germination. (See the January feature, page 285.)

Seedling   A very young plant that's been started from seed.

Setting The development of seeds or fruit after pollination.

Setting out Transplanting a seedling into the open garden.

Skips Empty spots in garden rows where plants failed to survive.

Thinning Pulling or clipping the weak seedlings in a pot or row in order to leave the others room enough to develop. (See the May feature, page 96.)

Tilth Soil broken down into fine crumbs.

Transplant Solution A mixture of foliar fertilizer and water poured onto newly set-out seedlings to get them growing quickly.

Transplanting Moving a plant from one location to another.

True Leaves All the leaves that a plant produces above the seed leaves. (See the January feature, page 285.)

Tuber The natural swelling of an underground stem.

Virus Microscopic organism that causes diseases in plants.

INDEX

Numerals in italics indicate an illustration or photograph of the subject.

A

acidity, soil, 47, 128, 246, 249
aeration: of plants, 99, 284–285; of soil, 246
African violets, 230–232, *231*; taking cuttings of, 232
ageratum, 8, *273–274*, 290
air circulation: in compost, 181; for seedlings, 285
air-layering, 261–*262*
air plants. *See* epiphytes
alchemilla, 206, 207
alfalfa, sprouting seeds of, 274–275
alkalinity, soil: correcting, in garden soil, 246, 249; correcting, in lawns, 47
All-America Selections, 267
all-purpose spray, 156–157, 206
alpine strawberries. *See* strawberries, EVERBEARING (ALPINE)
alyssum, 206, 207, *289*, 290
amaryllis, *233–234*; forcing, 252
American Orchid Society, 279
annuals: flowers, *184–185*; herbs, 19–20, 40; starting seedlings, 273, 289, 290; planting, 102, 307; transplanting, 102; list of, grouped according to length of time between seed sowing and transplanting outdoors, 290
anthracnose, 127, 162
ants, 151, 152
aphids, 86, 109, 151, *152*
apple trees: forcing branches of, 288; grafting, *15*. *See also* fruit trees
apricot trees. *See* fruit trees
arborvitae, propagation of, 257–258. *See also* evergreens
Army trenching tool, *304*
artemisia, 208
artificial light, growing seedlings under, 283

asparagus: preparing soil for, 71; spacing rows of, 65; planting, *71*; fertilizing, 71, 72, 98 (also adding side dressing to, 126–127; adding top dressing to, 234); pests of, 153; hilling-up, 71 (also 127); weeding, 178; maturation of, 70–71; harvesting, 71–72; wintering-over, 234
aspidistra, 245
aster, 208, 209
aubergines. *See* eggplants
azaleas, *9–10*, 93

B

baby's breath, 209, 272
Bacillus thuringiensis, 153, 155, 157. *See also* broccoli (and related crops)
balled and burlapped plants, 85, 216
balloon flowers, *150*, 207, 208
bananas, growing, 283
basil, *72*; planting, 73; transplanting, 103; thinning, 103; pinching off, 103; drying and freezing, 160–161; growing, in perennial border, 209
beans: bush (snap), 73–74, *103*, 127, 162; diseases of, 73, 103, 127, 157, 162; fava, 73; Italian, 268; kidney, 178; lima, 73, 103, 162, 212; pests of, 154, 155; pole, 73, 74; preparing seeds of, 74, 103; protecting, from frost, 186; purple-podded, 268; scarlet runner, 73, 161–162; shell, 73, 267; varieties of, 74, 268; yellow (wax), 268
bean sprouts, how to grow, *274–275*
bee balm, 207, 208
bees, pesticides toxic to, 110, 157
beetles: Japanese, 86, *153*; Mexican bean, *154*
beets: starting seedlings, 290; planting, 32 (also 104, 128); transplanting, 32–33 (also 74,

290); fertilizing, 32, 98; thinning, 74 (also 104, 125, 162); watering, 32, 104; pests, of, 75, 104, 128, 154, 162; harvesting, *33*, 104 (also 128, 162, 212); varieties of, 268
Begonia semperflorens. See begonias
begonias: fibrous-rooted, 290; Rieger, 290, *291*; tuberous-rooted, *213*; planting, 290; transplanting, 291; wintering-over, 213–214; wax, *10–11*, 275
bellflower, 206
Benemyl, 156, 157
biennials: flowers, 43, 137, 148; herbs, 19; ordering seeds, 102; starting seedlings, 102; vegetables, 63; winter protection of, 252
birch trees, pruning, 14
birds: protecting corn from, *132*; protecting fruit from, 121; protecting sunflowers from, 225
bitterness (in cucumbers), 133
black spot, 86, *156*
blanching: cauliflower, *107*; celery, 188; endive, *111*; leeks, 113
blanketflower, 208
bleeding heart, 207, 208
blemishes (on tomatoes), 149
blight, leaf, 109
blossom-end rot, *120*, 147–148
blossoming: inducing, in pear trees, 179; inducing, in poinsettias, 200
blueberries, protecting, from birds, 121
bluegrass, Kentucky, 48, 194
bolt, 49
bone meal, 98, 198, 203, 206
borer: European corn, 110, 157; iris, 16; squash vine, 146–147; stalk, *155*
botrytis blight, *156*
bottom-watering, 118, 285
brassicas, 11
breadfruit, 262
broccoli: starting seedlings, 11 (also 102, 128); hardening-off, 11; planting, 75, 128; interplanting, with lettuce, 33, 128; transplanting, 11 (also 33–34); fertilizing, 33–34 (also 75, 128, 163); thinning, 75 (also 163); diseases of, 33, 75; pests of, 34, 75, 153; harvesting, 104–105 (also *128*, 212, 230); varieties of, 268

browallia, *253–254*, 290
brussels sprouts: starting seedlings, 105; transplanting, 128; interplanting, with lettuce, 128; diseases and pests of, 128–129; harvesting, 187 (also 212, 230); pinching back, 187; varieties of, 268
bulb planter, *203*, 204, *302*
bulbs, spring-flowering: planting, 203–204, 276; naturalizing, 226–*227*; fertilizing, 98; fall growth of, 245; wintering-over, 8; forcing, 218–219 (also 224, 252, 272, 288)
burlap, 85, 151, 216
Burnett Brothers, 267
Burpee, W. Atlee, Company, 267
butternut trees, 25
buying: plants, 77, 102, 284; seeds, 102, 103–104, 224, 266

c

cabbage: starting seedlings, 11 (also 106); hardening-off, 11; transplanting, 34–35 (also 106); interplanting, with lettuce, 34; planting, 76; fertilizing, 34, 76; thinning, 76; watering, 106; diseases of, 34, 76, 106; pests of, 34–35 (also 75–76, 153); harvesting, 105, 106 (also 212, 230); preventing splitting in heads of, 106; varieties of, 268
cabbage maggots, *152. See also* root maggots
cabbageworm caterpillar, 34–35, 75, 76, 128, *153*
cactus, 292, *293*, 294
cage method (of growing tomatoes), *91*, 92–93, 176

cage traps, 132
calcium, 120, 193
calla lilies, 23, *235*, 236
calliandra, 262
camellias, *295*–296
cantaloupes, 50, *167–168*, 269. *See also* melons
Canterbury bells, 130
canvas hoses, *97*
"Cape Cod Weeder," *99*
Cape primrose. *See* streptocarpus
captan, 21, 55, 103, 157
caraway, 209
carbaryl, 86, 110, 153, 154, 157
carrots: planting, 35 (also 76, 107); sowing radishes with, 35; growing, in containers, 122; fertilizing, 35, 76; watering, 76, 107; thinning, 76 (also 106–107); splitting of, 76–77; harvesting, *76*, 106; varieties of, 268
cast-iron plant, 245
catmint, mauve, 209
cattleya (orchid), *278*
cauliflower: starting seedlings, 11; hardening-off, 11; transplanting, 11, 35–36; planting, 77; interplanting, with lettuce, 36; fertilizing, 35–36; diseases and pests of, 36, 77, 107, 108, 153; blanching, *107*; harvesting, 214; purple-headed, 107–*108*, *214*; varieties of, 268
celeriac, 205
celery: requirements of, 108, 296; starting seedlings, 296; transplanting, 11, 108; fertilizing, 108–109 (also 188); watering, 188; diseases and pests of, 109; blanching, *188*; harvesting, 212, 230; varieties of, 268
chemicals, 47, 155, 156, 157
cherry trees, 121, 179. *See also* fruit trees
chervil, 209
chestnut, horse, 179
chick peas, 274–275
Chinese cabbage, *129*–130, 212, 268
Chinese lanterns, 179
Chinese pea pods, 53
chionodoxa, 8, 204, 226–227
chives, 11–*12*, 207
Christmas plants, 252
Christmas trees: planting live, *255*–256; 272
chrysanthemums: dividing, 78 (also 215); planting, 78; in perennial border, 207, 209; pinching back, 78 (also 109, 164); transplanting, 126 (also 130, 160); taking stem cuttings of, 164; mulching, 77 (also 163); wintering-over, 215

cineraria, *130*, 164, 272
clay pots, 122, 284, 292
clay soil, 246
clematis, *37*
climate zones, *map 306–307*
cloche, 22–23, 239; how to build, *29*
clover, white, 281
clubroot, 33, 34, 36, 76, 77
coffee, 9
cold frames, 26–28; fall crops in, 212, 239; forcing bulbs in, 218–219; hardening-off in, 8, 28, 298; how to build, *26–27*; propagating evergreens in, 258; wintering-over in, 28, 212, 215, 242
collards, 130–*131*; harvesting, 188–189, 212, 230; varieties of, 268
columbine, 208
compost: adding, to soil, 247; making, *180–182*; as planting medium, 116, 118
composter, 3-bin: how to build, *182–183*; how to use, *180–181*
containers: for growing sweet potatoes, 89; for growing vegetables, *122–123*; for sowing seeds indoors, 284; for terrariums, 298
cool-weather crops: brussels sprouts, 187; Chinese cabbage, 126; endive, 41; fava beans, 73; kale, 138; lettuce, 18; parsnips, 241; peas, 170; potatoes, 57; radishes, 57; rutabagas, 146; spinach, 23

Class Plan

week 1 - April 30
6 - 1 - 2 - 1

week 5 - May 24 ☆
6 - 2 - 2

week 2 - May 3
6 - 1 - 2 - 1

week 6 - June 1 ☆
2 6 2

week 3 - May 10
6 - 1 - 2 - 1

week 7 - June 7 ☆
2 - 2 - 8 6

week 4 - May 17
6 - 1 - 2 - 1

week 8 - April 4
1 - 1 - 2 - 6

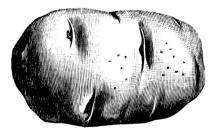

2